America's
Covert Warriors

Related Titles from Potomac Books, Inc.

Special Forces Today: Afghanistan, Africa, Balkans, Iraq, South America
—Alexander Stilwell

Chasing Ghosts: Unconventional Warfare in American History
—John J. Tierney, Jr.

Losing the Golden Hour: An Insider's View of Iraq's Reconstruction
—James Stephenson

Overcoming the Bush Legacy in Iraq and Afghanistan
—Deepak Tripathi

Through Veterans' Eyes: The Iraq and Afghanistan Experience
—Larry Minear

Inside the World of
Private Military Contractors

America's
Covert Warriors

SHAWN ENGBRECHT

Potomac Books, Inc.
Washington, D.C.

Library of Congress Cataloging-in-Publication Data
Engbrecht, Shawn.
  America's covert warriors : inside the world of private military
contractors / Shawn Engbrecht. — 1st ed.
      p. cm.
  Includes bibliographical references and index.
  ISBN 978-1-59797-238-3 (hardcover : alk. paper)
  1. Defense industries—United States. 2. Defense contracts—United
States. 3. Contracting out—United States. I. Title.

  HD9743.U62E54 2010
  338.4'735500973--dc22

                                                    2010030257

Potomac Books, Inc.
22841 Quicksilver Drive
Dulles, Virginia 20166

First Edition

10 9 8 7 6 5 4 3 2 1

This book is dedicated to all those who, in uniform and out, stepped forward when their nation asked. To those who muddled through, doing right as best they could, ordinary souls displaying extraordinary courage and self-sacrifice. This one is for all of you, who went over . . . and never came home. Your sunny memories give me strength during the blackest of nights.

Be not afraid.

Contents

Acknowledgments

Writing a book is not dissimilar to preparing for a military operation in that there are dozens of people behind the scenes contributing to the success of the one at the sharp end. So it is with this volume. In my particular case the entire chain of support, from agent to production editor was female. They were collectively intolerant of fools, honest in their criticisms, and invariably right. I cannot imagine a more humbling or constructive experience and am grateful for their unfailing guidance. To that end any undiscovered errors in this tome are my fault alone. All credit belongs to them.

Thank you, Jodie Rhodes, my agent who discovered barely discernable nuggets of potential in my early writings. To Hilary Claggett, editor, friend, and ruthless master of red ink in rewrites. To Vicki Chamlee, whose copyedit was as detailed as it was consistently impeccable. To Kathryn Owens, who turned a digital mass of words into an amazing entity called a book. Thank you all.

And to Dr. Charles Springer, surgeon extraordinaire, who, on an afternoon not so very long ago in a trauma ward, reassembled a shattered and broken wreck that was my body into the one that I currently call home.

The wheelchair is long gone, along with nearly all the pain. And since the collection of titanium rods, nuts, plates, and screws used to remanufacture me is lighter than the bone it replaced, the sole legacy is that I am now able to climb higher and run faster than ever before. I reflect on that every time I am high above the clouds, gazing down at the earth far below. For what turned out to be the best afternoon of my life, I thank you.

Preface

I have discovered, since the start of the Iraq War in 2003, grave truths that lend credence to antiquated clichés. The tired old phrase "Good men need only to do nothing for evil to prosper" is now a constant companion, inevitably strolling alongside my memories of Iraq.

That the world is a dangerous place and becoming increasingly so, there is no doubt. The terrorist attacks of September 11, 2001, provide cogent rationale for maintaining a highly trained and superbly equipped military, which far too often serves as the only bulwark between peaceful democracy and malicious jihad. U.S. military forces will comprise uniformed men and women as well as private military contractors (PMCs) for the foreseeable future. That fact is not going to change anytime soon. So those hoping to find in this book a frenetic, left-wing rant about mercenaries tearing apart the fabric of American foreign policy will be sadly disappointed.

But those who dwell on the far right, whose unspoken motto pertaining to all things Iraqi or Afghan is "Kill them all and let God sort them out," will find this volume equally sour to their literary palette. That leaves the silent majority of us, neither completely comfortable with nor dead set against the two conflicts the United States is engaged in half a world away. We are the same silent majority whose sons and daughters do nearly all of the fighting and dying.

The preponderance of those of us who have served in Iraq or Afghanistan, be it with the military or with contractors, have truly done the best we could in always difficult and often dangerous circumstances. As Winston Churchill proclaimed,

"We have muddled through." And just as the silent majority in which many of us are rooted, we have not had much to say, forfeiting our share of laudable, honest-toil headlines to one lunatic fringe element or another—elements, whose only common ground is intolerance and a penchant for shouting down the other side. In their views, private military contractors have been portrayed as either mercenaries or super patriots. It was black or white, while the best color, the one of truthful gray, was missing. The headlines, both for the military and private contractors, grew larger as the war deteriorated.

It should come as no surprise that those headlines have not always been positive. The egregious conduct of those in charge of the dungeons at Abu Ghraib hogged the editorials that rightfully should have been describing how the American soldier, at great risk, was building schools and befriending a hostile populace. With the media ever more focused on the "booms, bangs, and bloodshed of war," the superlative, day-by-grinding-day conduct of our men and women in uniform has been shunted to the editorial sidelines until the next bloody paroxysm of combat pushes them back to center stage. For those who depend on the wire services and the mini sound bites of television for information, one would presume the armed-forces have not had a good war after hearing incessant reports of suicides, spiraling casualties, and unit fatigue.

The private military companies, by comparison, have endured an exceedingly splendid conflict. Operating with near-total anonymity, these personnel, drawn mostly from the silent majority of America, deployed overseas for myriad reasons. Some volunteered, truly believing in the legitimacy of delivering democracy to Iraq. Many came because they supported their government in time of war. For them, it was "the right thing to do." The first wave of private contractors arriving in 2003 was exclusively ex-military, professional, and extraordinarily competent. In short order, less talented others were lured by financial opportunity, which is certainly not against the law. The truth is that very few contractors arrived with the intent to massacre unarmed civilians, just as the military police running rampant in Abu Ghraib never deployed with orders detailing how to connect an electrode to a penis.

But somehow or other, amid the fog of war, we permitted the proliferation of wanton killers, a consortium of "Thugs-4-Hire," whose only move faster than pulling the trigger was cashing the paycheck provided by the U.S. taxpayer. Just as with the military, it was only a small percentile of outright murderers that existed in the ranks of the PMCs. But they found homes in companies such as Blackwater, who tolerated it and whose employees conducted the awful civilian massacre in 2007. It was unprofessional conduct such as this that brought the moral roof crashing down on the heads of the majority of contractors who were trying to do the right thing. And for those of us in the know, the Blackwater massacre wasn't really that bad compared to other such massacres; the participants just happened to get caught. Much worse occurred on a near-daily basis, far away from the prying eyes of the media. Blackwater got what it deserved, but the others didn't, successfully side-stepping the ugly aftereffects of dead civilians and drunken contractors throughout the theater.

The U.S. Army has learned its lessons. As of the summer of 2010, the war being waged in Afghanistan (where I just returned from a lengthy embed with combat units) is a far cry from Iraq, though sadly the bloodshed continues. Civilian casualties are a shadow of what they used to be, intelligence gathering has improved, and the army is far smarter at counterinsurgency than it was in 2004. That the U.S. Army was able to evolve so rapidly is a function of a discerning public that observed its every action with grave scrutiny, for it was the children of the silent majority who formed the army's maneuver brigades. Defects in tactics and equipment, when arrayed under the glare of publicity, were quickly remedied. Lessons learned are already paying dividends in the form of saved American and Afghan lives. By admitting to failure, reorganizing, and applying cutting-edge tactics with such a renewed sense of purpose, the U.S. armed forces have come to embody many of the ideals I cherish as a citizen of the great republic to which I belong. Our men and women in uniform serve as living examples of all the best that we strive to be, and spending time among combat troops reaffirms my belief that all things are possible in America.

Private military companies, by contrast, have done nothing to improve their lot, except slither as far away from the public eye as possible. They lurk in the shadows, faceless, and desire to remain there. Both the attitude and modus operandi are wrong.

The harsh truth is that I didn't sign up for this garbage. I really, really believed in America and all that it stood for. I parachuted into Panama in 1989, fought behind Iraqi lines in the Persian Gulf War, and deployed to Iraq again in 2003, 2004, 2006, and 2007. So the supposition is that with all that combat experience I should have known better than to keep my mouth shut when confronted by the waste, fraud, death, and plain old stupidity that embodied the American occupation of Iraq following the invasion. I, more than my peers, should have displayed the intestinal fortitude required to step forward and shout from the highest rooftop that the "emperor has no clothes." In this case the "emperor" represented the occupation policies of the United States, which were, from the viewpoint of the little man on the street, bereft of both common sense and sanity. But integrity dictates that I must admit to never having muttered in dissent, far less yelling from the rooftops. I took my place alongside hundreds of thousands of other contractors, good folks all representing the backbone of America and trying to build a better future for Iraq. Together, we silently observed rigged contracts, bribes, and theft, along with the occasional murder. We knew Iraq was a grotesque miscarriage of common sense, that the lunatics had in fact taken over the asylum, and were cognizant that the actions many of us observed on a daily basis went against the grain of everything we had grown up believing in. A few spoke out and were promptly fired for their honesty and integrity. The decent Americans on the bottom of the food chain would scratch their heads, mutter, "That's just plain wrong," and continue to muddle through as best they could, just as I did. If any of us had tried the same stunts in hometown USA, we would have become instant pariahs in our neighborhoods and communities. The house of Iraq was plainly burning down, but few of us reached for the fire hose, opting instead to play it safe by listening to misguided leadership that said in effect, "Fire? What fire? Leave those water spigots alone." So we continued to play with moral and ethical matches. Sadly, it was the Iraqi civilians who provided a cameo role as tinder and gasoline, their lives destined to be consumed in the conflagration.

What far too many of us saw was wrong. Far worse, we knew it was wrong and did nothing about it. We were the mob at the lynching, rationalizing, making wisecracks while shifting guilt sideways, and submerging our own individuality into the collective whole; meanwhile, we were still permitting murder against the dictates of common sense. But that behavior is not representative of my neighbors, friends, or the small town where I live. It is not representative of the United States of America or at least not the one I believed in and fought for.

So it's time to make a stand. Not for the private military companies, which I really don't care about in the big scheme of things, but rather for the everyday masses of humanity that served in them and did their collective best with what they had because, just as I do, they believed in America. Many feel more than a little let down, with a lingering bad taste in their mouths after their year's rotation through mayhem, waste, and carnage. The most frustrating part is that until some little guy stands up with a spotlight and illuminates both the good and bad, nothing is ever going to change because institutional inertia is the status quo of the industry. And if we don't insist on changes, then we are still condoning actions that, in a roundabout way, contribute to the deaths of American service personnel abroad.

And that consequence is not acceptable. I have many friends who will never go bald, never gain weight, and will be forever young in my mind's eye, for they are all dead, killed in Iraq. Security contracting is a dangerous occupation, and I can live with that. Such is the life many have chosen to lead, with death as a possible consequence.

But if we do not learn from our mistakes, if we, as contractors, fail to evolve such as the Army has, then to a degree my friends will have perished in vain, and others will later fall prey to identical circumstances. And silently permitting the repetition of calamity is contrary to everything I have ever been taught in America.

Just because I looked away once before, I will not do so a second time. I am one tiny voice, but this book casts light upon a wiser path. This time I stand fast, buttressed by the silent support of dead friends whose ideas on how to improve the industry are encapsulated later in the book.

The volume you hold serves not to judge but rather to explain why. It does not preach and is just as quick to point to the good as to the bad. I hope it serves as a testament to honor the silent majority, few of whom were willing to be identified by their real names, whose words and personal experiences in the cauldron of Iraq lend a human element to many of the dramas contained herein. Each anecdote pays homage to the silent majority who have somehow muddled through.

It is time for America to shrug off the fatigue of 9/11, Iraq, and Afghanistan, and to cast a long gaze upon the challenges of the future. Our world is ever more interconnected, competitive, and asymmetrical. The greatest challenge to our future prosperity and security does not lie with sleeper cells of al Qaeda, nor even with the growing conventional power of China. Instead, it revolves around our internal capacity to build a nimble and powerful counterweight against evil, combining the efforts of strange bedfellows such as the State Department, USAID, and the Department of Defense. In the future this republic will be confronted with more asymmetrical conflicts, not fewer. To that end, the need for private security companies to be integrated into the grand scheme of things is critical.

The U.S. Army is learning and adapting. Private military contractors, so integral to the future war-fighting machine, are not.

These pages, containing both lessons and solutions, were paid for at great cost in blood and treasure. They show the way forward, providing a roadmap to a better operational tomorrow. Failure to learn from the past is prelude to failing on the morrow. How we choose to study and apply the lessons of recent history will dictate whether those who have fallen in Iraq and Afghanistan have perished in vain.

We should remember that.

Chapter One

The Dogs of War

This story is very simple. If it didn't involve leaving a trail of dead Americans, Iraqis, and a host of other nationalities scattered all over Iraq, it would never make the news.

The premise is straightforward. The American taxpayer, via the federal government, has entered the coliseum of corporate warfare in a literal sense. A multitude of private companies are now in the killing business, previously the exclusive domain of the highly regulated military, which does not operate according to a profit motive.

Lacking even the most basic oversight, the private military contractor (PMC) industry rakes in huge profits predicated upon the private firms' ability to end other people's lives as cheaply as possible. The old name tag for this type of service provider was mercenary, but with the advent of public relations spin, these firms have intentionally opted for increasingly vague descriptors. Private military companies, private security details, private security companies (PSCs), and military provider firms are all kinder, gentler nomenclature for organizations that do business over the barrel of a gun. The new monikers have successfully blurred the public's perception of how these firms operate. In today's world of sound bites and fifteen-second interviews, the difference between perception and reality continues to narrow. The public finds it increasingly difficult to disassemble the spin doctors' filters placed to hide the truth.

The media have settled on "private security contractors" as a catchall term. The left-leaning fringe of American society has labeled them mercenary killers while the far right has hailed them as international patriots fighting freedom's war in Iraq and Afghanistan.

1

Many Americans first became aware of the widespread proliferation of these firms in March 2004 when they observed on television the gruesome images of the dismembered and charred bodies of four Blackwater contractors swinging from a bridge in Fallujah, Iraq. In newsreel footage eerily reminiscent of the mutilated American soldiers dragged through the streets of Mogadishu, Somalia, in 1993, the victims of such Iraqi barbarity were hailed as American heroes. But when employees of the same company ruthlessly gunned down innocent civilians in September 2007, they were denigrated as killers for hire. It is indeed true that one man's terrorist is another man's freedom fighter. The wheel has spun full circle.

As with any "overnight" sensation, the gestation period for PMCs has been decades in the making. The industry's origins hearken back to post–World War II Africa, as large tracts of the continent suffered the birth pangs of newly gained independence wrought from former colonial masters. One high-profile cause célèbre was the pseudomilitary antics of one Col. Michael Hoare.[1] This South African, a self-proclaimed soldier of fortune, recruited a few hundred Caucasians to deploy and fight in what recently had been the Belgian Congo. His undertaking was lauded in the European press for saving scores of Europeans, including children and nuns, from a grisly fate at the hands of the irregular militias that had thrown the country into a bloody civil war after gaining its independent.

The early standard had been set. Africa, as sadly is the case with so many activities relating to bloodshed and violence, became a guinea pig upon which early PMCs did their experimenting.

Four decades later, and still in Africa, private military companies brought peace and stability to war-torn Sierra Leone. Tens of thousands of innocent civilians owe their lives to a handful of South African mercenaries who rescued them from certain genocide and kept Freetown from falling to the Revolutionary United Front during the Sierra Leonean civil war in 1995.[2] During the same time frame in Europe, an American logistical firm called Kellogg Brown & Root (KBR) performed a similar feat, saving the lives of thousands of Albanians in the closing days of the Yugoslav civil war. Both events are examined in great detail in chapter 3. Such examples are proof positive case histories that demonstrate the system of outsourcing logistics or carefully defined combat operations to private contractors can work when implemented correctly.

More recently, however, other PMCs have butchered countless innocents in Iraq. Hundreds of cases of rape against American women will never go to trial as the perpetrators are beyond the reach of the law. These garden variety, mostly American, thugs were protected by a sweeping decree promising "immunity from prosecution" that spawned every criminal activity imaginable. The American taxpayer has been defrauded of hundreds of millions of dollars while security contractors are involved in arms dealing, bootlegging, and cold-blooded murder in the fiasco that is the Iraq War.

The examples are legion. One Egyptian American contractor was documented as having brutally shot a thirteen-year-old girl in the face following a firefight during which he had spent most of his time cowering on the floor of a vehicle. Another, a British national, machine-gunned a ten-year-old boy in the back after the child hurled rocks at the contractor's truck. Neither man will ever be prosecuted. Those murders are only two confirmed incidents from one small, now defunct Kuwaiti company that occurred over a three-week period in the summer of 2004.[3] The period's grim statistics fail to include the company's non-reported incidents, which represent the majority of cases of human rights violations. Currently more than 180 of these private security companies are plying their trade in Iraq, and as of this writing, they have been operational for some seven years. Even with the drawdown and tighter regulations, dozens of PMCs still operate on the streets of Baghdad, while at headquarters, focus has shifted to the new financial Eldorado that is Afghanistan.

The total tally of collective prosecutions ending in convictions that have been amassed against all security contractors since the war began is zero. Even after the highly publicized investigation initiated by the congressional Committee on Oversight and Government Reform in October 2007 following the Blackwater massacre,[4] there has been no serious attempt at overhaul save for the Department of State dumping Blackwater as a service provider. Even that change is primarily cosmetic, as most of the operational staff simply transferred to the companies that took over the contract. Granted, five Blackwater employees were indicted on criminal charges in December 2008, and a sixth employee pled guilty to manslaughter,[5] but after more than a year of legal wrangling, all charges against the five contractors were dropped because the evidence was obtained improperly (their statements were given under the promise of immunity).[6] Perhaps it never really mattered because on June 25, 2010, the company formerly known as Blackwater secured a $100 million contract with the CIA for support services in Afghanistan. Zero prosecutions is a rather impressive number when one considers that as of December 2006, according to the

Pentagon's first counting of civilians operating in Iraq (not including subcontractors), there were more than 180,000 contractors hailing from dozens of nations.[7] Every one of them was working in a completely unregulated environment where the sole common denominator was a total lack of oversight.

By comparison, that PMC prosecution rate would be equivalent to the city of Ft. Lauderdale not having had any criminal convictions in some six years. It would be even more impressive if every citizen of this Florida city had been actively engaged in a war zone and was exempt from prosecution for any crime perpetrated, should they have engaged in an illegal enterprise.

Why were they exempt? Because in 2004, L. Paul Bremer, then head of the Coalition Provisional Authority (CPA), signed Order #17.[8] This decree effectively absolved all PMCs from prosecution stemming from their conduct in a war zone. In short, they were provided with a legal, U.S. government–sanctioned license to run amok without redress of any grievance. This colossal carte blanche is fully explained in chapter 4, but it is critical to immediately understand that the George W. Bush administration essentially placed tens of thousands of armed men beyond the reach of any law.

The obvious question on the lips of the silent majority of Americans is, why doesn't the government do something about this directive?

One reason is that the full extent of the problem is known only to a tiny slice of the general populace. The U.S. government cannot easily dismiss PMCs as the regular armed forces are now so dependent upon private contractors that the U.S. Army would break down without them. The sheer numbers that follow underscore this point.

In 2006, during some of the heaviest fighting, private contractors *outnumbered* the U.S. military in Iraq. The shortfall "missing division" often alluded to in Iraq was in fact composed of private military contractors whose numbers were greater than that of the entire British Army deployed to that barren country.

The same is true in Afghanistan, where as of March 2009 contractors represented 57 percent of the force, according to a congressional research group. A citizen of Afghanistan has a greater chance of interacting with an armed, U.S. government–employed individual attired in civilian clothes than with a U.S. soldier in uniform. Even more astounding, when averaged out for the two previous years, the number rises to 65 percent.[9]

Because they are politically convenient to utilize when an official military presence can be construed as embarrassing, private military companies have undergone explosive growth in seven short years. While few details have been released about the amounts involved in specific contracts, it is estimated that of the $18.6 billion the Bush administration allocated for Iraq's "reconstruction," at least 10 percent was used to pay security companies. David Claridge, a security expert based in London, estimated in 2004 that Iraq contracts have boosted the annual revenue of British-based PMCs from $320 million to over $1.6 billion, a fivefold increase in only one year.[10]

To date, it has not been a successful expansion. The private military companies were once the exclusive bastions of former long-serving Special Forces (SF) types. Today they have been swamped by a tsunami of rank amateurs seeking easy money to accompany a government-issued license to kill.

The clients have fared little better. The clients in this case are legitimate companies tasked with the reconstruction of Iraq. Part of their budget is dedicated toward hiring PMCs while they undertake U.S. government–directed and taxpayer-funded reconstruction operations. The U.S. military is also considered a client when it outsources food, buildings, and other infrastructure. These name brand American client companies, however, are paying outrageous sums for totally unqualified personnel whose conduct is closer to an ill-disciplined street gang than to a professional fighting formation.

According to highly placed sources, it is suggested that more than half of all client companies in Iraq switched security providers in 2004, providing mute testimony to poor service. The audit trail of responsibility leads directly to 1600 Pennsylvania Avenue. It was the Bush White House that had the unenviable task of trying to explain to the American public why things had gone badly awry. After all, it was Vice President Dick Cheney, one of the primary architects of the war, who originally conceived of the military contractor Frankenstein project over a decade earlier when he was secretary of defense. As the PMC machine ran amok in a war Bush had long ago declared "over," the occupants of both the White House and the Naval Observatory had every reason to obfuscate the reality of operations on the ground. George Bush was presiding over a growing insurgency that consumed American lives at an ever-increasing rate while Dick Cheney was earning millions in delayed payments as former chairman of Halliburton, which was pulling in one "no bid" contract after another. Both of these unpleasant realities were politically untenable and resulted in enormous pressure from the White House to squash realistic military appraisals of the situation on the ground halfway around the world. The insurgency needed to be extinguished, posthaste, and the administration had little time to expend on the regulatory process overseeing a few thousand armed contractors. Owing to this predetermined "failure to listen or regulate," PMCs were often labyrinthine in their complexity, rendering any form of regulatory overhaul nearly impossible to implement. Here is a typical case study the author encountered upon his arrival in Baghdad.

When an elderly Iraqi female is shot dead by a Nepalese machine gunner in a sport utility vehicle (SUV) manned by a South African team leader and driven by a Fijian, the organizational flow chart becomes difficult to explain. The challenge is increased when the public then learns the team is employed on a contract landed by a twenty-three-year-old Canadian whose claim to fame is that he fixed torn tents in Kuwait for a living. He was penniless but walked into the office of a rich Kuwaiti who had the money to bid the security job. The Canadian entered the office as a repairer of fabric and emerged as a security project manager with a six-figure income. This transformation is all compliments of an engineering firm hired by the U.S. Air Force and funded by the American taxpayer. The auditing is performed by Indian nationals for a Kuwaiti living in Switzerland who has bank accounts in Dubai. The SUV's occupants hailed from South Africa, Fiji, and Nepal. None of those countries were involved in the Iraq War. Neither was Germany, France, Ireland, Canada, Russia, Uganda, New Zealand, Chile, Senegal, India, or myriad other nations, but their citizens were clearing upward of $200,000 a year with all expenses paid for slinging guns in Baghdad. As an added bonus, the CPA had granted every man in every firm immunity from all prosecution.[11] This is a polite way of stating that the contractors had license to kill. Or indulge in arms trafficking. Or commit rape against an American female, or smuggle booze for 700 percent profit. The best one I found was being on the active payroll in Baghdad while taking your also-on-the-payroll girlfriends to party the night away in jet-set Dubai. All of these incidents have occurred in recent years, and every single individual involved has gotten away with them.

The greatest overall losers in the equation are the citizens of Iraq. They have perished by the untold thousands, often for a crime no greater than being an unaware driver or holding a cell phone when somebody else's improvised explosive device (IED) went "boom." The true number of fatalities will never be known. Private military companies, unlike the army, are loathe to report shootings and go to great lengths to avoid documenting them, even though they are instructed to report all incidents. The reasons are strictly financial. When the army dispatches a civilian in error, an immediate investigation is launched and the family is compensated from a government fund. I saw this firsthand in Afghanistan and Iraq.

When a PMC is forced to compensate a family for a "bad kill," the money has to come from the profit margin of the PMC. As PMCs are "for profit" entities, there is every incentive to drag feet, lose paperwork, and simply deny that the event even occurred in the first place. It was always easy to blame "another security company" as so many operated in the same battlespace. The old proverb of "Dead men tell no tales" took on a whole new meaning in Iraq.

On the professional side of the equation, the biggest loser is undoubtedly that small cadre of highly competent contractors who struggled in a marginal occupation for many years prior to the gold rush of the Iraq War. These men spent decades in the armed services of every Western nation, and their knowledge, integrity, and discipline were unimpeachable. A significant number of them had been in Afghanistan since 2001, and their services had adhered to the highest standard. It was their outstanding conduct in past conflicts, coupled with their deep personal knowledge of the military, that had convinced the Bush administration that their ranks could be increased twentyfold overnight without any loss of quality. So when the call came for Iraq, the amateurs trampled the old guard in the stampede to the trough of free taxpayer money.

Amazingly, this change was all destined to occur in Iraq a year *after* George W. Bush had declared victory aboard the USS *Abraham Lincoln*. Standing beneath a huge "Mission Accomplished" banner on May 1, 2003, he eerily foreshadowed the pending debacle when he proclaimed, "The United States upholds these principles of security and freedom in many ways: with all of the tools of diplomacy, law enforcement, intelligence and finance."[12]

It was in precisely these four areas of diplomacy, law enforcement, intelligence, and finance that the U.S. government, through no fault of the citizens who elected it, would sink to lows unparalleled in the lifetime of the republic. And leading the charge across the River Styx were the private military companies.

The Silent Expansion

In January 2008, ten men attired in civilian clothes arrived on a British Airways flight from London to Nairobi. Unbeknownst to the handful of tourists and businessmen on the aircraft, the ten mute Americans were in fact private military contractors. Long thought of as only hired guns in Baghdad, private security firms silently expanded to all four corners of the globe while the media remained transfixed on the debacle of Iraq.

Away from the glare of publicity, and under the umbrella of legitimacy granted by the Coalition Provisional Authority in Baghdad, the PMCs wasted no time in lobbying to expand their sphere of influence. Based on the premise of replacing noncombat military personnel with contractors worldwide, the PMCs found a receptive audience with the military. The U.S. Army brass were thrilled at the concept of plugging civilians into noncombat slots, for it would allow active duty military to be concentrated in the battle areas of Iraq and Afghanistan.

■ ■ ■

In December 2007, Kenya exploded into ethnic violence after allegations that its presidential election was rigged.[13] Long-simmering tribal tensions erupted in the Rift Valley, and on January 1, 2008, some fifty members of the dominant Kikuyu tribe were burned alive in Eldoret. Young males from some of Kenya's forty-two other tribes had herded them into the local church and torched it. Over a thousand died in the fighting, a quarter million were displaced—all ultimately categorized by the Red Cross as homeless. Most of the fatalities were the result of machete and arrow attacks, providing some insight to the barbarity of the fighting. Private military companies wasted no time in getting there, arriving less than a fortnight after the outbreak of violence in Nairobi.

A government representative awaited the ten Americans as they debarked in Jomo Kenyatta International Airport in Nairobi. Weaving through darkened corridors, the contractors were guided through a different channel at customs and did not receive the normal entrance stamp on their passports acknowledging their arrival in Kenya. In layman's terms, there is no record of their ever having been in the country. On paper, they never existed.

Even as these specialist advisers boarded the minibus to take them to their $250-a-night Nairobi hotel, similar teams were en route to other equally exotic locales. Other missions under way were to upgrade Special Forces in Hungary, to establish a school for senior noncommissioned officers (NCOs) in Poland, and to train infantry leaders in Indonesia. Contractor Internet employment boards were rife with adverts for Lebanon, the Sudan, Liberia, Kazakhstan, Georgia, Colombia, and the Congo.

Of the ten contractors skirting customs in Nairobi, the oldest was sixty-three and the youngest thirty-two. They had collectively fought in Vietnam, Grenada, Panama, the Persian Gulf War, Afghanistan, and the Iraq War. A sample passport from just one of the men produced visas for Ecuador, Burma, Indonesia, Kazakhstan, South Africa, Turkey, Iraq, Kyrgyzstan, Ukraine, Zimbabwe, Egypt, and Jordan. Almost all of their passports had the Coalition Provisional Authority's stamp from the American occupation of Iraq.

The group represented a fairly close cross section of the society they served in terms of their views on the war. The oldest, a long-serving, retired command sergeant major of some renown, was poorly educated. His interpretation of the war was reduced to the groupthink concept that the best Iraqi is a dead one. He had found a happy home with Blackwater, where he had spent a year on the original security detail protecting Paul Bremer. He had never previously traveled outside the United States save on military deployments. He was extraordinarily right wing, considering George W. Bush a "liberal." In short, he was loud, badly prejudiced against all things not "made in the USA" (even though he was born in Canada), and a living example of the Ugly American. The youngest was a veteran of four mediocre years in the Marine Corps. He didn't seem to care about anything but his three girlfriends, his hundreds of thousands of dollars in the bank, and his steroids. He constantly bragged at every opportunity about how many people he had killed. For him, life as a contractor was a wonderful adventure novel where he got to write the script, and if that entailed machine-gunning the locals, so be it. Just as most of the shoot-everything-that-moves crowd, he had spent little time in the regular military. Extremely bright, he saw the work as an exciting, legal way to amass a fortune, and he was sufficiently predatory in nature to take full advantage of the opportunity.

Both the oldest and the youngest were violently opposed to any sort of federal oversight on contractors, but they represented the extremist point of view. The remaining eight men were more moderate, and six had been to Iraq. They acknowledged that grave lapses of judgment had occurred in the daily interactions between armed contractors and unarmed civilians, where far too often the endgame for civilians was death. Some of the men had been employed by highly professional companies such as Military Professional Resources, Inc. (MPRI), or DynCorp that took good care of them and enacted strict policy controls to safeguard civilian lives. Others had been the hirelings of the many fly-by-night firms, which were nothing more than the employers of killers for hire in every sense of the word. Several men had left in disgust, appalled at what they had seen and vowing never to return.

The thoughts of these ten men regarding the resolution of the Iraqi conflict were just as complex, divergent, and mundane as those of the rest of America. The ultra hard neocons opted for victory via annihilation while the majority, just as their fellow Americans, believed that there had to be a better way. A powerful minority, true to the contractor ethos, could have cared less either way, provided they got paid. Only a couple of the men had the intellectual capacity and the background to realize that the whole contractor experience was, in its current garb, irrevocably flawed. And they kept their opinions to themselves, not wanting to risk instant ostracism from their peers.

The truth is there are no simple answers. The debate over the validity of the Iraq War will forever shadow the Bush administration as it recedes into history. Its most enduring legacy will be the expansion of Arlington National Cemetery. Any accomplishments undoubtedly will be examined through the prism of failed military adventurism. Even today, nobody can predict the final outcome of the Sunni-Shia battle that is still being fought in the back alleys of Baghdad, seven long years after "Mission Accomplished" was proudly proclaimed on the USS *Abraham Lincoln*. A simple answer in response to anything about Iraq is an open confession of having failed to grasp the enormous complexity of the issues.

Afghanistan: The Six Year Invisible War

PMCs have undergone a different evolution in Afghanistan. Irregular Afghan militias such as the Northern Alliance, supported by American Special Operations Forces, conducted the initial invasion. The overthrow of the Taliban and the fall of Kabul in 2001 brought an extended peace upon the land, until the return of the insurgency in recent years. So while Baghdad spiraled into chaos, the other theater of operations remained relatively placid.

No one can say that atrocities did not happen in Afghanistan, for they did. But nowhere was the loss of life comparable to the scale of events in Baghdad. There were two reasons for this reduction in civilian casualties. The first was the sheer scope of work in Afghanistan. Most of the PMC contracts initially brokered were for training the Afghan security forces. Trainers, as a general rule, don't engage in combat. Or if they do, they are supervising the actions of the Afghan "trainees." Either way, this type of activity reduced the odds of direct combat between PMCs and the Taliban.

There were a few high-profile, lucrative personal security detail (PSD) jobs available, such as serving on President Hamid Karzai's team, but they remained in the minority.[14] As Afghanistan was more or less "calm" during the conflict's early years, the majority of the work (and the money) was to be found in the wilder west that was Iraq.

However, today, with the focus and the moneyshifting to the Hindu Kush, the equation is beginning to change yet again. It is interesting to note that as of December 2009, with a spike in violence and a surge in Coalition casualties, PMCs are beginning to replicate what was Baghdad's experience in 2004, with their increased presence, overt aggression, and lowered professional standards.

Brian Williams, in his nightly blog for NBC News, wrote on November 2, 2009,

> Our last moments in Kabul left an indelible impression, and I'm afraid not a good one. While we were at the airport, waiting in the parking lot to be "processed," two SUV's full of American contractors arrived: all wearing visible body armor, many with thigh-mounted ankle holsters for their 9mm handguns, and still others with conspicuous automatic weapons held across their chests. They are not alone — this kind of thing is now ubiquitous there.
>
> There is a dynamic developing in Kabul which is reminiscent of Baghdad: Highly visible American security contractors, operating aggressively in Afghanistan. They are aggressive in traffic, they are threatening-looking in public.[15]

There is the distinct threat that Kabul will become what Baghdad was.

The second issue impacting Afghanistan was one of supply. The logistical challenge of deploying a training team to Afghanistan, equipping the members, and then supporting them for 180 days until the U.S. government paid up (it is not unusual in government contracting to have to wait that long to be compensated) defeated all comers save for those with very deep pockets. This environment was quite unlike that of the Coalition Provisional Authority in Baghdad, where a contract could be awarded one day, paid in cash the next, and implemented on the morrow.

Because of the financial operating parameters, only the well-established service providers such as DynCorp, MPRI, KBR, and others had the necessary capital in reserve to allow them to bid on tenders. These large, often publicly held companies had shareholders and boards, and both groups maintained the power of stringent oversight on errant individuals at the ground level. In simplest terms, the trigger-happy amateurs so prevalent in Iraq were mostly excluded from operating in Afghanistan. It was the first step to reducing civilian casualties from PMCs.

This is not to say that Afghanistan was a success story, because it wasn't. Several smaller companies did manage to infiltrate the system and were contracted for armed security in road-building operations. Staffed largely by South Africans, these entities extracted a punishing toll from the Afghan civilians to whom they were exposed on a daily basis, but the death toll never approached the levels in Iraq.

Another key difference in Afghanistan lay with the mobility of the PMCs. With the exception of modest convoy security and road-building contracts, the majority of Afghan security contracts were brokered for either training missions or static (fixed-site) security. The result was that the Taliban, should they wish to engage in combat, would have to bring the fight to the immobile PMCs. This combat template proved to be, after the first few skirmishes, very much a losing proposition for the Taliban. Eventually an uneasy truce stalked the land. Neither side "won"; rather, the Taliban generally steered clear of areas where history, in the form of fixed PMC bases, had proven to be immune to ground attack. As the Taliban has emerged resurgent in 2009–2010, the fight is once again returning to the compounds of the occupying powers, which does not bode well for the United States and its allies.

This situation is the polar opposite of what transpired on the ground in Iraq. During the author's deployments there in 2003, 2004, 2006, and 2007, there was not a *single incident involving firearms while the contractors were in fortified base camps.* Every combat action occurred while the teams were in transit or at locations "outside the wire." PMCs in Iraq were highly mobile and thus more likely to encounter insurgents and civilians unexpectedly, resulting in casualties to all parties.

These circumstances recall the old joke about two grizzly bears in the forest. Each knows where the other lives and thus judiciously avoids trespassing on the other's front lawn. Until 2009, such was the case in Afghanistan. In Iraq, the mobility and missions for the PMCs made for a high number of unexpected nose-to-nose encounters with predictably bloody results.

The last factor contributing to the positive PMC experience in Afghanistan is one of lessons learned from Iraq. Defense Secretary Robert Gates has little in common with his predecessor, one Donald Rumsfeld.

Under Gates's tenure, the cloak of immunity from justice has since been stripped from private military contractors. They have been brought under the Uniform Code of Military Justice (UCMJ), the same set of rules applicable to the military. Uniformed commanders were granted sweeping powers of control over PMCs located on terrain the military owns.

Although not a perfect fix, it is generally considered a step in the right direction, even though effective prosecutions still remain at zero.

Additionally, the State Department has dramatically improved its Worldwide Personal Protective Services contract, which raises the bar for those who wish to sling guns for the U.S. government. Applicants can expect to undergo background checks that include criminal and credit checks, urinalysis, physical fitness exams, and so on. This protocol is a galaxy away from what once existed in Iraq. The lessons of Iraq have not yet, as of press time, been repeated during round two in Afghanistan. Drawing on inside sources, it is the author's subjective opinion that PMCs will play a huge, and in some areas, combat-focused role in Afghanistan. However, oversight has been increased, along with at least limited accountability. Those who interact directly with the U.S. Army and are supervised by armed forces personnel will properly maintain the necessary professional standards. This expectation is especially true for organizations that have a high density of former top-end military personnel such as Triple Canopy. The great risk still exists in the vast unregulated area where private companies hire private security based solely upon the predicted profit margin. This sector is still ripe for abuse, corruption, and substandard operating protocols.

If the PMCs are fully cognizant that their performance in Afghanistan lays the groundwork for a sustainable future (or lack thereof if they blow it), I expect to see a quantifiable improvement over the fiasco in Iraq.

Beyond the Scope of the Law

Utilizing private military contractors on the battlefield represents a minuscule fraction of the big picture, but it poses some of the most vexing questions to emerge from the wars in Iraq and Afghanistan. The United States of America, for the first time in its history, has funded nonindigenous Caucasian and third world personnel to conduct combat operations on its behalf in direct action roles where U.S. forces are active combatants. In addition to playing the role of paymaster, the U.S. government granted immunity from prosecution to all U.S. citizens and foreign nationals serving in Iraq in private security companies.[16] As explained previously, this decree entrusted greater lethal power in the hands of PMCs than the government does to the highly regulated military.

Immunity from prosecution is normally a tool the Department of Justice employs to let the small fish escape, regardless of guilt, in order to go after the big ones. Immunity from prosecution is only trolled in waters where all who swim in them are already guilty. There is no value in dangling the bait in front of the innocent, for no crimes have yet been committed worthy of prosecution, thus rendering the whole process meaningless. To grant immunity from prosecution before the commission of any crime by irregular hired guns in Iraq was just begging for trouble.

In the author's experience, the overwhelming majority of Americans who work as security contractors in Iraq are either ex-military or blue-collar workers attracted by large financial incentives. They do their best to be law-abiding citizens and try to do the right thing when the situation permits. They are not mercenaries, killers, or super patriots. They are rather average Americans who are attempting to pay off mortgages or debt incurred by medical care. They are trying to send their kids to college, or are supporting their parents in a retirement home, just as families all over America are. However, as in all societies, the challenge lays with the extremists. Every municipality in America has those who swing wildly to the left or the right of the moderate majority. The dysfunctional caveat with private military contractors is that they provide an opportunity for all who reside on the fringes of normal society to take up arms and be counted, too often in a fatal way. These individuals have radical beliefs that would never be granted legitimacy in a pluralistic democracy; or rather, they would be allowed to hold their beliefs, but they would not be given opportunities to act upon them at will without being subject to prosecution.

Any armed conflict draws in psychopaths, deviants, and the sleazy underbelly of any nonviolent, democratic society. Normally these individuals are only permitted access to the battlefield via the conventional armed forces. The U.S. Army does a thorough job of screening out the lunatics and denies undesirables entrance during the recruiting phase. The handful that slip through the cracks are forced to regulate their battlefield actions under strict military protocols. They face harsh penalties under the UCMJ for any atrocity committed on the battlefield.

The widespread, deeply entrenched reliance on private military companies has short-circuited the whole military system, which is based on centuries of professional experience. Contract companies maintain no formalized recruiting process designed to screen out deviants, so the potential for committing atrocities is high. However, even with zero prerequisites for filtering out the nutcases, a PMC cannot run amok unless two key government provisions are in place. These qualifiers are both profoundly negative and have never been previously implemented in the history of the United States. The first is the issue of implied endorsement while the second pertains to the lack of deterrent, which in turn is a direct function of granting immunity from prosecution. The Bush White House provided both, effectively enabling contractors, for many years, to conduct their business beyond the scope of the law.

Implied Endorsement

The issues of implied endorsement and lack of deterrent can be framed in a historical perspective. Societal norms begin to fray when the state either quietly endorses the pejorative actions of a few and/or arbitrarily suspends any disciplinary process against the common foot soldier.

Adolf Hitler's SS is the classic example of the former. Germany could hardly be called a primitive country by any measure in the 1930s. Its populace was well educated and cultured, and it led the world in many technologies, including aviation. When Hitler became chancellor in 1933, what sane person could possibly have envisioned that a farm boy from Schwabia assisted by a shopkeeper from Hamburg would be herding naked grandmothers and six-year-olds into gas chambers less than a decade later? During the intervening years the Nazi Party had endorsed the Final Solution of the Jewish Question on a national level, thus legitimizing genocide in the eyes of the German public.

In so doing Hitler and his henchmen had paved the way for the small fringe of psychopaths, sadists, and criminals who naturally exist in any society to assume positions of undreamed-of power. One would think that any normal citizen would find the crimes of the Nazi era morally repugnant to the point of refusing to partake in them. Yet because the Nazis empowered the lowest strata of the human species that had no such qualms about committing what came to be called genocide, otherwise "normal" Germans behaved in appalling ways or were complicit by their silence. A well-disciplined, intelligent society ran completely off the rails predicated upon the thought processes of the handful in power. Implied endorsement from the highest authority in the land is a powerful persuader to the masses gathered at the street corner.

Hannah Arendt observed the war crimes trial in Jerusalem of the faceless Nazi bureaucrat Adolf Eichmann and coined the phrase "the banality of evil." She could have been writing about the actions of PMCs today when she noted, "The sad truth is that most evil is done by people who never make up their minds to be good or evil."[17] She also penned that "there is a strange interdependence between thoughtlessness and evil."[18]

Removed from the Nazi context and examined carefully, these comments could well describe the Blackwater employees in the Baghdad massacre. The majority of those six men had superior military service records and had never had any serious encounters with the law. But the group mind-set prevalent at the time in Baghdad allowed intelligent, law-abiding young American men to become killers in the same way that the SS inducted sharp, outstanding Germans under the Nazi reign. These Germans, similar to the Americans in Iraq, would have balked at any thought of transgressing the law except the all-powerful atmosphere at the time not only permitted it but also encouraged it.

Another example closer to home that precisely illustrates this condition is the My Lai massacre, which was conducted by American GIs in Vietnam in 1968. Lt. William Calley, the officer in charge, represented the vested authority and power of the U.S. Army. Under the military rank structure, Lieutenant Calley had the same command authority over his infantry platoon that Gen. William Westmoreland himself would have exercised if he had been standing in that provincial village. The military is structured in this manner to ensure junior officers have the power of higher authority behind their novice rank and commands so that discipline is maintained throughout the force. A lieutenant is viewed as a representative of command presence stretching all the way back to the commander in chief, the president. Lieutenant Calley did not overtly prohibit his men from wantonly killing the My Lai villagers. Instead, he aggressively murdered many of the villagers himself and ordered his subordinates to do the same. It was therefore safe for the lowest-ranking private to assume that he had the implied endorsement of a much higher command authority, of which Lieutenant Calley was a legitimate if junior spokesperson, to commit a crime. If it was wrong, the officer in charge would tell the men to stop for he was commissioned by the president, wasn't he? Calley, however, morphed into a cold-blooded murderer as he summarily executed civilian after civilian. His men, now floundering in an already stressful environment where their leader was flagrantly breaking every rule of law in warfare, could only assume these actions were both desirable and endorsed. The result was a very dark stain in the annals of American arms, due to the foot soldiers' perception of implied endorsement from above. Likewise, the implied endorsement of the Bush administration, via funding and expansion of the PMCs, set the first of two preconditions necessary for human aberration on the battlefield and potential war crimes.

Lack of Deterrent

The removal of effective deterrents is the second facilitator of atrocities committed on the battlefield. The absence of a deterrent is indicative of indifference from a higher authority that cannot be bothered to prosecute. It can also be a systemic policy authorized to exist if it serves the perceived interest of those in power. As a general rule, *the preponderance of battlefield atrocities occurs only in an environment where the individual believes himself exempt from prosecutorial retribution.* The more disciplined and transparent the military organization is, the fewer acts of disreputable conduct will occur. The U.S. Army, both disciplined and transparent, has actually done a good job of admitting to its lack of oversight in such circumstances as the Abu Ghraib scandal and the rape or murder of Iraqi civilians. A total of ten soldiers were convicted via courts-martial, sentenced to federal prison sentences of various lengths, and dishonorably discharged, following their appalling conduct at Abu Ghraib.[19] As those convicted soldiers will attest, the sword of Damocles encapsulated in the Uniform Code of Military Justice is a powerful tool to ensure soldiers adhere to the highest standards of conduct even when tasked with the killing of an enemy.

The Balkans conflicts of the 1990s provide a clear-cut example of a situation characterized by the complete absence of deterrent. Atrocities in the form of organized rape, the sniping of innocent civilians in Sarajevo, and the outright massacres of other human beings were commonplace on both sides. Concentration camps were reestablished, and Europe was plunged into its worst genocide since the Nazis' reign some fifty years earlier.[20] The Serbian soldier operated in an environment in which he believed he would not be held accountable for his actions. In other words, he perceived himself to be immune from prosecution. According to Hague prosecutors, Slobodan Milosevic and Radovan Karadzic (both later indicted for war crimes) fostered an atmosphere of extreme violence predicated toward an often civilian enemy. This brutal campaign included a plethora of extrajudicial killings and rape camps in addition to normal military objectives.

Sadly, post-conflict events have supported the supposition of the average Serbian soldier. As of February 2010, the International Criminal Tribunal for the former Yugoslavia had formally concluded 121 trials of the 161 individuals indicted for war crimes, with proceedings ongoing against the 40 remaining accused. When viewed in light of the hundreds of thousands of deaths suffered by a civilian populace, the handful of prosecutions is a drop in the proverbial bucket.[21]

Would the Serbian soldiers have been as keen to kill if they knew they would spend decades in jail or be hanged from the nearest lamppost if caught, even by their own side? The author's subjective analysis says no.

Immunity from prosecution is the equivalent of removing the governor from a powerful engine. Without it, the driver can easily red line the entire mechanism. Private security contractors found themselves operating precisely in this type of environment in Iraq from 2003 to 2007, the period during which they had immunity from prosecution. The government of the United States, in granting immunity, met all the necessary preconditions to support an environment conducive to the rogue actions perpetrated by contractors in Iraq.

The PMC Organization

As of January 2009, over 150 private military companies were operating in Iraq. The evolution of these organizations is closer to the tribal structuring of the group of castaway schoolboys in William Golding's *Lord of the Flies* than to any intelligent process. Each company has acted in a regulatory vacuum and has thus evolved predicated upon the dictates of its own conscience in the absence of any formalized standards.

To their credit, some have done well. Virginia-based DynCorp deployed contractors to Afghanistan in 2002 shortly after the fall of the Taliban. Combining a large base of institutional knowledge coupled with an intelligent set of checks and balances, DynCorp has implemented a set of protocols, developed since 2004, to ensure professional conduct. There is a mandatory procedural checklist to follow before any operator may pull the trigger, resulting in much tighter Rules of Engagement. A review board automatically follows any shooting, and the person behind the weapon is well aware that he will be discharged and sent home if he fires without cause. A few other firms, staffed with a high volume of former military personnel, such as Triple Canopy and MPRI, have also prospered.

As a rule, large companies that can eventually be held accountable to either a board of directors or shareholders have managed to avoid most of the fallout from egregious contractor conduct. These boards and shareholders have provided a modicum of deterrent and have not unilaterally consented to unsound practices. They have thus been able to partially self-regulate in a highly deregulated environment created by the Bush administration.

Blackwater, the largest PMC, is the exception to the rule. This company, which is most guilty of succumbing to implied endorsement and lack of deterrent, finally fell into political hot water over the wanton killing of Iraqi noncombatants by its employees.

The Congressional Committee on Oversight and Government Reform states it best:

> Incident reports compiled by Blackwater reveal that Blackwater has been involved in at least 195 "escalation of force" incidents in Iraq since 2005 that involved the firing of shots by Blackwater forces. . . . In addition to Blackwater, two other private military contractors, DynCorp International and Triple Canopy, provide protective services to the State Department. Blackwater reports more shooting incidents than the other two contractors combined. Blackwater also has the highest incidence of shooting first, although all three companies shoot first in more than half of all escalation of forces incidents.[22]

As all PMCs are loathe to report shootings, these numbers must, in reality, be considered as only a minute fraction of what really happened.[23]

The notable point is that Blackwater, at the time, was privately held. As such the company lacked both a corporate board and shareholders. This setup allowed the owner, Erik Prince, free reign when it came to the operational protocols he implemented for his organization. This lack of accountability contributed to the abuses perpetrated by his employees against the Iraqi populace.

This abject lack of accountability has haunted Erik Prince's company from its earliest days. The reading public will doubtless remember the horrible incident where four Blackwater contractors were ambushed, dismembered, and their body parts hung from a bridge in Fallujah. Public sympathy ran high and George Bush ordered in the Marines to pulverize the city. What is less well known are the results of yet another congressional investigation, this time aimed at discovering precisely what went wrong on that fateful day.

The documents reviewed by the committee indicate that Blackwater embarked on this mission without sufficient preparation, resources, or support for its personnel. According to these documents, Blackwater took on the Fallujah mission before its contract officially began and after being warned by its predecessor that it was too dangerous. The company sent its team on the mission without properly armored vehicles and machine guns. And it cut the standard mission team by two members, thus depriving them of rear gunners. Blackwater took all of these actions before sending the team into an area known to be an insurgent stronghold.[24]

It is interesting to note that DynCorp, a publicly held company, has not suffered similar pitfalls though it operates in the same environment as Blackwater. MPRI, which is run by a former chief of staff of the U.S. Army and has training units throughout the world, has also never been investigated for egregious conduct. The overwhelming majority of those in management are former career military and its professionalism reflects its pedigree.

With the exception of Blackwater, the gravest issues lay with smaller, amateur companies lacking experience, depth, and the prerequisite sets of checks and balances. They also do not have boards, shareholders, or a high concentration of career military. These new entrants, in a quest for unheard-of profits, are content to push self-engineered standards aside in light of two powerful persuaders—implied consent from higher authority and lack of deterrents for wrong doing. These companies have zero incentive to improve when there are zero penalties for subpar practices.

That human rights violations against Iraqi civilians have not been higher is proud testimony to the professional conduct of the thousands of contractors who do uphold standards of ethical conduct. Just as the ten contractors deployed to Kenya did, the vast majority of the men and women currently working in the combat theater have done their best to provide exemplary service in an exceedingly difficult environment. These individuals have attempted to keep civilian casualties to a minimum. It is a record they can be justifiably proud of. Sadly, it is always the case that a few on the fringe spoil it for the vast majority who press on and try to do the right thing.

The Role of PMCs at the Strategic Level

Nation building is one of the most difficult challenges imaginable. The restructuring of a failed state requires long-term financial commitment, along with guarantees of security and improved infrastructure. The effort to win hearts and minds may well take decades before final "victory" is declared.

The nation builders must operate within tight specifications to ensure collective success. There is scant room for turf battles, and all elements must work in a carefully choreographed effort to ensure government entities are striving toward a common goal. A failure in one area creates a ripple effect across the entire occupied population and reduces the overall chances of success.

What nation builders do *not* need in the process is an international conglomeration of armed security companies completely exempt from guidelines applicable to all other organizations involved in the rebuilding effort. These companies are at cross-purposes with the final goals of peace and prosperity. PMC profit margins stem from continuous strife. As such, they have little incentive to closely follow protocols that will eventually result in their own demise.

Imagine how the citizens of Los Angeles would feel if a foreign occupying power permitted some twenty thousand armed civilian contractors to run roughshod over everyone without any legal recourse whatsoever. In this scenario, every one of those twenty thousand men would be his own judge, jury, and executioner. And what if thousands of these paramilitaries were from other nations not even involved in the war but had powers identical to those of the occupier? By failing to invoke regulatory oversight at the national level, this situation was exactly what happened for the crucial first few years in Baghdad. Granting contractors immunity from prosecution only exacerbated an already bad situation further. The contribution of the PMCs in terms of diplomatic and logistical security roles must be viewed in light of their destabilizing influence on the overall effort at nation building. Several high-ranking, anonymous sources at the State Department I interviewed personally contend that private military companies' biggest contribution to the rebuilding of Iraq was the role of loose cannons on deck. Any objective onlooker would surmise that U.S. foreign policy as it pertains to Iraq is built on a foundation of double standards. Conduct that would never be remotely appropriate in a Western democracy is deemed acceptable in an occupied third world nation. Oddly, this doctrine runs precisely opposite to that of U.S. Special Forces, whose role is to win the hearts and minds of the local population.

America's Reputation

The international image portrayed by the private contractor has badly damaged the world's view of America. We are proving to be as capable of performing just as shoddily as the rulers of Myanmar do when it comes to our inability to restrain the state-sanctioned security apparatus.

By outsourcing applied violence as a marketable commodity, the Bush administration has legitimized an industry considered anathema to the rest of the world. America, with Bush at the helm, chose to chart a course where final victory was the only yardstick that mattered. Dubious moral and legal practices involving the use of PMCs have severely eroded America's standing as a beacon of legitimate business practices in an already dark world.

The Human Cost

In times of war, the most grievous damage is not done to physical objects composed of brick and mortar but rather to organisms composed of flesh and blood. That private contractors are operating outside the bounds of the conventional armed forces raises grave concerns about their mental health.

War fucks people up. It is the most profound experience on the planet, and the stressors upon one's mental equilibrium are directly proportional to one's proximity to and the intensity of combat.

When mature societies go to war, they recognize that the demands placed upon the young men and women who volunteer to fight them are extraordinary. To that end, armies are created that, with state funding, study and practice war. Armies are specifically designed to kill the enemy as quickly and efficiently as possible. Modern armies also have a well-thought-out series of checks and balances defined in the regulations pertaining to soldiers in combat. Military support includes psychological screening services, counseling, medical attention, and the treatment of posttraumatic stress disorder (PTSD). All of these actions are designed to allow the individual soldier to eventually re-assimilate into society as a cognitive, functional human being. Intelligent societies have no wish to send sons and daughters off to war and to have hardened, amoral killers return.

PMCs, however, have created a conduit to precisely that nightmare. PMCs provide a shortcut to the horrors of war and create a petri dish for the evolution of the individual bereft of national controls. How the fringe elements of these organizations eventually cope with the normal world remains to be seen. PMCs present a channel for idealistic young men, along with deviants and sadists, to assume a life-and-death power over a populace that is often unable to fight back.

Insurgencies are the most difficult conflicts in which to engage. Without enemy uniforms and front lines, insurgents are indistinguishable from civilians, placing a serious mental burden on the occupier. The insurgency that U.S. forces face in Iraq is similar to what it experienced in Vietnam.

The contractors are working in a vacuum devoid of all the cultural yardsticks that Americans associate with progress. We are a quantitative society and feel most comfortable with numbers, charts, and graphs. All of those elements are poor evaluators for a nebulous war of hearts and minds, especially one that is fought in a broiling foreign landscape in the midst of a totally alien culture.

Lacking battle lines that can be drawn on a map, the soldier or contractor has difficulty in determining who in fact is winning the war. The situation often appears hopeless, lessening the combatant's desire to push forward. Losing friends to enemy action further alienates and lowers the morale of personnel engaged in sporadic combat. Lacking the means to identify quantifiable gains, troops begin to question their mission as their presence seems to make no difference in the big picture.

In Vietnam, Afghanistan, and Iraq, Americans were confronted with an irregular force that dressed and acted exactly like the civilian populace. This blending exacerbates the difficulty of winnowing the insurgents out from the broader civilian population. As a result, the soldiers and contractors, unable to communicate in the corresponding foreign tongue, begin to regard every civilian as "hostile." This view further alienates the contractor from the society where he should be striving to win hearts and minds. The result is a destructive, self-fulfilling prophecy whereby the contractor's actions become overtly hostile, thus fomenting the same from the civil populace in return. Far too often the endgame increases the ranks of the insurgent enemy.

Confronted with an invisible enemy who employs IEDs and snipers to randomly kill, the military and PMCs retaliate by gunning down everyone in the vicinity of the explosion to avenge their dead and wounded comrades. It is the only time they get to shoot back at an invisible enemy who is everywhere and nowhere simultaneously. When viewed as a whole, this maneuver box is extraordinarily destructive for the human psyche.

The results are predictable. Suicide rates for the U.S. Army are double what they were in the mid-1980s. On June 11, 2009, CNN's senior Pentagon producer had a solemn announcement: "The Army said the total number of potential or confirmed suicides since January stands at 82. Last year the army recorded 133 suicides, the most ever. Earlier this year, army officials saw the suicide numbers moving up, and by February said the service was on track for a record year for suicides."[25]

In addition to the penchant for self-extermination, the problems of alcoholism, PTSD, domestic abuse, and failed social reintegration are all ugly by-products of those fighting a counterinsurgency war. Statistics are only available for the armed forces, however, as PMCs do not maintain records of personnel issues. Mental health concerns are not tabulated by PMCs as that would entail additional expenses incurred against the profit column. But what is known is that a hard core of military contractors has been in combat since the beginning, with tens of thousands of others having come and gone.

We know how much difficulty the army is having in coping with stressors initiated by combat in an asymmetrical operating theater. What is not known are the stressors carried by private contractors, many of whom have been in combat since 2003. It is safe to say that the stress of seven years of continuous warfare must be profound.

Private contractors who admit to suffering from "combat stress" will invariably lose their jobs. Any who choose to vocally oppose the brutal policies condoned by many companies are told in no uncertain terms that they "lack the intestinal fortitude" or that they "are cowards" who are no longer capable of "doing what needs to be done." In this way management is able to redirect the focus from the company's policies and to the contractor in question. This dodge is a common ploy; even I have been exposed to it on more than one occasion throughout my career. Other individuals interviewed for this book have encountered similar experiences, and several examples are examined later in this volume.

The grotesque reality is that individuals suffering from severe psychological issues are permitted to continue to work because the cost of replacing them is greater than paying compensation for any Iraqi family member who a contractor may have killed. These problems are all by-products of profit-driven entities where the bottom line is the dollar as opposed to the individual on the front line.

Tens of thousands of young men, contractors in Iraq and Afghanistan, are maturing under the mistaken assumption that the law of the gun supersedes all else. The impact that these hardened individuals will have upon society should the fighting ever end is a point of serious concern.

"War is Hell," William Tecumseh Sherman once stated. Just ask any reticent grandfather who still suffers nightmares stemming from the action he saw in northwest Europe over sixty years ago.

The paradox is that by permitting the existence of PMCs we are removing all the societal controls on human exposure to combat. Professional armies built these regulators laboriously over a span of centuries. In discarding them, we are directly exposing our youth to the most destructive process on the planet without any form of societal oversight. And we are doing so all in the name of corporate profit.

Now What?

The reality is that private military companies are here to stay. How we choose to integrate them into a national war-fighting plan says as much about us as a society as it does about those we permit to serve in the ranks of PMCs. With appropriate oversight and training, PMCs have the ability to become a prized asset and play a vital supporting role in the future crises of this country. By permitting the status quo, which is a disaster of the first magnitude, we are trumping morals with dollar signs. We are selling off our long-cherished beliefs in justice, equality, and habeas corpus to the highest corporate bidder. President Dwight D. Eisenhower, in 1961, urged his fellow Americans to "beware the military-industrial complex." PMCs are simply a new offshoot of the same entity.

The unregulated use of military contractors has proven to be a grave liability for the just and lawful foreign policies of the United States.

On October 31, 2007, the unlikely coalition of Senators John McCain, Lindsey Graham, and John Warner drafted a powerful letter to the attorney general nominee, Michael Mukasey, attacking the use of waterboarding as a form of torture.[26] Colin Powell, in an open letter to John McCain, quietly noted, "The world is beginning to doubt the moral basis of [America's] fight against terrorism."[27] The former secretary of state also alludes to how it will "put our troops at risk."

As the United States is a great democracy, it is up to its people to clearly express what they will and will not tolerate. Silence is often interpreted as implied endorsement and fuels the propaganda of our enemies by allowing them to proclaim that we do not care.

The issue of how to treat private military companies should be employed as a litmus test to determine the moral character of the United States. Is this republic prepared to utilize any means necessary in warfare? And if so, are private military contractors, regardless of motivation and nationality, a prized national asset to be deployed with pride in future conflicts? Do they truly represent all that is good concerning the United States of America?

The American public is unaware of the vast majority of contractor abuses that occur in Iraq and, to a lesser extent, in Afghanistan. If the reality were made known, the industry would go bust tomorrow. It is disturbing to consider the possibility, however, that most contractor abuses have gone unreported because the American public no longer is concerned enough about anything in Iraq/Afghanistan to attempt to redress the grievance.

Is it perhaps that the reading public is too fatigued over the despondent process of fighting two wars to really care about a handful of civilians armed with assault rifles who are shooting up civilians who many Americans consider the enemy anyway? And the media won't touch the story as it no longer sells?

If so, then the future of the world's most powerful democracy looks dim indeed.

Moreover, if our leaders cannot overhaul this issue of enormous national importance in a bipartisan manner, our international standing will sink even lower than what it is today.

The good news is that the policies of the U.S. government do not always accurately reflect the feelings of its citizens. The American people are proud, noble, and generous. They have carried more than their share of the burden of freedom and have given profligately, in terms of blood and money, to other nations engaged in legitimate struggles for freedom. Eventually, it will be the American people, who clearly understand right from wrong much more so than the government that rules them, who will implement reform at the grassroots level. It will finally percolate upward. Positive change will come. But before change can take place, the people must seek knowledge. Knowledge, the catalyst to promote change, is in the pages of this book.

Chapter Two
The Contractor Experience: Iraq

The personal experiences of contractors in Iraq since 2003 are as diverse as those of their grandfathers who served in the Second World War. Every year since the invasion of Iraq both the intensity and location of fighting have varied. Fallujah in 2004 was a death trap for contractors. Three years and two massive attacks later, it was one of the most peaceful locations in the country. Men serving in convoy escort roles began their service in soft-skinned trucks armed with a pair of cast-off AK-47s. As the insurgency intensified, the same gunner would have transitioned through perhaps three different series of escort vehicles, each one more heavily armored than the last.

A contractor could deploy for a year and never hear a shot fired in anger. The next man could expend hundreds of rounds of ammunition on a daily basis and consider it completely routine to be shot at four or five times a week. Any given day in any location could be blissfully calm or deadly violent or both.

The contractor's war is different from that fought by the military, though it is equally life threatening. Although contractor casualties cannot be accurately compiled without federal assistance, all individuals well connected to the industry agree that employment as a private security contractor is one of the most dangerous jobs in theater, with casualty rates higher than that of the regular U.S. armed forces.

Steve Fainaru of the *Washington Post* concurred: "Private security companies, funded by billions of dollars in U.S. military and State Department contracts, are fighting insurgents on a widening scale in Iraq, enduring daily attacks, returning fire and taking hundreds of casualties that have been underreported and sometimes concealed, according to U.S. and Iraqi officials and company representatives."[1]

Human conflict is a difficult enterprise to document, for every person observes the fighting through the filter of his or her own observations, past experiences, and thought processes. A relatively minor skirmish to one experienced veteran may seem utterly terrifying to a newcomer. By documenting the furnace of combat through the eyes of many, a sort of collective experience begins to emerge. The accounts that follow are diverse enough to underscore the individual recollections but similar enough in nature to enable the reader to discern that of the collective whole. It may come as a surprise to many that these anecdotes lend credence to the Bush administration's initial statements that Iraq was ripe for liberation. The truth is that the Iraqi people secretly longed for freedom from tyranny just as any other enslaved nation does. The personal narratives of those who arrived early in the occupation, during 2003 and early 2004, do not paint pictures of growing insurgencies and violence; rather, they encountered a populace delighted to be delivered from the evil caprices of Saddam Hussein.

Intelligent interpretation of these personal case histories points not to a flawed invasion, regardless of the existence or lack thereof of weapons of mass destruction, but to an utterly botched plan for the rebuilding of Iraq's national infrastructure. Had the Bush White House paid as much attention to the rebuilding of postwar Iraq as to the military plan to conquer it, there is ample evidence to suggest that the Middle East would be radically different than what it is today. Bush's plan for a placid democracy in the Middle East may have been much closer to fruition than his detractors will ever give him credit for. His Achilles' heel proved to be his lack of wherewithal and desire to implement assertive nation building immediately upon the cessation of hostilities. All of the accounts encapsulated here suggest that for up to a year, from April 2003 to April 2004, there existed a golden window of opportunity for the Americans to peacefully reconstruct vital services.

James Stephenson, the director of the United States Agency for International Development (USAID) in Iraq and a veteran of twenty-five years of post-conflict reconstruction in such locales as Lebanon and Serbia, would agree.[2] This expert in nation building had the following to say about the Bush team sent to oversee Iraq's reconstruction and, in fact, referred to the Coalition Provisional Authority, the de facto government of Iraq for over a year.

"Many of them spent only three to six months in Iraq and were on their first trip overseas. Few had any overseas development experience, and many were former Republican Party campaign workers, supporters, and fund-raisers or Bush administration political appointees."

He goes on to state that "but most advisers were learning on the job, with an astounding lack of preparation in either life experiences or training. More than a small number could only be described as 'loons,' who pursued pet agendas, oblivious to the damage they could cause. Unfortunately, all were generously empowered to run Iraq on behalf of Ambassador Bremer and the CPA. It was their 'most excellent adventure,' and we were along for the ride."

Many of the personnel at the "boots on the ground" level who were interviewed for this book consider the Iraqi insurgency was a natural reaction to two problems that transpired during those first invaluable twelve months. The first was the chronically lethargic pace of American-directed reconstruction. Most Iraqis were worse off a year after the invasion with regard to basic water and electrical power services than they had been under Saddam Hussein's rule. This situation was not what had been promised and stirred considerable resentment, resulting in violence. Overpromising without delivering is a poor format for nation building.

The second concern was the appalling conduct of private security contractors who often left a huge swath of dead civilians behind them whenever they drove out of their heavily armed compounds. It is also true that the American military also occasionally fell prey to the "shoot first, ask questions later" syndrome. But the army personnel were nowhere near as trigger happy as their civilian contractor counterparts, who seemed to feel a compulsive need to pull the trigger at every opportunity. The first security contractors to arrive were extremely professional, but the nearly overnight expansion of their ranks, especially in 2004, resulted in a dramatic decline in quality and respect for human life. For every Iraqi civilian who was needlessly killed, a family unit of insurgents was instantly born. How many opted to pick up arms against the occupiers after burying an immediate family member will never be known, but the numbers must certainly be in the thousands.

The insurgency was practically nonexistent in 2003, however, when the first contractors arrived on the heels of the victorious American Army. Baghdad was a much different city then, as these narratives show.[3]

■ ■ ■

In the beginning, during the late spring and summer of 2003, private contractors were a rare breed and nearly invisible on the landscape. Small in numbers and highly professional in quality, the early stories are a far cry from the disaster that was to befall the country in the months to come.

One man, a former American Special Operations soldier whose real name is Jon Tripp and whose life would later be shattered by an IED, recounts the earliest days, only weeks after the regime was toppled. He provides a different view from what was seen in later years on American television.

For me, the whole thing kicked off on August 4, 2003, when I arrived in Jordan. So it was still less than six months after Saddam had fallen. From Amman, we traveled in soft-skinned "Dolfeens" [Chevy Caprices] from Jordan to the Baghdad Sheraton Hotel. For the entire move we carried neither weapons nor body armor. We had no protective gear of any kind. We didn't need it.

Within three weeks of arrival, my company was moved to the Al Safeer Hotel, about a mile from the Sheraton and outside the official Green Zone. That was before it was known as the Red Zone. It was actually just another neighborhood in Baghdad and lacked any formal security measures. At the time, this was not a problem. Those who stayed there were mostly Iraqis, a few Kurds or Turks now and again, and a Westerner or two. We would all meet in the dining room for dinner and talk about the current info within Iraq. It was quite the eclectic and opinionated group. As I got to be friends with them, I started to receive better and better inside info on whether or not an attack was going to happen that day or the next. I stayed at the Al Safeer for about four months. One of these gentlemen, Iraqi born, is still a friend of mine. In fact, with my wife, we have traveled throughout Europe together on vacations. Of course, I can no longer admit to knowing him as now I would be considered fraternizing with the enemy and my security clearance would be subject to review. But back then we did everything possible to integrate with the locals.

Eventually, as the security situation began to deteriorate, I would stay away from the hotels and live openly in the city outside the Green Zone in homes with local staff. I did this for ten months. During this entire time we were completely at the mercy of the locals should they have harbored any ill intent toward us. I was never attacked, never accosted, and generally treated with the utmost courtesy for that period. Every now and then they would whisper to us that we should avoid such and such a place tomorrow. More often than not, like clockwork, there was an attack or a bomb where they predicted.

During my year living on the local economy, usually between six to seven o'clock every evening, all of the private security contractors would get together in the Sheraton near the pool to share intel. I had a Coalition Provisional Authority [CPA] card so I could also go into the Green Zone and get the military's intel. Our intel was usually more accurate and up-to-date than the military's. However, I would share it back and forth between the Personal Security Details [PSD] and the military head of security. We were all working for the same side in those days, and the level of cooperation between the military and private contractors was still very high.

Jon goes on to recount the history of his Iraqi staff in 2003.

My staff consisted of two former generals of Saddam's military. The first, Aziz, had fled Iraq after the first Gulf War and ended up advising the British during the current invasion. Fateh, the other, had his men surrender to the first U.S. troops they saw, and he then served as an advisor to the U.S. military as they advanced. I had forty other Iraqis working for me. Twenty-five were utilized as stationary guards for our client, and fifteen were used as escort security for the client when they moved around. One of the escort team members, a sharp-looking Iraqi called Ramsi, was a former bodyguard to Saddam. We used to joke about it together in front of a client or someone like that. I would say, "Ramsi, what would you have done if someone had shot at Saddam while you were protecting him?"

He would turn away and step to the side like he was getting out of the way of the bullet and letting it hit Saddam. My clients loved it and would just end up in tears laughing so hard.

This former paratrooper, a tall, gangling, ultraprofessional by the name of Leonard Toon, arrived in 2003. He had similar, positive impressions of the locals.

I trained all my locals in security, ate with them, and became friends with them. As an African American it was a bit of a challenge to begin with, but both sides adapted quickly. The highest compliment they can pay you is to invite you to their house for dinner. I went several times to the homes of my employees to meet their families and have dinner with them. Unfortunately,

I ended up sick each time due to the water and how the food is prepared. Afterward I would have to be on antibiotics and Imodium for a week due to evil diarrhea. Of course, as soon as I was better, another would invite me to dinner. I went as it was an honor, so I could not possibly say no. However, my abdominal tract paid the price for about a month until I had visited everybody at least once.

The value of endearing yourself to the local population in the early days becomes evident in this anecdote from another early arrival.

Also at this time I was traveling throughout Baghdad meeting potential clients, both Westerners and locals, and even the U.S. military. I was in negotiations to provide trained security details for them. I met with the UN (car bombed four days later), Food for Oil, COTECNA Inspection S.A., ABT Associates, Citicorp, the Danish Embassy, the Bank of Baghdad, the Jordanian Embassy (car bombed the next day), the UAE Embassy, etc. I would also try to meet with some of the more important Iraqi leaders in Baghdad. Just trying to foster a good relationship. I let them know who we were and what our client did so they knew we were not here to hurt but help. We ended up with a lot of good warnings to stay out of areas at certain times, which I would pass on to the CPA.

This American, a Special Forces NCO, recalls a similar level of professionalism and enthusiasm among fellow contractors in the early days.

I loved it. I was working with total pros. There were no personality conflicts, everybody worked together, and a lot of things got done. I have no doubt that we would back each other up. I actually looked forward to getting out of bed every day. The sense of teamwork and camaraderie was awesome, and I have never seen anything like it, before or since, save for combat with a military unit. I had a great time doing something worthwhile. I spent nearly two years there and left only when it was evident we were going to totally screw it up. I have nothing but good things to say about most of the early contractors, the military, and the majority of the Iraqi people. I am proud to have served and if the circumstances were identical would be honored to do it again. I knew what I was getting into and have no regrets.

In the late spring of 2003, several companies utilized Iraqi staff without any ensuing security problems. This Pole, a former member of their ultra-elite Operational Mobile Reaction Group (GROM) unit and now serving in Afghanistan, remembers:

> I was also using the escort security teams to run border missions to and from Jordan and Kuwait, either bringing people in or taking them back out. At this time there were no passenger flights in or out of Baghdad. So you had to come in through Kuwait or Jordan and drive in. We also ran the odd job for business or government personnel already in Baghdad. They didn't have enough people to cover them in all their travel, so I would supply a team or two of Iraqis with vehicles to help escort them throughout Baghdad. The Westerners were always surprised to begin with by the arrival of a crew of armed Iraqis but none ever complained afterward.

As the summer of 2003 turned to autumn, a schism slowly developed between security companies that employed local Iraqis and those that did not. It all boiled down to a matter of trust. These reflections come from two contractors who allied themselves with the Iraqis, trusted them, and used Iraqis for security details as opposed to the ever-increasing number of foreigners flooding into the country. Their recollections suggest that a different course could have been pursued much earlier in the budding insurgency with very different results.

Jon Tripp again remembers:

> It was easier and much more pleasant to visit with the local establishments and Middle East embassies than with the Western ones, even as an American and former serviceman that I am. The Westerners treated us like a nuisance, especially when they found out we used Iraqis, at which point most wouldn't talk to us at all. In comparison, the local businesses/leaders treated us like friends. It was rough on the health though. Every time we met, first I would have to leave all my weapons and no guards could come with me, only my interpreter. Then we had our formal greetings, and then a cigarette and a cup of tea half filled with sugar would be put in front of me. Normally they smoked hand-rolled or Turkish cigarettes, which are very harsh. But for me, they brought out the best, Marlboros. The more affluent Iraqis could afford a few packs on the black market and would produce them on special occasions.

I was invariably a special occasion, and they were very proud to be able to do this. We would smoke and drink the tea, then talk about pleasantries, then another cigarette, and either more tea or Turkish coffee, which is closer to varnish than Starbucks. If they liked you, after tea and cigarettes they would set up a second meeting to discuss business. That was fine, but I don't smoke or like sugar. I would go to two or three of these meetings a day in the middle of Baghdad, no weapons, and smoking and drinking sugary tea. I would feel sick by the end of the day, but that was the way they did business. I learned how to speak all the basic greetings and their replies, learned their customs, and did things their way. I studied Islam and the Koran. Why? I was in their land, in their homes, and I truly wanted to help and be friends. Also, accordingly to Sun Tzu, and [Special Forces] doctrine, "The fastest way to destroy an enemy is to make him a friend," and this was the fastest way to do precisely that. Back then, though it sounds stupid now, we were winning.

Another American contractor also had a Special Operations background. Adhering to its winning-hearts-and-minds methodology, he had a similar experience.

I guess it would have been September or October of 2003. I regularly went to local restaurants and shopping down the streets of Baghdad. I trusted my local employees to advise me and keep me safe. I never stayed longer than thirty minutes, and I never went back to the same area within the same month. The locals at these establishments, and the ones who lived on these streets, loved it. So many people stopped to talk and laugh with me. They welcomed me, said Allah bless the U.S. for saving them, kissed my hands, took pictures of me with their arms around me. They all wanted to know where I was from in the U.S. and what it was like. Most said that they hoped they would get a chance to visit the U.S. in the future. When I did start having expatriates show up to work for me, or any other Westerner I became friends with, I would take them to one of these restaurants. The food was excellent and the people were all very nice. Once I even had an Iraqi family at the restaurant pay for our meals just to say thank you for liberating them.

As the winter months arrived, the first premonition of the chaos to come slowly began to trickle down to the men in the field. This observation by an American who has requested anonymity describes the confusion between the military and the initial wave of contractors, resulting in the first forays into the black market for the purchase of weapons.

When private contractors first got to Iraq, the U.S. military didn't know what to do about them. They wanted to help, but had no guidelines on civilians with weapons and such. However, if you already had a weapon, they didn't ask you about it. It was so difficult to bring any equipment in that we had to start using the black market. The only exception was Blackwater, but they were with the CPA mafia and could do and get whatever they wanted. Everybody knew they were Bremer's Praetorian Guard and were first in line for everything, including arrogance, immunity, and ego. Anyway, I used to do deals for trucks, weapons, ammo, and anything else we needed down the backstreets of Baghdad at night. My teams would have to stay several blocks away. I brought an interpreter with me and had large sums of money on my person as everything was cash on the barrelhead. It was a big risk, but it was what I had to do to get the job done. I did not ask who they were, or where they got the weapons. For that night we were friends, dealing with each other as such, and who knew what would happen tomorrow. Maybe they would have to shoot at me, or I at them. It was understood.

But even with the deteriorating security situation, the early professional contractors still stood firmly behind the winning-hearts-and-minds campaign. This excerpt is from Hamish Burling Claridge, a New Zealand Army platoon sergeant who had served in East Timor, Bosnia, and the Solomon Islands. As of this writing, he is still in Baghdad, years after the events described here. He still recalls the early days with something approaching fondness.

At one point I was traveling throughout Baghdad conducting route and site surveys with a small expat team coupled with local Iraqi support. I was lucky enough to be working with guys I had served with in the military. Over time, the needs of our client, a civilian U.S. company tasked with reconstruction of power plants, had changed and required more traveling. So we needed several full expat-run Iraqi teams going every day. Everyone treated everyone else well. No problems. The expats brought in were all professional, ex–Special Ops types, or at least extensive military and security backgrounds. They were from New Zealand, France, England, USA, etc. Everybody had the same idea about "hearts and minds." We considered ourselves in their country as guests, and should act like it. We were all getting paid top dollar. None of us "wanted to" nor were we "itching to" kill Iraqi people. We were there to protect our clients. To prevent something from happening. We felt that if we had to shoot, it was the last resort. We were not the military; therefore, our job was to protect the client by running away and only advance toward the fight when [we were] caught in a corner and had no place to go.

One of the advantages the initial wave of contractors had was their vast experience. Part of that pool of knowledge enabled them to keep things in perspective and to make the best of a bad situation. War is a very wrenching experience emotionally, and the ability to crack a smile at the right time can go a long way to maintaining morale, as Jon Tripp recalls. The newcomers were found to be lacking this strength.

November 21, 2003. The Baghdad Hotel is hit with a suicide car bomb. It is one street back and a few blocks over from my hotel. The military shows up and puts razor wire around it, and stations U.S. military guards in vehicles inside the wire. Neal and I thought we would liven things up for them. So out of the dark, a couple blocks away, here we come, holding hands and skipping down the street. At first they locked and loaded, then when they figured out what we were doing they just all busted up laughing. We made their night. Neal would be killed one year later in Basrah.

Times began to change. What was once a closed circle of professionals in a niche industry was rapidly going mainstream with the expansion to match. The days of everybody knowing each other in the tiny contractor community were coming to an end. As the demand for private military contractors increased, so did the need for recruiting fresh personnel. The standards varied widely, depending upon the need and professionalism of the company.

A former Green Beret recalls,

When I got the call and spoke to the recruiter about Iraq, it was like old home week. I had served with over 50 percent of the employees when they had been in the military with me. It was the easiest ramp up ever. They said, "Can you be in Kuwait City in three days ready to go?"

I said yes and stepped off into theater that very weekend. That move was smoother than any I had done with the Special Forces.

Others placed on a standby basis found the waiting to be frustrating. One slated for Baghdad, a civilian with little relevant experience, remembers:

I was told to plan on deploying the following Friday, twelve days hence. So I quit my job, spent over three thousand dollars on extra personal items I thought I would need, and waited. No airline ticket and no call. I phoned them and they told me to stand by as it could be delayed. I waited for nearly six weeks, being informed each Friday that it was sure to be the next. By then I was fed up and finally went with another company that seemed to be better organized.

Another, interviewed and hired over the phone by an individual he never met, had to turn down a contract because he was unable to deploy the very next day.

Very few companies provided packing lists. Most flew by the seat of their pants and simply stated, "Bring what you think you will need."

The old hares, men with decades of military service and years spent on deployments, arrived in country with exactly what was expected of them. Others, especially those with police or civilian backgrounds, lugged in an amazing collection of personal articles totally unrelated to operations in a war zone. If nothing else, this mass of material underscored how completely ill prepared some of the civilian contractors were for Iraq. One attempted to bring in golf clubs, hoping to knock out a few holes in war-ravaged Baghdad. Another, a self-proclaimed redneck from the South, fought a losing battle in an attempt to fly over his favorite hunting dog so it could "get" some Iraqis.

A British contractor with time in the commandos and already with nearly a year in country explains the arrival of a civilian recruit in the summer of 2004:

He arrived with an awkward suitcase inside of which was a Stetson cowboy hat. He had no neutral-colored clothing in tans or browns. But the best was when we discovered a set of really expensive fishing tackle. He had been planning to spend the evening hours fishing from the bridge over the Euphrates.

Doubtless he would have been killed in minutes, but I was gobsmacked by the level of unpreparedness displayed by so many individuals who only had to watch the news to understand what exactly they were getting into. It never ceased to amaze me.

The means of arrival into the theater were limited. One drove overland from either Kuwait or Jordan or one flew into Baghdad on a charter flight. The following anecdote is from the author's personal experiences of Iraq, where he served in 2003, 2004, 2006, and 2007.

The narrative picks up after he arrives in Kuwait City the evening before and departs for convoy escort duties to Baghdad just a few hours later.

Just like many millions of Americans, we began to prepare for the morning commute. The gun trucks, in this case radically modified and armored Chevrolet Tahoes, rolled up to the front of the hotel with military precision at 4:30 a.m. All black, with massively reinforced chassis complete with armor and turret, each displayed the warning sign in large red letters "Danger, stay back 100 meters!" in Arabic and English.

With a last sip of stout Arabic coffee, I settled my bill at the hotel in Kuwait City, and we rolled north to the frontier, averaging about 90 mph [miles per hour].

The American checkpoint was brisk, efficient, and polite. We were soon marshaled and in less than an hour were guided over the border into Iraq.

A short 400-meter drive took us to our own compound, in this case a couple of metal sheds and a pair of mobile home–type trailers.

Inside could be found the usual array of lockers, beds, and a washroom familiar to all whose jobs require transient quarters in remote environs.

The supervisor, after introducing himself to me, pointed to a locker and indicated it was mine. I pulled out body armor, radios, medical kits, and all the other paraphernalia of war.

Showing me to another trailer, he opened the door and simply stated, "Help yourself."

The trailer was literally stuffed to the ceiling with AK-47s, rocket launchers, Western assault rifles, submachine guns, hand grenades, and other assorted sundry that specialized in going "Boom" on command. In the corner were propped a pair of 20mm cannon, no less. I settled for a Belgian FN heavy assault rifle, a smoke grenade, and a fragmentation grenade as I was responsible for manning the belt-fed machine gun on the Tahoe. There was no point in carrying too much.

I asked him if I had to sign for anything.

"No," was all he said in response. "There is no accountability required here."

Another inbound American, a former Marine whose name is Dan Tucker and whose heroic actions are described in chapter 8, spoke of the airplane flight. It was a newly established Royal Jordanian Airlines charter into Baghdad from Amman, Jordan.

As I strolled toward the gate it was not difficult to identify those on my flight. There was an overabundance of clothing in tans and grays, mostly with labels like North Face, Columbia, and Marmot. Nearly all wore some type of desert boot. Few were clean shaven; most were sporting a few days' stubble while several cultivated the Fu Manchu goatee so popular with contractors at the time. Every form of English accent imaginable could be heard: English, American, Canadian, Australian, New Zealand, Swedish, Norwegian, Fijian, Nepalese, and even a Ugandan. I remember they kept to themselves, and other passengers in the terminal avoided them like the plague.

The flight itself was on a small Jordanian charter with perhaps fifty seats. There were no women passengers. There wasn't any service either. There was a marked difference in the demeanor of those flying into the city. The veterans spoke of this and that and were very nonchalant. The fresh meat inbound for the first time were as silent as the grave some of them would eventually find.

The plane maintained a high altitude until we were directly over Baghdad International Airport [BIAP]. Then, without warning, the pilot pushed the stick over, the nose diving for the ground, and we fell like a stone, maintaining tight spirals all the way. The veterans laughed and the newcomers looked just plain terrified. Of course, we were descending rapidly to present the least possible amount of time as a target. More than one newcomer thought the plane had been shot down. This acrobatic descent continued until we were only a thousand feet or so off the ground. The only time I ever got slightly queasy was the last five hundred feet with wheels down and flaps deployed. We were banking onto final approach near a few buildings, and a competent insurgent with an RPG [rocket-propelled grenade] could probably nail us with a lucky shot. Perhaps that is why the Americans always had attack helicopters patrolling the sky when civilian aircraft arrived.

The only other thing worthy of mention that I recall was there was no type of taxiing to speak of. Our plane made a beeline for the terminal, and the bags were unloaded with the utmost haste. The engines never stopped for if mortars started dropping bombs the plane could depart instantly. No sooner had the last inbound backpack come off than the first outbound one replaced it. The aircraft would reload for the flight out in minutes. Fifteen minutes after touchdown it was taxiing out at a speed that would send the pilot to jail in America. It reached the end of the runway, applied full power, and was aloft again within twenty minutes of having landed. Those lucky souls heading for Amman held their breath for the first five thousand feet or so and then sighed with relief for they were out of gunfire range. That was Baghdad in 2004.

Upon arrival in the terminal the inbound contractor would theoretically be met by his company representative though it didn't always work this way. There were delayed flights, unexpected arrivals, and so forth in a country where communications were still primitive. There were cases when individuals were stranded at the airport for a day or two, unable to get word out of their arrival. They were reduced to sleeping on the floor by the luggage belts and scribbling notes to passersby, asking for them to be delivered to the company they were to work for.

For a few, their first intimation of the magnitude of violence that awaited them proved more than they could bear.

Leonard Toon, the African American operator who had been there since the earliest days of the invasion, provides this revealing anecdote.

We were waiting on the tarmac for a group of a half-dozen new personnel. The head office had warned us that one of the new hires was a point of concern as he seemed overly bloodthirsty. This was always an issue for us as we had found that those who had really been in the shit up to their ears rarely spoke of it.

We needn't have worried in this case. The aircraft arrived and the new men off-loaded. The individual in question, a young man in his early twenties, seemed very agitated.

It was just then that a massive car bomb detonated several miles away. It was a bad one, and we could feel the concussion as jet-black smoke billowed into the air. I knew instantly that a lot of people had been killed.

The new kid was as white as a sheet. He never said a word but just turned around and got right back on the plane. He had seen enough and wanted nothing to do with it. He flew out ten minutes later, having spent a total of perhaps three minutes on the ground in country. We divided the contents of his luggage among us, each man taking whatever he wanted. We knew he wouldn't complain. We never heard from him again.

During his conversations with the author, Leonard expressed the feelings of many others who were interviewed when he commented about many of the young men flooding into Baghdad from all over the world in the summer of 2004.

We had a lot like him, you know. Guys with wild haircuts and "Kill them all" T-shirts, bragging to all within earshot about how many ragheads they would personally dispatch to Allah. It was all bullshit, of course, as if they were trying to prove to themselves how brave they were. They were always the first to come unglued when the bullets started flying. We were to discover that it was the quiet guys, those who most resembled "normal" society, who were the most dependable when the shit hit the fan. Eventually we became very leery of self-proclaimed heroes, and if one seemed too aggressive or trigger-happy during the interview in the United States we made sure he was quietly turned down. Assholes all, and eventually I left the industry because I met too many "cool" people who were proficient at killing civilians but weren't quite "cool" enough when it came to the heavy lifting like that practiced by the regular military. They were jerk offs and most would be in jail if they stayed at home. I never want to see them again.

A former garbage collector from Chicago turned security contractor has a different memory of arriving in Baghdad.

Our team leader met us in the airport and escorted us to the underground parking garage. In the back door of the crew cab were weapons, helmets if we wanted them, and body armor. We put on the armor, loaded the weapons, and climbed aboard while the bags were tossed in the back. Five minutes later we were gone, headed for our encampment. The driver kept the accelerator floored as we zoomed down the road from BIAP to the Green Zone. The media later called it the most dangerous strip of road in the world. I would agree. About halfway there I heard a bang, and then everybody started firing toward an apartment on the right. I couldn't see anything to shoot at, but I fired along with everybody else in the same general direction. I assumed we were being shot at. The truth was I didn't have a clue but just kept pulling the trigger as it seemed to be the right thing to do. I have no idea what I hit. The shooting lasted for maybe fifteen seconds before we were gone. About twenty minutes later we pulled into camp. I had been shot at on my first trip out from the airport. I realized then that this was going to be one hell of an adventure tour. No regrets, though I did lose several friends. But no regrets.

In 2004 the security situation in Baghdad was beginning to deteriorate. It was also a time when the insurgents were still willing to stand and fight in conventional shoot-outs, a far cry from the hidden bombers and snipers of today.

There were times Baghdad itself was more akin to Dodge City than a modern metropolis. The U.S. Army, the only real authority, could not be everywhere at once. The result was frontier justice, as this contractor from California recalls.

It had been a very quiet day, and we were in transit home after dropping off our engineers at another location. It was just the two gun trucks. We were driving home, minding our own business, when from across the open median a couple of insurgents in a beat-up white sedan opened fire on us. It was a single male in the back who gave us a quick burst of AK-47 fire before they sped off. As per usual, they missed.

We had had enough, and Chuck, the team leader, yelled, "Turn around and let's get them!"

Both our vehicles U-turned and sped across the dusty median, accessing the other highway maybe two hundred meters behind the sedan. We increased speed, starting to weave in and out of the traffic. We closed the distance to fifty meters and both SUVs pulled up alongside the other, occupying both lanes. Everybody who had a clear field of fire leaned out of the windows and commenced to engage with rifles. It is hard to fire from a moving vehicle, but we were scoring hits. Of course, the civil populace on the road was terrified, and cars were smashing up all over the place trying to avoid the gunfight. The insurgents maybe fired a burst or two back, but mostly they tried to escape by outdriving us. With our big V-8s that wasn't going to work. We were closing and scoring more hits. I could see bits flying off the sedan as our rounds struck home. There was no longer any return fire.

They finally tried to escape by driving the wrong way up an off ramp toward an overpass. That was a bad call on their part because one of our trucks was equipped with a pedestal-mounted machine gun, which fired to the rear when the gate was open. We hadn't been able to use it till now. It spun 180 degrees, stopping on the verge, and the former South African paratrooper manning it opened up.

That sedan looked like it got hit by a five hundred–pound bomb. It was all over in an instant, but the gunner raked it for another ten or fifteen seconds, practically sawing it in half. I have never seen such a mess, before or since, and the results could hardly be identified as human. As there was nothing further for us to do, we left the wreck and bodies where they were and continued on our way, still minding our own business. The sedan burned behind us.

Upon occasion contractors would employ covert tactics in order to move unnoticed. A common trick was to dress like a woman in a full-length burka, the black robes concealing all but the eyes. This tactic was a dangerous one as it increased the odds of being shot by American forces if they suspected any males in the vehicle were possibly insurgents. However, by riding in non-SUV-type vehicles, the contractors could swim in an insurgent sea without undue attention. In this particular instance it probably saved this New Zealander's life. He picks up:

In this case there were two of us in an old, battered Chevy Caprice, which seemed to be every third car in Baghdad. We were poodling along but had weapons pressed against the doors ready to shoot through them if problems developed. A few minutes later a small car pulled up alongside. It was a single male and he seemed wary but at peace. He gave us a long, hard look and for an instant our eyes met before he glanced elsewhere. He slowly pulled forward and slid in the lane ahead of us. It was no major drama and I thought nothing of it.

A few minutes later we could hear the sirens and see the flashing lights in the rearview mirror as another contractor company approached with a three-vehicle convoy. It was one of the firms protecting the State Department. I could tell because nobody else used sirens back then. They roared past us in three black SUVs, guns out the windows and lights flashing. About thirty seconds after they had passed us, the same guy from before stepped on the gas and drove into the middle of them.

The explosion was huge, and I distinctly recall watching a black SUV pull a cartwheel in the air. It wasn't until then that I realized that I had been looking at the suicide bomber. I often wonder if he knew we were infidels and was simply waiting for a juicier target or whether we had actually deceived him. I guess I'll never know. But I still wonder.

The author personally recalls a close brush with death at the hands of the American military. No protocols regarding military-contractor interface had yet been developed, sometimes leading to fatal confusion.

It was our first mission at night, in the summer of 2004, and we were returning from BIAP after delivering one of our static guard contractors to the airport. His father, also a contractor, had just been killed and the son was flying home with the body. It was just a few days before the official handover, though the dates would be moved forward at the insistence of the CPA.

It was maybe one o'clock in the morning. The roads were empty and we were running without lights. You use your headlights only when you have to; otherwise, it makes it too easy for the insurgents to target you. Anyway, we came barreling off the elevated highway, and lo and behold, maybe two hundred meters ahead was an army checkpoint. The Joes were scrambling into the prone while the barrel of a M1 Abrams locked on to us. It was like staring into the Manhattan tunnel, even at that range. The guy on the Humvee with the .50-caliber was also tracking on our windshield. We were about to get blown to kingdom come by our own side. They must have thought we were suicide car bombers.

Our driver saved the day when he flipped on a set of flashing blue and red lights we had purchased for precisely this situation. Both vehicles slowed way down, and we crawled up to the checkpoint with windows open but guns in. After conversing for a moment they waved us through. I think they were just as relieved as we were at not having shot up friendlies. Neither side was used to seeing much traffic at night, and we were the first contractors they had encountered during the hours of darkness. It was only afterward that my knees actually trembled for a second or two as I realized how close I had been to dying. It was just one of those things, and there was nothing you could do about it. But that was the way it was, and if you didn't like it you could always go home.

The risk of being shot by your own side was an ever-present danger even during the daytime. The author was on a convoy escort mission from the Kuwait border to Abu Ghraib, which is located in the suburbs of Baghdad. He records the approach to Baghdad and the ensuing confusion.

An hour later we penetrate the environs of southern Baghdad. The evidence of recent fighting is everywhere. The first thing I see are twisted guardrails, road signs hanging at crazy angles, and a glistening pile of 5.56mm shell casings. Military presence abounds with the Iraqi Army and police out in force. Bright pennants are flying from their new Humvees and Dodge trucks, courtesy of the American taxpayer. Bradley fighting vehicles and Abrams tanks still occupy the critical intersections, lurking behind concrete barriers with only the gun turrets visible. It sucks for them as the absolute lethality of the vehicles condemns the crews to a year's rotation of total boredom. No insurgent would ever even begin to contemplate anything under the gaze of those far-reaching cannon. Off to the right, a pair of Apache helicopters circle like birds of prey, ready to fall upon those who make even the slightest miscalculation. From the center of the city, a lazy pillar of thick black smoke gently boils up into the light blue sky. I can discern the blare of sirens near the base of it. So it is a Wednesday morning remarkable only in its total anonymity when compared to all other Wednesday mornings in this violent city. It is a cookie-cutter copy of the last two years of Wednesday mornings and doubtless will remain so for all the Wednesday mornings of the foreseeable future.

The only difference is that there will be fewer and fewer people around to see them as the death tolls continue to climb.

As we turned off the highway and began the final five-mile drive into Abu Ghraib, the turret machine gunners, of whom I was one, become very busy people. We are transiting a residential neighborhood, which is a rabbit warren of houses, alleys, and roofs. This is insurgent country. Iraqi military posts dot the area, but they are poorly marked and generally best identified by the gun pits. The Iraqi Army now uses Humvees à la Americans, but still ride around in the back of pickup trucks à la insurgents. Insurgents often wear blue shirts à la Iraqi Police. Private Security Companies use Iraqi gunners in the back of pickup trucks à la the Iraqi Police à la the insurgents. Insurgents wear civilian clothes à la civilians, of which 98 percent of the residents of Baghdad are. A large number of civilians drive pickup trucks, à la police, à la insurgents, à la everybody. And everybody's greatest terror is the suicide bomber with a car packed with high explosives, randomly cruising the streets, figuring out who he is going to take with him when he meets Allah.

And finally, dear Joe, through no fault of his own, tends to shoot at everything that is not obviously American military. Sometimes it is better to just keep driving when some insurgent takes a couple of potshots rather than risk unleashing a mini version of World War III if all the main players are in the neighborhood. We gunners have only a split second to determine friend from foe and take the appropriate action. I am utterly beggared that the so-called friendly fire incidents are as rare as they actually are.

The narrative continues once inside the city.

We are now in Baghdad proper, and as the road becomes more congested with city traffic the gunners have to switch tactics. Leaving the machine guns [MGs] ready to go, we all reach into the turret box and pull out small arms. My personal choice is a twelve-gauge pump action shotgun. Now the problem is that if the insurgents are literally in the car next to us I cannot depress the MG quickly enough to engage. Hence the shotgun. The drill remains the same. We scan the rooftops and then peer into cars, looking for hands. If I can see their hands it doesn't matter what the rest of the body is doing for I am safe. I continue to curse the idiot who invented window tinting to keep the heat out, for it reduces my ability to see into the backseat. The insurgents know this, of course, and thus keep most of their shooters in exactly that location. They don't care if we shoot civilians by mistake. But we care so must take the extra second or two to confirm before pulling the trigger. Some good people have died trying to make sure it was indeed the bad guys, only to react a hair too late. Of course, this results in shorter tempers on our side with a correspondingly higher casualty rate for civilians who didn't react fast enough. There is no workable solution to the problem short of outright peace. Thankfully, tinted windows are still something of a rarity in Iraq.

We grind to a halt at the Ministry of Transport. The place is covered in concrete blast barriers, and the walls are festooned with machine gun positions. The Kurdish guards are happy to see us, and we get waves and smiles. Turning into the approach lane, I wave my hand at all following traffic. To a man, they apply brakes and stop, leaving some two hundred meters between us. Nobody tries to creep forward as to risk doing so is inviting a burst of MG fire through the radiator. The noise diminishes and it gets very, very quiet as we clear the barriers. I remove the ammunition belt as we pass under the watchful eyes of the sentinels.

For the next two hours we try to stay cool under the blazing sun. It is about 130 degrees today, nowhere near as bad as next month will be. There is a covered shed with an old billiard table so a few of the boys take turns playing pool. The local Iraqis, all male, sit on each other's laps and hold hands. These gestures are considered far too intimate in the Occidental world but quite the norm here. We are used to it and don't even bat an eyelid. Such is another afternoon in the life of a convoy protection dude.

The Untold Fight for the Supply Lines

PMCs were eventually tasked with the protection of the ponderous supply trains. The resupply routes for the military were broken down into a number of selected highways, or main supply routes (MSRs), and each bore a different code name. Most of the fat, slow convoys that kept the massive American presence in Iraq supplied originated from Kuwait. Foreign nationals such as Indians, Pakistanis, and Filipinos constituted the drivers. The American Army lacked the manpower to protect all but the most critical of cargo so private military companies picked up the slack.

The MSRs themselves were advantageous as they provided specific routes with known checkpoints. Quick reaction forces (QRFs) in the form of motorized American infantry were available as were helicopter gunships if the tactical situation permitted it. The convoy vehicles carried the global positioning system (GPS) and the security contractors were linked with the military's monitoring system. This software marvel, when coupled with GPS, allowed the real-time identification and location of every unit on the move. If contact with insurgents or IEDs was made, the team leader needed to only push a panic button and his location and identification would immediately start flashing at the nerve center manned by the military. The appropriate response could then be initiated. The glitch was that the PMCs had to register with the military and obtain a "trip ticket" to be entered into the system. Many of the fly-by-night crowd abstained from doing so, and thus when they were engaged it took forever to get the military to intervene.

A final advantage of using specific routes was that combat support center (CSC) stations were set up to provide overnight laagers for the convoys. A combat support center is similar to an interstate interchange with hotels, restaurants, and gas stations all located in close proximity. The convoy personnel could eat, sleep, refuel, resupply, and be provided updated intelligence all at one heavily fortified location.

The CSC's sole disadvantage was predictability. By transiting only a few well-established main supply lines, the Coalition forfeited the element of surprise in favor of efficient response. The insurgents were cognizant of this shortfall and realized that it was only a matter of time until Coalition vehicles appeared. Thus all insurgent attacks were focused on what is really a narrow corridor of road links connecting the country.

Among contractor circles, some of the routes are notorious. MSR Irish was the name given to the Baghdad Airport–Green Zone run, dubbed the Highway of Death and made infamous by the media. MSR Tampa was the big one, linking Kuwait to Baghdad. It was a three-day trip and involved stopping overnight at CSC Scania, located about ninety minutes south of Baghdad. Everybody stayed at Scania as the next day meant only a short hour-plus drive to Baghdad, and then you had all day to deliver your supplies. The Iraqis were not the most efficient, and lengthy (meaning all-day-long) delays were the norm. Nobody wanted to get stuck in Baghdad after dark, so all elements, following delivery of the cargo, would make a short high-speed beeline back to Scania. That meant a good feed in the army chow hall followed by a solid night's sleep and roll out in the wee hours of the next morning for the long drive back to the Kuwaiti border. It was a highly popular routine with most crews.

MSR Tampa supports the highest percentage in terms of total supplies carried to U.S. forces and was therefore the scene of particularly ferocious fighting, especially in the southern approaches to Baghdad. These overlooked battles were noted for a lack of prisoners taken on either side.

It was only a matter of months after the official war ended before the move-countermove sequence began for the unheralded battle of the resupply routes. To start with, the insurgents would crawl up to the ditches on both sides of the highway to emplace IEDs under the cover of darkness. The Americans strung razor wire in the ditches in response.

Then the Iraqis cut the wire and moved into culverts beneath the highways to bury bigger bombs. The Americans welded the culverts shut and placed tanks on the overpasses, which allowed them to utilize thermal technology to detect human activity at great range. Many insurgents died unknowing because an Abrams tank's heat sensors had been tracking them from thousands of meters away.

The Iraqis, now wary of tanks, avoided placing bombs near overpasses and focused on the empty areas between them. The Americans inserted sniper teams armed with .50-caliber sniper rifles and night scopes with a range of 2,000 meters in every direction. These teams were stationed at intervals covering the dead spaces that the tanks could not.

The Iraqis turned to pressure-activated devices that exploded when a vehicle rolled over them. The Americans developed a "sweeping" device, mounted on the front bumper of a Humvee, that prematurely exploded the bombs and minimized damage. The Iraqis added a time delay to the IED's timing mechanism to explode a second or two *after* the sweeper rolled over them so they were directly beneath the vehicle at time of the explosion.

Eventually there were so many bomb craters and potholes on the road the Iraqis stumbled onto the next trick. They inserted IEDs in the bottom of the craters and filled the holes with oil. Cement dust was applied and mixed until the color of the mixture matched that of the road.

The private military companies responded to these threats with superior armor, additional weapons, and better communications. Machine guns, which were originally able to fire only to the rear of the convoy, were repositioned in top turrets to achieve a 360-degree field of fire. The wooden stocks of AK-47s were removed and replaced with folding stocks to allow more maneuverability inside the cramped confines of an SUV. Laser sighting systems with holographic displays were mounted on weapons to support instantaneous target acquisition.

This system of punch and counterpunch continues to this day. It is over these highways that private military companies fought a campaign of ruthless skirmishes well away from the public eye, which was focused exclusively on official military casualties emanating from Baghdad.

This anecdote from a former Marine aptly details the savagery of these small unit encounters. A convoy is returning from a run into Baghdad and is approaching a notoriously dangerous overpass. However, the American Army began to station tanks there only the day before. As documented in this example, it is likely that the insurgents had not yet discovered this new tactic.

We approached the overpass. The recent sandstorms had deposited large sand dunes on the roads. To the amazement of all, an insurgent, either extremely brave or extremely stupid or both, had just been found digging a hole in the sandbank with a shovel to emplace a bomb. Joe was on the other side of the overpass and had promptly stopped traffic and taken a potshot at the bad guy with his M-4. The insurgent ran and was now some two hundred meters away, trying to traverse an open field toward a nearby village. If he made it to the hamlet, we knew he would disappear. Our guys wanted to engage, but Joe told all to hold fire. We understood why seconds later when an Abrams tank rumbled over the embankment. Without further ado, the driver stepped on the gas; the tank lurched forward and rapidly began to close the gap. The Iraqi glanced over his shoulder and must have known he was running for his life. The grim reaper was reaching out and already had the scythe on the back swing.

Not wanting to miss the show, several members of the PSD teams halted by the drama unfolding before their eyes were soon on the roofs of their vehicles, cheering like they all were attending a college football game. Only this was much better as for once we had actually found a real, living bomber. IEDs are cruelly indiscriminate. They kill wantonly. It could as easily be a family of four blown to bits as an American soldier. So the bombers get very short shrift from the security forces. We all hate the invisible enemy, and this one was, for once, out in the open.

In a matter of seconds, the tank had closed to barely fifty meters behind the wildly weaving bomber. The coaxial machine gun opened up, ripping huge divots of earth slightly to the left. The cheers increased to a thunder, as if the home team had intercepted the football. The Iraqi had zigged and the gunner had zagged. For his efforts, the bomber had bought himself a few extra seconds of terrified existence. He never tried to surrender, and we would never have taken it. He had opted to play a hard game and this time his number was going to come up and there would be no tears from us. The coaxial ripped off another burst of fifteen rounds. Rooster tails of dirt flew up just a hair to the right. The Iraqi, obviously starting to become exhausted, started another zigzag. Only this time the gunner matched him, fired a long burst, and tore him to shreds, large gobbets of flesh flying off as the rounds hit home, the dismembered carcass collapsing in the field. All those in attendance broke into a huge cheer of approval. The tank returned to rounds of applause, smiles, and plenty of thumbs-up signs. Nobody was overly bothered for the death of a human being, myself included. The corpse was left in the field. Perhaps the wild and ever-hungry dogs will have a good meal for a switch.

During the interview I asked this former Marine if he really wanted the fallen Iraqi to be consumed by feral dogs. He paused for a moment then replied, "Eat well, my four-legged friends."

An Australian of enormous legend, a true mercenary with combat time in the former Rhodesia in the 1970s, contributed this story of an IED attack on his convoy. At the time of the attack most of his peers were old enough to be at home living on Social Security.

Not five miles later we hit an IED. This time it was manually detonated, the team observing the fleeing pair of insurgents in the ubiquitous pickup truck. A thunderous report and a billowing mushroom cloud of black smoke from the center of the convoy was how the team leader described it. Explosive Ordnance Disposal [EOD] later determined it to be a pair of 105mm howitzer shells wired together so it was a pretty substantial affair. Lead gun truck turned around to count the dead and to assist the still living.

We were lucky. One transport flatbed had been near the detonation. Doubtless our way-above-average road speed had made the timing of the explosion difficult to gauge. The only damage was a few shell fragments through the front of the cab and a lot of splinter damage to the flatbed itself. Practically all of it was superficial, which was amazing. One tiny, jagged fragment had penetrated the rear window of the vehicle and pranged off the helmet of the Indian driver. He didn't even have a headache. The only damage was a bit of a smelly cab, as the driver, not used to being blown up in his day job as a taxi driver back in Delhi, had promptly shit himself. Not once, but six times he informed us with eyes still wide. Defecation is the body's way of naturally lightening the load prior to fight or flight and happens far more often in combat than many think. Well, the Indian was most certainly lighter.

The remainder of the trip was completed without further incident.

A German contractor with no military experience recounts this ambush from the early days of convoy protection, before the Iraqis had developed the tactical expertise that they soon were to display. He would go on, years later, to run his own security company in the Balkans. At last contact, he was entering the gray world of arms dealing.

We were approaching Baghdad from the south. We were also nursing a sick tractor trailer, and our speed was vastly reduced. We were averaging 25 to 30 mph so we were all a bit anxious. IEDs weren't all that common yet but there had been some, and we didn't wish to add to the list of people blown up by roadside bombs.

From out of nowhere we got ambushed from the right side. It was the most bizarre thing I ever saw. They were maybe fifty meters away, and all of a sudden up popped eight or ten guys from shallow slit trenches where they immediately opened fire at us.

Like that of most Iraqis, their shooting was pathetic. They just go to full automatic, and after the first shot the rest go straight up in the air. The AK-47 is a pig of a weapon to control on full automatic, and these guys were useless. But the most amazing part is that they stood up, in broad daylight, in full view of our riflemen and machine guns. The truth is that had they remained in their slit trenches and engaged us from behind cover, we would have been in deep shit. There is no doubt we would have had some people hurt.

Our guys returned fire from inside and it only took a couple of seconds for the machine gunner in the rear to traverse around and open up. It was like knocking over bowling pins. They didn't move, didn't try to take cover, just stood there and slugged it out. Not one of them went for cover, even when the guys on each side were shot to pieces. I do not question their bravery, but their stupidity is beyond comprehension. Thank God they were thick as bowling balls; otherwise, we would have been in serious trouble.

The war continued to degrade, with fewer and fewer of the main supply routes considered safe. Eventually the southern part of the country, that of the British-occupied enclave near Basrah, would turn violent. The Shias who inhabited this area were among the most peaceable in the country. That was no longer the case as evidenced by this anecdote, recounted by a former London policeman turned contractor for one of the many U.K. firms in action in Iraq.

In another completely unrelated incident, another friend in a different company was hit. The driver lost his arm, and the man behind him was killed. Errol had a piece of shrapnel punch through his helmet, leave a bloody furrow across his forehead, and tear out a jagged exit hole on the other side of his helmet. The frightening part is that the attacks are now occurring in the south, areas that once were deemed relatively safe. There is no answer to these huge IEDs currently being employed. One's only hope is not to get hit. The resources required to effectively defend the highways would require two-thirds of the army. Just last week a conventional rocket was fired into a tanker truck at Safwan. Safwan was once as safe as London as it is within spitting distance of the border of Kuwait and is the staging area for a huge cross-border resupply operation.

The first time we got lit up was pretty amateurish. We were just leaving Safwan when we were attacked from the edge of town. Thankfully the "towel heads" [Iraqis] were first timers as they engaged us from point-blank range. The RPG rockets didn't detonate as we were too close for the warheads to arm. But there was a loud thud, the truck shook, and you could see a tail fin sticking out of the rear quarter panel, which was a pretty hairy occurrence for all concerned. The perpetrators were dispatched to Allah with the utmost haste.

The next lot tried it again about a week later and managed to hit a big fuel tanker. The black billowing smoke was visible for miles. The common consensus was that for them to shoot up a fuel tanker at Safwan is something akin to being robbed at gunpoint directly outside FBI [Federal Bureau of Investigation] headquarters in Washington. The base of the flagpole is no longer considered safe ground. We knew then that this was going to be a long haul war and all the talk of victory in the near future was rubbish.

The situation around Safwan continued to deteriorate throughout 2005 and into 2006. Much of the fault laid with the various militia groups, mostly Shia, who took to playing both ends against the center. The British military were slowly withdrawing, leaving contractors to fend for themselves. The situation was becoming increasingly ugly. Another British contractor recounts:

We had two of our Fijian drivers kidnapped a couple of weeks ago. A vehicle with black balaclava-hooded men with AK-47s jumped them just outside the compound and bundled them into the backseat. It proved to be a short kidnapping. Our lads weighed about 250 and 280 pounds, respectively, and both were well over six feet. So they cracked a pair of heads and exited the vehicle at about 20 mph. Both survived the impact with the gravel and immediately were on their feet, moving as quickly as possible. The Iraqi Police were in the area and came across our running pair. They gathered them up and took them to the local station. Problem solved, or so it seemed to us when we were notified. We sent over a vehicle to pick them up.

It was in fact only the beginning. The major in charge, an individual of dubious reputation, refused to release them. Robert, our project manager, was appraised and drove over to speak to said major. The police were not budging and refused to cut loose the Fijians. They began hinting about the huge amount of paperwork these two had caused, which is Iraqi-speak for bribe time. Robert asked to see the charge sheet. There wasn't one. It was a shakedown, pure and simple. They spoke for eight hours and were no closer to resolving the issue than when they started. Robert excused himself and stepped outside. He called the British Special Forces compound in Basrah, explained the situation, and asked for help. It didn't hurt that Robert had spent twenty-odd years with Special Forces previously, and one of his former soldiers was now in charge of the squadron. Within minutes, a pair of Sea King helicopters stuffed to the gills with Special Forces was en route to the prison with intent to break Iraqi heads.

Back inside the jail, the phones began to ring off the hooks in a matter of minutes. The British Army had liaised with the locals and kindly informed them that the wrath of God was about to arrive at the Safwan jail via Sea Kings and wished all a pleasant trip to eternity. The major's cronies, anticipating serious depletion of their ranks, were all calling in to urge the major to release the Fijians without further ado.

Two minutes later the Fijians walked out, the helicopters about-faced, and Robert was left with a rather exorbitant bar tab at a Special Forces Mess.

However, as in all things Iraqi, it didn't take long for the corrupt police to strike back. The story continues with the same set of players.

About a week later, while we were all up country in Iraq, a group of policemen overwhelmed our own security at our compound in Safwan. They threatened to kill the families of our guards if they didn't comply. Sadly, when the local constabulary are in bed with the militia and they are leaning on you, most locals don't have much choice. They complied. As a result, many of our remaining weapons, to include machine guns, were confiscated. The militias also helped themselves to GPS's, portable electronics, and some very nonwarlike things like iPods, sat [satellite] phones, and personal laptops. The official reason was that the documentation from the Interior Ministry was lacking. This was bullshit as the Interior Ministry didn't have any documentation to follow in the first place. So it was a setup.

Around the same time frame, several other private security companies were stopped by the same gang of some forty-odd policemen and had weapons, vehicles, and everything else stripped. They were left standing on the side of road, several miles from home, with nothing more than the clothes on their backs. It is illegal for any Coalition elements to fire up the police, so the militias have flooded them with their own people. The majority of the police are nothing more than legalized militia gangs. They are effectively exploiting a judicial loophole in order to bully and steal outright for their own (and their militias') personal gain. Protests from the private security companies to Baghdad just enter the black hole of Iraqi government, never to see the light of day again. So one night we all sat down and figured out what we would do when our turn came. We didn't have long to find out.

It was less than a week later when the militia halted the company in question on the highway. Thankfully, the company had rehearsed for precisely this occasion as the continuing narrative demonstrates.

Robert was in charge of our three gun trucks, returning in the early afternoon. As if by magic, a swarm of Iraqi Police, many wearing balaclavas, emerged and blocked the road. Our favorite major was at the head of the mob, smoking a cigarette and doubtless preparing to add to his collection of vehicles and weapons. They were anticipating another bloodless coup and had not really deployed in a tactical formation, which was a mistake.

Robert never missed a beat. Speaking rapidly and quietly into the radio, he instructed the other two gun trucks to deploy into an L-shaped position so as to have the Iraqis covered in a lethal cross fire if necessary. The vehicles dispersed accordingly. The militia postured, threatened, and waved weapons, but did not fire.

Robert debussed, I tagged along, and we met the major halfway. The conversation went something like this.

Major: You are being detained and as a result of violating Iraqi law must immediately surrender all your weapons and vehicles in accordance with Iraqi law. You lack the necessary paperwork from the Ministry of the Interior to operate legally.

Robert: Our current contract is for the Ministry of the Interior. What is the specific paperwork you wish to press charges against?

Major: Your weapons cards lack the necessary Interior Ministry Stamp.

Robert: No, they don't.

Major: Yes, they do.

Robert: No, they don't. No weapons cards in the Coalition have approval stamps yet as the Interior Ministry have not standardized them.

Major: Enough of talk. You are under arrest. Lay down your weapon immediately.

Silence for about twenty seconds.

Then very precisely, Rob reached up and pushed the transmit button on his radio three or four times. This creates a squelching noise in the earpieces of other listeners. This was the prepare for combat signal. Machine guns were tightened into shoulders, laser sights turned to full illumination, and all the vehicle teams save for the turret machine gunners debussed and took up firing positions in the sandy soil. I could hear the safeties being switched to Fire and flipped mine at the same time.

The militia became very agitated. Some took cover on the ground while others ran to the vehicles. There was a lot of screaming. The major was incensed.

Major: I said, YOU ARE UNDER ARREST! LAY DOWN YOUR WEAPONS IMMEDIATELY AND MY MEN WILL NOT FIRE.

With that, the major tried to push past Robert and walk back to his semi-hysterical police/militia. Rob followed squarely behind him and intentionally began to step on his heels with every pace. The major was very distraught. This game continued for another twenty meters or so, Rob deliberately stepping on the man's heels harder and harder. Finally the major had no choice but to do something. He was practically screaming when he turned around.

Major: WHY ARE YOU WALKING RIGHT BEHIND ME AND STEPPING ON ME? I COULD HAVE YOU SHOT!

Robert (in a very clear, calm voice): I just want you to understand that at the sound of the first shot, you will never hear the second as it will already be in your head.

And with that, Robert cleared his Glock 19 and, lightning fast, ground it into the major's ear before anybody on either side could react.

Had the world ever held a competition for people to act as if frozen in place, this group would have been medalists. The only visual motion during that eternal half minute was the rapidly increasing stain on the major's trousers as he urinated all over himself.

By sheer happenstance, at that point in time an American military convoy was beginning to grind by. The lead Humvees, recognizing the Mexican standoff for what it was, rapidly covered the hundred meters of dirt and brought a pair of .50-caliber machine guns to the party. They aimed them squarely into the thickest mass of Iraqis and the gunners had their gloved fingers on the butterfly triggers. That scared the shit out of the militia as Joe was much faster to shoot than his British counterpart and was far less concerned about either paperwork or prisoners. An American officer could be seen speaking into a radio through the bulletproof glass, and it didn't take a rocket scientist to figure out the cavalry, both British and American, would soon arrive at a full gallop. Though the private and military sectors have their squabbles, when the chips are down, there is absolutely no question as to who is going to support who. We share the same mess halls and most of us are former army and we share a common contempt of the corrupt police. The Iraqi mob were markedly less enthusiastic about the whole thing than they had been just a couple of minutes ago.

The major's shoulders slumped perceptibly as the pistol continued to reside in his ear.

Robert: Tell your men to move to the police vehicles, weapons pointed towards the ground.

In return all he got was a stony stare. Rob never said a word, but in response ground the muzzle into the militiaman's ear so deeply it drew blood. The major turned, barked out a command in Arabic, and the police began to sullenly withdraw back to their vehicles, the .50-caliber heavies of the Americans covering them the whole time.

There we waited. About twenty minutes later several vehicles with British Army markings pulled up. Out popped a pair of officers, one British and the other a fairly distinguished-looking Iraqi light colonel. It would appear that the police major and the army colonel had met before as no time was spent in introductions. The colonel walked up, pistol drawn, grabbed the police major by the hair, and threw him into the backseat after tossing his pistol into the dust. Just as rapidly as they had arrived, the vehicles pulled away with hardly a word spoken. Our people packed up and pulled in behind Robert. We boarded up and left along with the Americans who also drove off, heavy machine guns covering the Iraqi Police until the last. The leaderless Shia mob eventually drifted off, doubtless happy to be alive.

We found out later that the Coalition had been aware of the major's little racket for some time, and that we were the first ones to have refused to buckle under.

As for the major, his outcome bore grim resemblance to the larger war that swirled around us all. An easy case for prosecution, one mistake was made after another. Some two weeks later, doubtless due to influence, he was back at his post, arrogant as ever, though he rarely meddled with us anymore. It was then that I knew the war was lost.

A Polish paratrooper cum contractor, working farther north in the country, also reflects upon the Iraqi Police. His story repeats a common theme among contractors: the police

were corrupt and in league with the various militias. The author witnessed this person-
ally on many occasions.

We could always tell the legitimacy of any police checkpoint simply by looking at the police manning it. If they were dressed in rags, barefoot, and had
absolute shit weapons, they were probably real police. If they were wearing
black masks to hide their identities, they were invariably allied with us. They
knew that if they were identified their families might very well be murdered.

But if they had fresh uniforms and really good equipment, you had to
be careful. The Americans had given them thousands of brand-new Dodge
extended cab 4x4s complete with police paint job. If you came across one of
these at a checkpoint, manned by healthy, well-equipped Iraqis without face
masks, you knew you were dealing with the militias. They didn't give a shit
who saw them as they were the bad guys to begin with. They had the best
of everything whereas no legitimate cop would ever have a truck like that.
When we saw the militias at checkpoints we never even slowed down and
were ready for a shootout in any given instant. After a bunch of them got
pretty shot up, they didn't bother us much after the first few attempts. They
did their thing and we did ours.

There was another checkpoint by the bridge in Nasiriyah that was legendary among
convoy contractors, but for a very different reason. This American recounts why:

The Italian Army was tasked to guard the bridge. They were well dug in,
had armor, and excellent fields of fire. To attack them was a form of sweaty
suicide. They were equally well prepared for car bombers and had multiple
rings of security to deter any attack. So they were pretty safe, which made
it pretty boring for them. Imagine sitting on your ass for a year behind a
machine gun that you pretty much knew you would never have to pull the
trigger on. Boring.

But they did have a handful of females as the Italian Army is gender
mixed. Two in particular were drop-dead gorgeous, at least by the standards
of thousands of guys working in Iraq, where women were nonexistent. For
an hour before we arrived, the topic of conversation was nothing else. It was
the only time everybody prayed for a hot and calm day, because then the girls
would remove their fatigue jackets and be clad in their T-shirts. I suppose it

was every male's fantasy. You would see them, long legged, dark haired, with voluptuous figures, reclining behind a belt-fed machine gun. They were the only Western women many of us would see for three months. We all pretended not to stare but everybody did. Everybody waved to them, every time we crossed the bridge in either direction.

Surely they must have been sick to death of waving to five thousand sex-deprived males every day, but they never let on. They always waved back and seemed to manage a smile. Rumor has it one Christmas Day they donned Santa hats and threw candy canes to every convoy that rolled by. I regret missing that.

They became a landmark for many of us. It was a way to mark time. Those women probably didn't know it, but they had about five thousand personal bodyguards who were deeply concerned about their welfare. Funny how little things like that assume such major importance in times of war. If you had a bad day, it became better when you saw them. They were a definite boon for morale. I am sure they must have been propositioned about twenty million times, but they never accepted any offers that I know of.

The Italian Army eventually pulled out, and, of course, they went too. The checkpoint at Nasiriyah was never quite the same again. It's sad, I never even knew their names, but felt as if I had become quite close to them over that year of freezing cold and baking heat. War does that, I suppose. I would have loved to have met them in Rome or somewhere in Italy, you know, like in a classy square, and wearing nice civilian clothes. Buy them an ice cream and see them all dolled up, not in the sexual sense or anything like that. Just to let them know what a difference they made for all of us heading up country. Just talk and hear what they had to say as people. Of course, it could never happen, but I still occasionally wonder what they would have been like in the real world. They were great in Iraq, and I wish them well wherever they are.

The author, who many times crossed over the Nasiriyah bridge, concurs wholeheartedly with the preceding account. They were gorgeous and always smiled and waved.

Not every moment in theater is spiked with adrenaline and the crackle of small arms. Since time immemorial, all combatants spend excessive time simply waiting. Firefights are still the exception as opposed to the norm, and there are interludes of beauty, peace, and humor even in the most desolate corners of the world. This account by a Canadian requesting anonymity exposes a very different side of the contractor experience in Iraq.

We arose at three o'clock in the morning for the drive back to the Kuwaiti border. Normal working hours are meaningless in war. Troops were moving and vehicles were echeloned on the road just as if it was three in the afternoon. We quietly rolled out of bed fully clothed, laced up our desert boots, gathered our packs, and strolled to the vehicles. It doesn't take much. Coffee is brewed over tiny stoves set up abutting the shrapnel barriers. Beside us armored Humvees growl by, returning from another patrol of the highways. The Nepalese prepare the weapons and turrets while we Westerners check the S-2 (intelligence) shop for updated information. Like a good neighbor they are always there, always open, and always do their best to help. We study the map. The route north has a red box beside it. There have been several minor firefights and one suicide car bomber. Now is not the prime time to move through the area. The route south back to the Kuwaiti border and into Shia country has a green square hanging beside it. It is all clear save for the usual sporadic pot shots around Nasiriyah. In short, same old stuff. We filch a cup of real coffee; joke with the staff, whom we all know well; and wander back through the blaze of generator-driven floodlights where our vehicles await. I hop into the rear and our Nepalese driver shuts the door. I am now effectively trapped in the back. I can only get out by going up through the turret or clambering over to the front seat, which is awkward at best. I ensure the belts of machine gun ammunition are correctly coiled. They are. I prepare my swing seat, check radios, turn on the laser sights on my rifle, and settle down to wait. I spend a moment of solitude sipping my purloined coffee.

Ten minutes later our convoy is shepherded and the manifest turned in. The mission briefing is complete, given by a young Scot called Charles. With that, in a last symbolic gesture, the entire team takes a last pee on the rear tires of the gun truck. I am told this is a hangover from the days of World War II. Apparently bomber crews performed the same load-lightening act on the rear wheels of the Lancasters and B-17s before lifting off for the terror-filled skies over Germany.

The analogy to aviation is an apt one, for ten minutes later I am in another world. We cleared the checkpoints and the last American sentry wished us good luck. Within a minute the glow of floodlit Combat Support Center

Scania is gone as if it never existed. I am the rear gunner of the last vehicle, and in all directions lay a vast nothingness. There are no lights, not even the flickering, dying embers of a Bedouin campfire. Gazing forward I can just discern the red taillights of the other thirteen vehicles. These red dots represent the sole sign of man's presence in the great void. I return my attention to the rear and only the empty desert beckons. The night air has cooled and blows over the top of my head. The desert smells clean and the air is pure. Glancing inside, I can see Charles peering out as he takes it in, face bathed in the multicolored reflection of the lights on the instrument panel. I can no longer see the driver as the armor plating prevents it. This is my only connection with the life I know, this small cocoon of humanity and comrades as we hurtle through the night desert at 90 mph.

As for so many who served in any capacity in Iraq, the tranquil night sky, filled with innumerable stars (for there are no man-made lights to be found), provides ample time for self-reflection. The Canadian continues.

Above me gazes down every star ever made, accompanied by a crescent moon. There is just sufficient astral illumination to discern the hard shape of the machine gun and the belt hanging from it. Beyond the muzzle, the sky and surface of the earth blend into one varying shade of gray. It is impossible to determine where one ends and the next begins. It feels more like I am flying than driving. I no longer have any spatial or depth perception and the bumps could equally be air pockets. Raising my head in the open turret, the chilled desert air flows over my bare scalp, furthering the notion that I am indeed well above terra firma. We are but the tiniest of entities, moving infinitesimally slowly against such a massive and impressive landscape. We are alone on God's vast sea, surrounded by only darkness. There is no up or down, backwards or forwards. Only my comrades and the millions of stars gazing down upon my pathetic efforts compared to the overwhelming power of the earth that surrounds us. It is very easy to feel small in the desert as we crawl through the endless spaces. The rhythmical bouncing of the truck, coupled with the darkness and the gently swaying seat, caress my brain into a semi stupor. One is apt to converse with one's maker at such times. What a fortunate man I have been to experience moments such as this. I feel very puny and very lucky indeed.

And so it goes for hour after hour, until finally the heavens begin to lighten ever so imperceptibly. With majestic grandeur, the stars bow out to be replaced by the golden hues of sand and shale as the sky continues to brighten. Far off to starboard, for I still have trouble thinking of us not being at sea or flying, a lone Bedouin emerges from a tent. He stoops over and stirs the embers of last night's fire. He gazes at us from within his black robe, AK-47 by his side. I wave but he fails to reciprocate. Doubtless we are as alien to him as he is to us. We hail from two different planets that, for a millisecond in time, crossed paths. Does he know that the person who waved to him will in twenty-four hours be in Kuwait City, forty-eight will see me in London, and seventy-two hours hence will have me partaking of lunch in downtown Toronto? He will still be tending his goats and sheep and brewing his tea over burning camel dung. What a strange world we live in.

A young Swede, formerly a bank teller, had a similar experience during the terrible first few months of 2006, when it seemed that all of Baghdad was burning.

It was a brilliant morning, absolutely stunning. The sun was slowly coming up in a clear blue sky with temperatures just above freezing. I was standing in my favorite fleece out in the yard, sipping coffee, to see the teams off. Perhaps I remember it well as I had survived an IED blast the day before and was still rather thankful to be around. The neighborhood was silent save for the muted clinks and clanks as the Fijians rigged the machine guns. The engines were tested while the teams loaded all the impedimenta of modern conflict into the armored gun trucks. Small vapor trails of condensation from breathing in the chilled air surrounded the head of every man. It was a serenely peaceful moment, a tableau frozen in time. I wished to be nowhere else in the whole world. It was as if this was all we had ever done and all we would ever do. I was in total bliss, with a grin from ear to ear as I sipped the scalding coffee. Far in the distance, the first car bomb of the day detonated, the only intruder in our peaceful valley. The crews gathered to chatter before departure, radios were checked, and the Fijians partook of Morning Prayer, standing in a circle and holding hands. A final briefing and they were off.

Regardless of the tranquil interludes, it does not take long for the reality of war to return. A former paratrooper records the arrival of a new man in the harrowing first months of 2007 when death tolls in the capital city were at their highest.

We picked him up from BIAP and rolled back to the villa in the Red Zone. We were off on a mission the next day while he got himself sorted out. Eight-hour jet lag can be tough so he had a light day and would go on a "milk run" escort detail the next day. That night after we got back he said hello and I caught his first name, though I don't remember it.

That was the only time I saw him. He was blown up the next day and airlifted to Germany for treatment before we all got back from a different mission. He didn't even have time to put his stuff in his wall locker before he was a casualty. He had been in theater for less than twenty-four hours so he had a pretty short war. But I guess that's the way it goes.

The situation would continue to deteriorate as the years flowed by with the nadir coming in 2006–7. Another American recalls that particular time, summoning up the feelings of many.

We had parked our vehicles in a supposedly controlled area. They were under the security of the Iraqi Police who were supposedly not in cahoots with the various militias. When we came back there was human shit on the hood of every truck. Some of our supposed "Allies" had taken a crap on the hoods and windshields of our SUVs. We knew it was them and they knew that we knew it was them, but there was nothing we could do to them about it. From that instant on, I knew, regardless of what the politicians proclaimed that it was going to be a long, long war. I was right.

The author recalls the winter of 2006–7 in Baghdad:

It got so bad that by January of 2007 I was reduced to filling my morning coffee cup only two thirds full. Every time a car bomb went off within a couple of mile radius I wound up spilling my priceless java brought from home. So in order to facilitate cohabiting in the same city with suicidal fucking lunatics who blow themselves up in vehicles packed with high explosives, I struck a compromise and never carried around a full cup of coffee. Welcome to Baghdad, baby.

Chapter Three
A History of Violence

The arrival of multinational teams toting heavy weaponry on the streets of Baghdad did not occur overnight. There was an incubation period lasting decades, replete with brilliant successes and abysmal failures. No single entity can be wholly held responsible for the ensuing disaster, nor can any claim the moral high ground. Private military companies have evolved to what they are today not because of competent design complete with a series of checks and balances but rather because of a total lack of them. There was no federal oversight at inception nor is there any currently save for a few cosmetic changes that have accomplished nothing. The congressional show of force over the Blackwater massacre of 2007 has been a waste of time, save for the sound bites. The charges against all six men were dropped on New Year's Eve 2009 for technical reasons.[1]

The PMC industry is specifically designed to kill human beings if necessary. Yet it receives less federal oversight than Kansan farmers applying for grain subsidies.

The history of the business is more one of accident than intelligent planning. American private military companies that occupy combat roles didn't exist a decade ago. In 2002, the largest PMC contract was a force protection operation at Camp Bondsteel, Kosovo, where a round was never fired in anger.

If the U.S. government opted for hired guns, it was invariably through third world proxy irregulars such as the Montagnards in Vietnam or the mujahideen in what was then Soviet-occupied Afghanistan. So exactly how did low-grade Department of Defense (DOD) decisions regarding the outsourcing of military logistics evolve into gangs of AK-47-wielding foreigners shooting up Baghdad? That these companies are on the payroll of the U.S. government is a shock to much of the American public, the majority of whom, even today, are still unaware of the full extent of these pseudomilitary activities.

To comprehend the byzantine miscegenation between the PMC industry and the Department of Defense, it is necessary to go back some three decades, when Ronald Reagan sat astride the helm of American policy.

The Beginning

When Ronald Reagan assumed the presidency in 1980 one of his primary missions was to restore the prestige and combat capability of the U.S. armed forces. Again and again, three key phrases were advanced to describe how to radically transform the world's greatest military. "Force multipliers," "cost control," and "concentration of combat power" represented the sacred triad of future battles propelling the country into the next millennium. All three were proven to be correct in concept and stunningly powerful in execution.

Force Multipliers

Force multipliers entail utilizing assets that generate more collective combat capabilities than the sum of their individual parts. A classic example is the introduction of Special Forces troops onto the battlefield. These elite soldiers train indigenous personnel to fight while the SF troops assume key leadership positions. The reality is that the SF unit no longer engages the enemy as a detachment of twelve men; rather, it is likely to be leading a company of 120 tribal warriors. The tenfold increase in combat power stems from the SF capacity to mobilize personnel not normally available to conventional commanders. The benefits are patently obvious.

However, not all multipliers pertain to the human side of the equation. The introduction of smart bombs has been a force multiplier of incalculable value. Today, all that is necessary is a grid reference and a cruise missile can literally be programmed to fly through a bunker's door before detonating. In the European theater during World War II hundreds of B-17 Flying Fortresses would be dispatched to destroy a particular high-value target. Today the identical mission is performed to a higher standard by a solo ordnance officer loading grid coordinates into a missile in the comfort of an offshore submarine.

A more exotic land-based example is the utilization of Predator drones. These unmanned aerial vehicles conduct surveillance and ground attack missions inside

Pakistan. The operation's unique feature is that they are remotely piloted by operators sitting in bunkers in Nevada!

Force multipliers were to have the most profound effect in Afghanistan. Here a comparative handful of Special Operations Forces (SOF) such as Delta Force, the Ranger Regiment, Special Forces, and U.S. Navy Seals led indigenous Afghan tribesman of the Northern Alliance into combat. Once these troops were able to call upon the awesome destructive capacity of American airpower, this mixed bag of forces trampled the Taliban on their home turf in a matter of weeks. Sadly, the success of the force multiplier theory in Afghanistan was to have a profoundly negative impact in Iraq. Under Rumsfeld's chiding, the Pentagon was urged to conduct a land campaign with far fewer forces than it would normally draw upon, based on the mistaken assumption that force multipliers would work as well in Iraq as they did in Afghanistan. During combat operations this assertion proved to be partially true, but the lack of boots on the ground made it difficult to enforce the peace once hostilities were terminated.

Cost Control

The Pentagon next reviewed the finances of war. During the Reagan era, escalating costs rapidly became a factor in combat. In 1944, the average GI to hit the beach in Normandy was equipped with about $179.00 worth of government-issued equipment in today's dollars. By the Vietnam War the price tag was $1,112 per head with flak jackets, early night vision scopes, and so forth added to individual hand receipts. As of 2007, the cost for outfitting personnel in Iraq was about $17,500 per head.[2]

But hidden costs really jack up the true taxpayer price of a service member. Not factored in to the financial equation are recruiting, salary, training, equipment, pensions, life insurance, housing, food, medical care, and all the other myriad add-ons that represent the true dollar cost that a soldier standing in a pair of boots actually represents.

The equation can best be compared to the simple analogy of running a restaurant. To recruit, house, feed, train, clothe, pay, and provide medical insurance for a line chef whose mission is to grill hamburgers is a daunting task to most commercial employers. The financial commitment increases when the chef is promised a pension after twenty years of faithful service. In the long run, or so ran the theory of those determined to change the Pentagon's ways, would it not be cheaper to hire a line chef only when needed? Even at a higher daily wage, the enormous savings reaped elsewhere would surely offset this expense. This "contracted" individual poses no financial drain on the organization, as the civilian contracting agency for whom the chef works is paid a turnkey rate for the company's services. The contracting agency is then responsible for transporting, feeding, and providing all other benefits for the line chef in question. At the end of the contract, this asset simply goes away until it is needed again, unlike the permanent army chef who must still continue to be paid, fed, housed, and so forth, regardless of the demand for his services. In the civilian world this form of subcontracting is so commonplace as to be virtually invisible. But for the more slowly evolving army, this practice was a total break in tradition that would produce highly controversial results.

Concentration of Combat Power

The last leg of the triad was the one area that received the most enthusiastic endorsement from all four branches of the military. No army unit engaged in operations wishes to dispatch soldiers for noncombat essential tasks, such as guarding bases, unloading supplies, or even filling the proverbial "kitchen police" (KP) assignment. This work represents a slow hemorrhage of the lifeblood of battle, manpower. Every soldier committed to other duties, be it peeling potatoes or escorting supply convoys, is one fewer man that the commander has in the front lines where he is urgently needed. There is no such thing as having too many soldiers in a combat environment.

The prevalent view in the E ring of the Pentagon in the 1980s was that by subcontracting out noncombatant tasks to private companies, the Pentagon would win what was for the planners a three-front war. First of all they would have more boots on the ground for combat. Second, the costs of maintaining a huge number of in-house logistical personnel could be reduced by hiring contractors only when needed.

A final advantage of contracting that all were acutely aware of but rarely discussed was political. Private contractors are low profile and quiet whereas the uniformed, conventional military is anything but. By removing the logistical tail from uniform, overseas deployments would be sharply reduced in terms of *military* manpower. This situation, in turn, would create a more politically palatable environment for the projection of force abroad. Even today, the public is generally unaware that as of late 2007 there were over 180,000 contractors (*not* including security firms) in Iraq to only 160,000 military.[3]

The result of all this study was the initiation of a new program designed to provide civil outsourcing assistance to the U.S. Army. It became known as the Logistics Civil Augmentation Program (LOGCAP).

Introduced in 1985, this program, born of intelligent foresight, has been the center of a firestorm of controversy regarding its implementation. Based upon interviews drawn from individuals in the U.S. State Department and DOD, it is the author's subjective but firm opinion that LOGCAP is the true grandfather of the PMC companies so prevalent in Iraq today.

Civilian augmentation to the military has been around for a long time. The absolute truth is that private contractors have supplemented the military dating back to the Revolutionary War. The task of making bullets was contracted out to local blacksmiths, allowing George Washington's men more time to shoot up the Redcoats. Leaping forward two centuries, contractors still played only a minor role in World War II. It was not until Vietnam that civilian contractors were employed on a large enough scale to merit the Defense Department's attention. During the conflict in Southeast Asia, contractors were employed on a nonsystemic basis depending on the logistical needs of the armed services.

In his book, *Inventing Vietnam: The United States and State Building, 1954–1968,* James M. Carter demonstrates how early contractor operations in Vietnam eerily foreshadowed those that eventually would pan out in Iraq. (It should be noted that the company called Brown & Root Services [BRS] described by Mr. Carter was the 1960s version of the modern-day Kellogg Brown & Root, which would achieve plaudits in Kosovo and notoriety in Iraq as one of the largest PMCs in theater.)

The Lyndon Johnson administration, according to Carter,

made the decision to breathe new life into a private contract with a limited construction consortium—made up of Raymond International and Morrison-Knudsen construction firms. These firms quickly brought on two others—J. A. Jones and Brown & Root—to form the RMK-BRJ. Together, these four firms represented an unprecedented resource base and possessed an unmatched global reach and expertise. This private giant quickly set about transforming southern Vietnam, dotting the landscape with fire bases, airfields, modern ports and harbors, supply depots, and fuel/oil/lubricant storage facilities, and turning it into a militarily defensible piece of real estate. In short, they carried out what they, marveling at their work at the time, termed "the construction miracle of the decade." . . . By the time the [eighteen-month] contract expired [in 1967], the "Vietnam builders" had put in place close to $2 billion in projects spanning the length and breadth of southern Vietnam.[4]

The results, in terms of value provided for dollar paid, ranged from excellent to horrible. The General Accounting Office (now known as the Government Account-ability Office [GAO]) raised questions when a consortium of which Brown & Root was a part won a $380 million contract to build airports, bases, hospitals, and other facilities for the U.S. Navy in South Vietnam. According to the GAO,

> In connection with the military construction program, totaling nearly $600 million up to March 1966, $504 million had been incurred under a single joint-venture contract for construction of air bases, port facilities, canton-ments and logistical and administrative facilities for United States and Viet-namese military forces, and other projects. Audits to date by the defense agencies having responsibility have been limited mostly to examinations of the contractors' cost representations as shown on vouchers presented for pay-ment. Insofar as we could determine, no management reviews or evaluations have been undertaken of substantive contract performance or of the broader control aspects of the construction program.
>
> The atmosphere surrounding the billion-dollar construction undertak-ing in Viet Nam and the conditions of urgency under which the work is proceeding are at best conducive to a large element of waste, some of it un-avoidable. Many of the management controls which are applied in a normal construction operation are precluded by the circumstances. In our opinion, this creates an urgent need for a counterbalance in the form of a searching management review and inspection function on a continuing basis to reduce avoidable waste without hindering the program.
>
> There appears to be a particular need for audits and inspections concern-ing the adequacy and timeliness of delivery, the end use, and the propriety of costs of the large amounts of equipment, spare parts, and supplies that are being provided under the program. . . .
>
> We found no audits being conducted.[5]

Brown & Root took a considerable lambasting from the press,[6] which believed the Texan firm had been the recipient of favors from another Texan, Lyndon Johnson, who then occupied the White House. That a near-identical situation was to occur some forty years later, with yet another Texan in the White House, is open to interpretation at the reader's discretion. It is also interesting to note that Brown & Root were publicly attacked by a young congressman, who delivered a passionate speech about the firm's construction of airfields in South Vietnam. The elected official leveled accusations of cronyism at the company. The name of the congressman was Donald Rumsfeld.[7]

One of the lessons emerging from Vietnam was the need for a more organized system for employing civilian contractors in far-flung combat theaters. The general consensus was that contractor operations needed to be brought under one central administrative umbrella, thus minimizing duplication and waste and ensuring unity of effort.

Some four years later LOGCAP was the result and in theory is a well-thought-out and forward-looking program. The original premise runs parallel to the wishes of the Pentagon in that LOGCAP allows for the concentration of combat power by alleviating the need for the military to execute its own logistics package. The scheme's intent was to contract out packets of work to commercial firms on an "as needed" case by the army.

When LOGCAP was created in 1985, it received only minor attention from the commercial sector. The predominant threat in 1985 was the Soviet Union, poised with its massed tank armies on the borders of the North Atlantic Treaty Organization (NATO). As Western Europe was highly developed in terms of logistical infrastructure, there was minimal application for the LOGCAP process.

The most viable potential for the outsourcing of logistics for Europe was the appropriation of commercial maritime and aviation assets in times of national emergency. This form of civil augmentation, however, was already covered under separate contracts between private companies and the U.S. government should massive reinforcement of standing forces in Germany become necessary in light of Soviet aggression.

LOGCAP was therefore shunted into the back alleys of power, as conventional wisdom assumed its only function would be to support an expeditionary force in some third world backwater. The imagined scope of LOGCAP's work was roughly equivalent to what the British undertook in their amphibious campaign to retake the Falkland Islands some three years earlier in 1982. The sole deterring issue was that for the foreseeable future the Pentagon had eyes only for Soviet T-72 main battle tanks massed on the edge of the Fulda Gap. The other potential flash point, Korea, was already well engineered with allied infrastructure designed to thwart the threat from the north. Based on the realpolitik of the late 1980s, few ever anticipated the invocation of the program on a substantial scale.

There was one other critical characteristic of the early LOGCAP programs. For the first seven years of operation, from 1985 to 1992, a separate LOGCAP existed for each active army. Thus, soldiers in the Pacific might receive support from a completely different contracting company than soldiers belonging to another army based in Europe. This arrangement is akin to having 50 percent of an air fleet maintained by Boeing in theater A and the other half serviced by Airbus in theater B, even though the force flies identical airframes in all locales. It is impossible to create a cohesive, consolidated logistics program as there are simply too many chefs in the kitchen. Worse yet, each one is directly competing with the other for a greater percentage of the pie.

This structure later created massive headaches in the Persian Gulf War of 1991 through duplication of effort and administrative entanglement over who exactly owed what to whom and why. The force mustered in Saudi Arabia was drawn from all over the world, and as units were amalgamated and repositioned on a global scale, this decentralized version of LOGCAP, with one service provider per army, came unglued.

The Global Security Organization phrases it succinctly:

> During the 1990–91 Persian Gulf War, LOGCAP was not used. Instead, contractors were hired on hundreds of separate contracts to provide logistics support with uneven results. There are numerous examples of contracts awarded with poorly defined or missing Statements of Work and unclear contract requirements. These situations led to inadequate contractor performance and customer dissatisfaction at significant cost. The contractors' payment vouchers still had to be honored, however, because the poorly written contractual requirements contained no basis upon which to reject their claims for payment. As a result, LOGCAP was revised to preplan for contractor support during any contingency or war.[8]

Thus, during DOD's after-action review of the Persian Gulf War in 1992, the issue of logistical contracting again came up in light of the spotty performance of individual companies supplying the troops in the desert. A number of changes were implemented to streamline the process.

The first amendment was based on a rapidly realigning world with U.S. military power as the centerpiece of international stability. The United States would not necessarily have the luxury of an existing logistical grid such as it had enjoyed in Western Europe during the Cold War. With the United States as the world's sole sheriff, contingency plans had to be formulated to deploy U.S. forces into hostile areas where the infrastructure to support them might be nonexistent. The question being asked at DOD was, "Does any private company have the ability to provide this level of service and if so what is the best way to proceed?"

Dick Cheney, then secretary of defense, approved a $3.9 million tender that would be awarded to the company that produced the best logistical plan to support the army's needs on a contingency basis. The hypothetical example was based on the deployment of twenty thousand troops to a hostile environment for an initial period of six months. A troop increase of up to fifty thousand had to be anticipated with combat operations continuing for an indefinite period of time. DOD wanted the transcendent plan ready for implementation should a hypothetical scenario ever become reality.

A total of thirty-seven companies forwarded proposals. BRS, specializing in the logistical support of remote oil rigs and whose work history already included Vietnam as described earlier, once again emerged the winner. The suggestions contained in the classified report were allegedly implemented and the first LOGCAP contract was born.

As a footnote to history it is worth noting that in 1995 Dick Cheney went on to become the chief executive officer (CEO) of Halliburton, which is the mother company of BRS. This unusual move became a point of some contention in political and judicial circles a decade later, especially when the vice president's stock options in Halliburton rose 3,281 percent in just one year shortly after the invasion of Iraq.[9]

The first reform was to centralize the LOGCAP under one umbrella. The miserable duplication of effort during the Persian Gulf War and the ensuing chaos validated the concept of consolidation.

In layman's terms, LOGCAP was about to become to the army what Walmart is to the consumer, a one-stop superstore where all the logistical necessities of life on the battlefield can be bundled into one package depending on the needs of the customer. The company holding the LOGCAP contract would be able to provide the necessary construction and logistics services that the army requested at predetermined prices with a fixed profit margin. This billing system is commonly referred to as "cost plus" and would become synonymous with "fraud" a decade later in Iraq. Every five years the contract itself would be up for bid, thus theoretically preventing a monopoly of the system. However, due to the enormity of the possible scope of work, only a handful of companies have the necessary depth to remain competitive in their solicitation of the LOGCAP tenders.

BRS won the first amended LOGCAP 1 contract in 1992. The company was to implement the plan it had designed only months before.

Later that year an additional $5.9 million was again paid to BRS to update its worldwide contingency plans in an attempt to streamline the efficiency of contractor operations. Logic dictates that the company was in fact producing contingency plans for specific scenarios at DOD's request. Future events would confirm this hypothesis.

Only a few months later, in December 1992, that proverbial call came from the Pentagon to implement the improved LOGCAP, and this time it was for real. The United States was deploying forces to Somalia in a humanitarian operation called Restore Hope. Brown & Root were tasked, under the LOGCAP contract, to provide food, accommodations, and other logistical services to the U.S. Army while it conducted operations in the Horn of Africa.

On December 9, 1992, U.S. Marines waded ashore on the desolate shores of Somalia near Mogadishu. The first BRS employees arrived the next day and without delay began logistical support to the military.

By every performance standard, the initial mission was a success. BRS provided food, accommodation, and all the other compendium of services necessary for maintaining a force in the field. The army was not bled of troops for noncombatant tasks, and the administration reaped the political gain of having fewer U.S. servicemen deployed overseas. BRS was focused on providing quality service and made heavy use of local labor. According to Peter W. Singer in *Corporate Warriors*, "The firm even hired local women to wash U.S. Army laundry because it was cheaper than bringing in washing machines."[10]

BRS employees stayed for the duration, departing the shattered country in March 1995. The trial run had proven successful even though the operation as a whole would later be seen as a failure in light of the mutilation of U.S. Army Rangers who were dragged through the streets of Mogadishu in 1993. It seemed that the LOGCAP concept was validated. The door was now open to future business.

Those contracts arrived in swift succession.

In 1994 BRS deployed to Kuwait to support U.S. forces in response to yet another Iraqi buildup on the Kuwaiti border. The contractors were dispatched to Africa again, albeit on a much-reduced scale, to support the assistance provided to Rwandan refugees of the genocidal campaign in 1995. Finally, they became involved in Haiti, where they provided support for the U.S. peacekeeping mission that began in the fall of 1994. Based on its performance, BRS slowly but inevitably crept forward, digesting larger and larger percentages of the army's support function.

The Balkans were next. Yugoslavia exploded into civil war in the early 1990s, and the United States finally became involved in 1995. The LOGCAP operation for this deployment practically followed a word-for-word copy of the initial tender. The U.S. Army required facilities and logistical support for twenty thousand men, with the option of additional troops to follow. BRS swung into action and produced. In a matter of a few months, small, self-contained cities were constructed from the ground up. Each one was self-supporting in terms of providing power generation, food, laundry, mail, and all the way down to American name-brand ice cream. It was as if a slice of small-town America had been air-dropped, literally brick for brick, into the Bosnian landscape. Even the big-screen televisions in the dining facilities were tuned in to American stations, albeit seven hours ahead.

For their efforts, Brown & Root Services were paid some $546 million. In commercial circles, LOGCAP now represented serious money.

In 1997, LOGCAP was due for renewal, and this time another multinational company, called DynCorp, beat out BRS for LOGCAP II. BRS pressed to keep the Balkans region under a separate contract under the justification of ensuring smooth continuation of services for the army. DOD approved this move. The next BRS contract for the Balkans was worth over $400 million and a five-year renewal until 2004 grossed another $900 million for the company coffers.

Fate is a strange mistress because from 1997 to 2001, archrival DynCorp held the LOGCAP II contract while BRS, now exempt from LOGCAP oversight, profited from the Balkans. DynCorp was not called upon during the four-year service time as BRS was in earlier years. In 2001, the contract was up for rebid, and BRS was able to wrest it back from DynCorp. This time LOGCAP III was for a term of ten years. Months later, the World Trade Center was attacked, and as so many things, the contracting world would never be the same again.

■ ■ ■

The military-contractor relationship as seen in its current guise has been in existence for nearly a quarter century. As evidenced in the Balkans and Kosovo, this symbiotic relationship is beneficial to both parties when implemented correctly.

The Persian Gulf War once again demonstrated the hazards of ad hoc sub-contracting, and LOGCAP was overhauled and validated. On a theoretical level, LOGCAP is a winner. When implemented correctly with the necessary checks and balances to prevent fraud, the outsourcing of military logistics to private companies has achieved the performance standard expected of it when the scheme was devised back in the Reagan administration.

Unbeknownst to most of America, the vast majority of financial disputes pertaining to fraud in the history of outsourcing logistics has been traced to the billing/accounting side of the house and rarely resides with the individuals on the ground.[11]

The current fiasco in Iraq is less an issue of implementation than one of too much money thrown at for-profit companies without appropriate financial controls. This topic will be discussed in chapter 5.

Unexpected Side Effects of Outsourcing: Private Military Companies

One of the by-products the Pentagon perhaps did not expect when it began to out-source logistics a quarter century ago was the birth of the private military companies. It is these firms, such as Blackwater, that have created such furor in the forum of American public opinion.

Private military companies can be classified into three separate subgroups, each with its own specialty. They are logistical, advisory only, and operational. A brief overview of the three types yields many insights.

Logistics

When the entire issue of privatizing portions of the military was raised in the early 1980s, the focus was to outsource the logistical tail of the military. LOGCAP was created precisely for this purpose. Logistics personnel are noncombatants and their applications are covered in the previous examples of Brown & Root Services' work in the Balkans and Somalia. Their utilization in combat theaters is now so commonplace it raises no eyebrows. Even such blue chip companies like FedEx have provided logistical support to the military in the Iraq War.

Advisory

Private advisory companies only advise and provide training to others; they do *not* permit their personnel to engage in armed combat. Advisory companies utilize former military men to train host-nation militaries. Two of the oldest firms are Control Risks Group out of London and Military Professional Resources Incorporated located close to the American capital. "Old" is a relative word in this case, as MPRI was created in the 1980s and is roughly the same age as LOGCAP.

Advisory companies are not totally independent entities and must still conform to the laws of the nations where they are headquartered. The overwhelming majority of advisory firms are based in either the United Kingdom or the United States. The bottom line is that the training company must receive at least an "unofficial" blessing from the administration in office at the time. This stipulation, in turn, entails that the State Department, DOD, and the White House all tacitly condone the mission, even if official status is lacking. This setup has proven to be convenient to the U.S. government on more than one occasion.

The all-time classic example is Croatia. When Yugoslavia began to disintegrate along ethnic lines in 1991, Croatia and Slovenia were the first to secede, both declaring their independence on June 25, 1991. However, a significant Serbian minority in the Krajina region of Croatia were not enamored with thoughts of independence, and Belgrade, capitol of the former Yugoslavia, was even less impressed. Civil war promptly broke out, and Belgrade deployed the federal Yugoslav People's Army (the JNA) to assist the rebellious Serbs. Arrayed against the JNA's T-72 main battle tanks was little more than a Croatian militia, appallingly equipped and deplorably trained. The results were predictable. The Serbs, allied with the JNA, drove deeply into Croatia, occupying a third of the country and nearly cutting the new republic in half. A United Nations (UN) cease-fire was implemented and enforced before all of Croatia fell beneath the tank treads of the advancing Serbs. UN arms embargoes were promptly slapped on both warring factions as were provisions prohibiting the training of either side by the *regular armed forces* of any third-party country. Croatia was thus reduced to a nonshooting backwater on the Balkans stage. The world's

attention was soon redirected to the long, drawn-out agony of the Bosnians be-
sieged in Sarajevo by atrocity-prone Serbs.

The United States was in a bind. It had no desire to send ground forces into
a European quagmire. But the world's only superpower also had no wish to be
reduced to a mere bystander while the democratic-leaning Croatians and Bosnians
were inundated by a wave of Serbian goonery. Bill Clinton's administration believed
the best way to end the bloodshed was to ensure the Bosnians and Croats had the
military capability to resist further Serbian aggression. To that end the Washington
Agreement was signed on March 18, 1994.[12] This agreement allied the two minority factions against the larger, more powerful Serbia. The next phase for the United
States in regard to the Croats was to stiffen the fighting qualities of their armed
forces and give them a reasonable chance of deterring the Serbs should hostilities
recommence. This work was not as straightforward as it sounded as the United
States had formally signed the UN resolution prohibiting third-power training of
any of the combatant factions. Officially, Uncle Sam's hands were tied.

A popular urban legend in contractor circles has it that when a small Croatian
military contingent arrived in Washington in 1994, the Pentagon, legally incapable
of assisting, provided a D.C. street map with a large X marking the whereabouts of
MPRI's headquarters.

Consultations were duly held and a bargain was struck.[13] This private military
advisory firm composed of retired generals and senior NCOs somehow managed to
obtain a State Department license meeting the UN's preconditions to teach a course
in "democratic principles" to the Croatian Department of Defense.[14]

The instruction of democratic principles was part of a curriculum to support
the Democratic Transition Assistance Program (DTAP). It was a vaguely defined
undertaking theoretically aimed at restructuring the Croatian military to adapt to
the Western style of civil-military interface. Democratic principles were taught to
allow the former Soviet-type military to move closer to a NATO model, thus enabling Croatia to enter the Clinton administration's Partnership for Peace program.
The course curriculum, as taught by MPRI, remains unknown and unavailable to
the public.

What is known is that in late 1994 the Croatian military was a rabble in uniform, little more than an organized militia. In August 1995, a mere nine months
later, the same Croatian rabble violated the UN cease-fire with an offensive dubbed

Operation Storm.[15] The disciplined formations swarming over the border to fall upon the dumbfounded Serbs were more akin to Hitler's Waffen-SS than the tattered pseudo army they had been less than a year before. Close coordination of armor, airpower, and artillery allowed the Croatians to bludgeon the hapless Serbs at will. As per U.S. Army doctrine,[16] the first to fall prey to air strikes and commando raids were the Serbian command and control elements. In one swift stroke, the Croats decapitated the military brain from the ponderous body. Croatian armored columns shredded the Serbian lines of communication while artillery pounded the latter's static infantry positions. Emphasizing maneuver over attritional warfare, the Croatians were able to mass quickly, annihilate a numerically and qualitatively inferior enemy, and disappear in the gloom of the Balkan forests as deftly as the wild wolves that used to live there.

Reeling from the ruthless blitzkrieg, the Serbian forces in the region collapsed in days. In less than a week practically all of the territory ceded to the Serbs in 1991 had been liberated. Those Serbs still capable of breathing fled for their lives.

Sensing opportunity, the Croatian Ground Army linked up with its Bosnian counterpart to pursue the common enemy, who was now in headlong retreat. The combined forces thrust deeply into Serbian-occupied territory, the reinvigorated Croatian Ground Army occupying some 22 percent of Bosnia in the process.

To quote a former MPRI staffer familiar with the situation, "Serbia then found itself in very deep shit."

Barely three months after Operation Storm crossed the line of departure, a badly battered Serbia agreed to the cease-fire accords known as the Dayton Agreement in November 1995.[17] For many in the war-torn Balkans, the end of the nightmare was finally at hand.

There is no serious opposition to the tenet that MPRI played a decisive role in reshaping the Croatian military. Exactly to what extent will probably never be known, though there are a few tantalizing clues that have since surfaced.

As Ken Silverstein noted in his 1997 article "Privatizing War" for the *Nation*, MPRI began offering "advice and training to the Croatian military" in April 1995. According to Silverstein,

> Just months after M.P.R.I. went into Croatia that nation's army—until then bumbling and inept—launched a series of bloody offensives against Serbian forces. Most important was Operation Lightning Storm, the assault on the

Krajina region during which Serbian villages were sacked and burned, hundreds of civilians were killed and some 170,000 people were driven from their homes. Roger Charles, a retired Marine lieutenant colonel and military researcher who has been honored for his work by the Investigative Reporters and Editors Association, is convinced that M.P.R.I. played an important role in the Krajina campaign. "No country moves from having a ragtag militia to carrying out a professional military offensive without some help," says Charles, who has closely monitored M.P.R.I.'s activities. "The Croatians did a good job of coordinating armor, artillery and infantry. That's not something you learn while being instructed about democratic values."[18]

This case is proof positive that a private military company can have an impact far beyond the number of advisers who are dispatched to remote regions on vaguely worded training missions. The Balkans example has also allowed the West to discreetly circumvent restrictive wording in official treaties, allowing private military companies to operate in locales where official ones are prohibited.

The role of the private military adviser over the last two decades has continued to grow and has seen a track record of considerable achievement. Prior to Iraq, one of the pillars of success has been the close if informal cooperation between the organs of state and the end service provider. The truth is that an organization such as MPRI cannot operate on an international scale without the tacit consent of the U.S. government.

Once again, Ken Silverstein sums it up best:

For the government, privatization offers a number of advantages. In addition to providing plausible deniability about overseas entanglements, it allows Washington to shed military personnel while simultaneously retaining the capacity to influence and direct huge missions. Firms on contract can train an entire foreign army. By contrast, the Pentagon's International Military and Education Training Program [IMET] generally provides instruction to no more than a few dozen soldiers. The largest current IMET effort is in Honduras, where 266 soldiers and officers are being trained. "Private companies augment our ability to provide foreign training," says retired Lieut. Gen. Larry Skibbie, now at the American Defense Preparedness Association. "We'll see more and more of this as we continue to cut back on our uniformed forces."[19]

In many ways, private military advisers are nothing more than Special Forces attired in civilian clothes. In both cases their mission is to train foreign indigenous personnel in military tactics. A final advantage the private firms bring is that their involvement releases active duty Special Forces for combat operations elsewhere.

Thus, the report card for advisory companies is a positive one. Being noncombatants, they still adhere closely to the defined policies of the country for which they work. When well supervised, such as MPRI in Croatia, they are able to become effective force multipliers striving for the same goals as the democracies they represent. The future of private military advisers, much like their logistical counterparts, seems assured and is removed from the moral fray that swirls around the last type of PMC.

Operational

It is the third member in the family of the private military companies whose report card has been perhaps irredeemably besmirched. "Operational" is the adjective used to describe private military companies that engage in combat. The more commonly used vernacular is the term "mercenary." The advent of the term "private military companies" was an industry-wide drive to adopt a vague euphemism to self-describe services as opposed to having the business category of "mercenary" appear in the Yellow Pages. The truth is that, in purely semantic form, wiggle room is limited. Dictionary.com describes "mercenary" as "working or acting merely for money or other reward; hired to serve in a foreign army, guerrilla organization, etc." All of the private military companies currently operating in Iraq would technically qualify as mercenary organizations.

North Carolina–based Blackwater, founded in 1997 and now rebranded as XE, is the most notorious of the operational firms, but it is by no means the first. Its historical precedent was formed shortly after the dismantling of apartheid in South Africa.

Executives Outcomes (EO) was a South Africa–based company that specialized in private, full-scale military operations. All of the soldiers were former members of the South African Special Forces, which included the much-feared 32 Battalion. The 32 Battalion was either tremendously combat capable or regarded with the utmost loathing. It all depended on which end of the rifle was aimed at you.

After several successes fighting in Angola in the early 1990s, the firm's capabilities became better known worldwide. Executive Outcomes, by its very name, was the first group to utilize Orwellian terminology to disguise its true role and the earliest to successfully manipulate the media to its own ends.

Sierra Leone

The country that was destined to play the role of petri dish for future armed contractor operations was the corrupt, war-wracked nation of Sierra Leone. The government was engaged in a prolonged struggle with a rebel faction that called itself the Revolutionary United Front. The year before, in 1994, Sierra Leone had finished 170th out of 173 countries in the United Nations Human Development Report.[20] The president was a twenty-six-year-old army captain by the name of Valentine Strasser. This juvenile leader had assumed power when the previous occupant of the presidential palace had fled with a significant percentage of the treasury.

The standing army deployed to save the populace from the insurgency was horrific, routinely press-ganging children into combat units. If possible, the rebels were even worse. Like the government, the RUF press-ganged children into its ranks, forcing them to gun down both the innocent and the enemy with equal abandon. Villages were pacified by the linear expedient of decapitating the village elders and impaling their heads on stakes posted at the villages' entrances. The RUF trademark was amputated limbs hacked off by machetes. One can neither pull a trigger nor vote if one does not have a hand.

The greatest losers were the general populace, trapped between predatory RUF elements and government troops only slightly less debased. By early 1995 the country had collapsed into complete anarchy. Life was brutal, cheap, and short.

The Strasser administration had pleaded for military assistance from any quarter but had been rebuffed on all fronts, including the United States, the United Kingdom, and the UN. Faced with a "nothing to lose" situation, Strasser signed a contract with a British company named Gurkha Security Guards to come in and train his army. The advisers, primarily Nepalese Gurkhas with Caucasian leaders, arrived and attempted to prop up the collapsed regular forces. Shortly thereafter the RUF managed to ambush the mixed bag of military advisers, inflicting heavy casualties in the process. The Revolutionary United Front celebrated the victory by dismembering and eating the body of the leader of the fallen trainers. This grisly event concluded the first attempt to import private military companies into Sierra Leone.[21]

Freetown, the capital of the beleaguered nation, was in chaos as embassies evacuated all foreign nationals. The RUF advanced to the suburbs as the reign of terror continued to envelop the doomed metropolis. It was not long before Strasser's government began to seek salvation in any direction, leading it, perhaps inevitably, to a rendezvous with Executive Outcomes.

The government of Sierra Leone lacked the necessary start-up capital so EO was funded in part by a shadowy firm that would be compensated in the form of diamonds after EO troops had liberated the areas that contained the mining concessions.[22]

Within days the logistics were arranged, and the EO troops deployed to Sierra Leone to link up with armored personnel carriers, (BMP-2s) transport helicopters, and a dreaded Mi-24 gunship. Taking full advantage of the helicopters' tactical capabilities, EO rapidly mounted an unconventional offensive against the ill-trained boy soldiers of the RUF. For the first time in living memory, a professional fighting force confronted the rebels. Night ambushes, raids, snipers, and point-blank assaults tore gaping holes in the rebel ranks. The RUF, lacking even the most rudimentary of military skills, were slaughtered en masse. The helicopters provided EO troops with a high degree of mobility. These aviation assets became force multipliers of the first order, especially in light of the difficulties involved when traversing jungle terrain on foot. In the space of a fortnight, the RUF absorbed an estimated several hundred dead, lost thousands in desertions, and was thrown back over eighty miles into the jungle's interior.

The next phase was to overrun the diamond concessions to ensure payment. Executive Outcomes required only a few days to accomplish this task. The moral issues of being paid in the same diamonds as those that fueled the RUF's ability to wage war is for the reader to decide. That the diamonds of Sierra Leone are truly "blood diamonds" is not in doubt. Executive Outcomes continued to punish the RUF for the remainder of 1995, driving the rebels to the very fringes of the country and rendering them incapable of sustained combat.

Sierra Leone again began to prosper as the military contractors brought stability to the country. Valentine Strasser was removed in a bloodless coup, and a general by the name of Julius Bio was inserted as an interim president. EO condoned the coup but did not proactively participate in it. International critics of EO assumed the worst, however, and issued provocative statements in the world media that a mercenary gang had taken over an entire country for personal exploitation.[23]

To the amazement of all, in February 1996 a legitimate, multiparty civilian election took place. Ahmed Kabbah assumed the mantle of president. Kabbah's first priority was to attempt to end the civil war, and peace negotiations commenced with the remaining RUF who still lingered in the southeast portion of the country. The guerrillas, facing a vastly reduced share of the national pie, pulled out of the negotiations that October.

Executive Outcomes was again unleashed. Utilizing multiple intelligence sources but focusing on aerial reconnaissance, the company identified the exact location of RUF headquarters. In a joint operation, supported by Nigerian artillery and the regular Sierra Leone army, the rebels were virtually annihilated during a three day attack. Facing extermination, Foday Sankoh signed the peace accords on behalf of the Revolutionary United Front a couple of weeks later. EO had unilaterally brought political stability to the country. Sierra Leone was able to celebrate Christmas 1996 as a nation at peace.

There is no question that the private military contractors restored stability to a war-wracked nation. For the villagers who were trapped between the mercies of the RUF and the government forces, the black and white troops of EO are considered saints. Many are alive today because of the effective actions of the private military company.

The final tally sheet was impressive. EO lost fewer than two dozen troops dead, wounded, or sick. The RUF's losses will never be accurately collated but are estimated in the thousands. The country had morphed from a tin-pot dictatorship to a budding multiparty democracy during the time EO was responsible for security. Thousands in Freetown had been spared a grisly end, and over a million displaced persons were able to return to their homes. Those are heady statistics for a private military company of just over 160 men.

What was the final price tag to restore democracy? The government of Sierra Leone paid the equivalent of what it costs the American taxpayer to purchase eight M1 Abrams tanks, or about $35 million.[24]

The case for using private military firms becomes even more pronounced in light of subsequent events. During the civil war the United States, the United Kingdom, and the United Nations had all declined to provide any form of financial or military assistance. In what can only be interpreted as a morally ambiguous move, once peace had returned to Sierra Leone, the international community applied pressure on the Kabbah administration to expel the "mercenary" units.

Executive Outcomes' justifiable rebuttal was that it was hypocritical to condemn the organization when it was in fact the only Western-style entity that had been willing to take on the job of securing the peace in the first place. Now having succeeded, it was being run out because of the international political uproar over the employment of contracted military forces to prop up a now functioning democracy. Furthermore, EO's intelligence wing predicted an internal coup led by the Sierra Leone military within a hundred days if the South Africans withdrew.[25] Lastly, the RUF, though severely mauled, was not completely finished as a fighting force, and the company feared its resurgence based on the continuing incompetence of the standing national army. Nonetheless, Kabbah caved in to a combination of internal and international pressure.[26] One of the provisions in the peace accord called for a termination of the EO contract signed by Strasser, and the last EO soldier flew home in January 1997.

Almost as soon as the last plane carrying EO troops lifted off the runway, the situation began to deteriorate. The much-touted and highly anticipated UN peacekeeping force failed to materialize when nobody was willing to foot the $47 million tab.[27] The same Western democracies so adamant in their demands for EO to go home were less than forthcoming when it came to providing for UN replacements after the South Africans departed. The best that could be arranged was for a Nigerian monitoring force to be deployed. It became known as the Economic Community of West African States Monitoring Group (ECOMOG).[28]

Five days before EO's hundred-day prediction expired, the coup occurred. The resurgent RUF had been secretly plotting with a number of army officers with the result that Kabbah's democratically elected administration was toppled in May 1997. The Revolutionary United Front paired up with the rogue army units and descended upon Freetown. The Nigerian troops withdrew behind their fortified perimeters and did little to alleviate the medieval horrors that were descending upon the capital city. In the most ironic twist of fate, many UN and Western nationals scrambled for refuge in the diamond mining concessions that were protected by a Western firm with connections to Executive Outcomes.

A period of prolonged terror for the civil population commenced. It would require five years and a major deployment of British Marines and Special Forces before the RUF was finally eliminated. UN involvement was also required before the country was stable enough to hold elections again in 2002.

The following observation from Human Rights Watch provides tragic insight into the anarchy that befell Freetown after Executive Outcomes returned to South Africa.

> The battle for Freetown and ensuing three week rebel occupation of the capital was characterized by the systematic and widespread perpetration of all classes of atrocities against the civilian population, of over one million inhabitants, and marked the most intensive and concentrated period of human rights violations in Sierra Leone's eight-year civil war. [29]

The article goes on to state that ECOMOG forces were not necessarily saviors either.

> ECOMOG troops also violated medical neutrality during a January 11 operation in which they stormed a hospital, proceeded to drag wounded rebels from their beds, and executed them on the hospital grounds. At least twenty-eight rebels, including two children and a few who had already surrendered, were executed.

In light of the appalling crimes committed against the civilian population of Sierra Leone, a strong case can made in favor of continued employment of private military companies such as EO based solely on humanitarian grounds. The reality is that the country's defenseless citizens paid an exorbitant price in blood to support the moral repugnance of the international community in the deployment of mercenaries. A similar situation exists today in the Sudan. The West has been dragging its feet in an attempt to solve the problem without inserting uniformed military forces. How many Sudanese have perished is open to speculation, but undoubtedly a professional, private military force would make as short a work of the Janjaweed militia as Executive Outcomes did to the RUF.

In Sierra Leone, the outlay of hundreds of millions of dollars, the infusion of UN and UK troops, and the lives of thousands could have been spared for a fraction of the cost had the country been supported properly once the South African company had stabilized the security situation in 1996. Through fear of involvement, the Western democracies have partially legitimized operational firms such as EO when the only bottom line for the host nation is one of success or failure. Less than a decade later this oversight would come home to roost in the fiasco that is Iraq.

The American Experience: Blackwater

Unbeknownst to the general public, Blackwater originally opened as a one-stop training facility, designed to draw in Special Operations teams and police units from all over the world to its state-of-the-art facilities in North Carolina. Blackwater is a bifurcation of LOGCAP. The theory at Blackwater's headquarters in Moyock, North Carolina, in 1997 was "if they privatize logistics, why not training?" In this case, the gamble has paid off. Subsidized by a $500 million cash inheritance of the owner Erik Prince, Blackwater was established as the world's premiere, cutting-edge training facility that could support every military specialty imaginable. If the mission called for free-fall parachuting skills for night insertions, the students went to Blackwater. If forced entry, door breaching, close-quarters combat, anti-kidnap driving, sniping, and surveillance training were on the menu, the teams deployed to Blackwater. Canada's covert Joint Task Force 2 (JTF-2) has trained there. So have many other secretive units from multiple allied nations along with a large number of metropolitan special weapons and tactics (SWAT) teams. The only unique spin on Blackwater was that founder Erik Prince had a half-billion dollars of his father's money to construct his own military theme park in whatever manner he so desired. Cost was not an obstacle in the pursuit of providing the world's best training facilities, and to this day Blackwater has no commercial equal in terms of physical quality.

There is no credible evidence prior to September 11, 2001, to suggest that the Moyock-based company ever considered any operational taskings similar to those of Executive Outcomes. The attack on the World Trade Center and subsequent invasion of Afghanistan led to an increased use of contractors, but they worked mostly on a logistical basis as Special Operations Forces in conjunction with the Afghan Northern Alliance conducted the fighting.

It was not until some two years later that the perfect storm for private military companies was created by the Iraq War. This unprecedented opportunity, unlikely to be repeated, was based on the precise confluence of three key factors. The first was the U.S. administration's abysmal preparation for the occupation, which created a window of opportunity for PMCs. The second was a complete lack of regulatory oversight coupled with unlimited funding. (This situation was the equivalent of providing the alcoholic with the keys to the distillery.) The third was the driving political pressure to complete the job as rapidly as possible, thus tacitly legitimizing marginal business practices. Nobody was too concerned about the details. With one corner of the triad feeding another, the storm grew in intensity. Eventually it reached the status of a category 5 hurricane as the initial success of the invasion gave way, in 2004, to a rising insurgency.

Chapter Four
The Perfect Storm

The Bush administration's lack of a cohesive plan for the postwar reconstruction of Iraq is well known and bears no need of repetition here. However, a number of events that occurred following the toppling of Saddam Hussein directly contributed to the proliferation of PMCs and are worthy of further examination.

The first was the paucity of American combat forces. Gen. Eric Shinseki, army chief of staff prior to the war (and now secretary of veterans affairs), testified in February 2003 that several hundred thousand troops would be required in Iraq for years after the initial invasion. For telling the truth, he was relieved of his job.[1]

This refusal to accept reality seeped upward to the highest levels of the administration. Speaking on National Public Radio in 1991 following the Persian Gulf War, then–secretary of defense Dick Cheney had stated,

> The notion that we ought to now go to Baghdad and somehow take control of
> the country strikes me as an extremely serious one in terms of what we'd have
> to do once we got there. You'd probably have to put some new government in
> place. It's not clear what kind of government that would be, how long you'd
> have to stay. *For the U.S. to get involved militarily in determining the outcome
> of the struggle over who's going to govern in Iraq strikes me as a classic definition
> of a quagmire.*[2] (italics added)

The Allied Coalition in Operation Desert Storm involved over a half million men, and Cheney was on the record as saying Iraq could not be realistically occupied. A dozen years later the same individual was part of an administration that instructed the same army to occupy the same country with a force only 40 percent of the size of the 1991 juggernaut. Simple arithmetic dictated the army would need every person in combat boots it could lay its hands on to succeed. To effectively concentrate its combat power, the army would have to rely on the outsourcing of logistics through the LOGCAP contract on a scale never previously imagined. This increase in outsourcing would widen the window of opportunity for PMCs in Iraq.

The second contributing factor was the Coalition Provisional Authority's contracting guidelines, which were ludicrously loose when compared to standard contracting guidelines in the United States. The CPA contracting guidelines ran for thirty-one pages as opposed to 1,923 pages for contracts based in the United States. "Small" contracts up to $25,000 were permitted to be solicited on an *oral* basis. Contracts of $500,000 were theoretically supposed to be reviewed by three officers but could be waived. Contracts did *not* have to be bid on a competitive basis. Contracts could be posted, bids tendered, and contracts awarded all on the *same* day.[3]

At best, the CPA ran an extraordinarily laissez-faire shop as far as keeping the books was concerned. Tasked with spending nearly $20 billion, it hired an obscure accounting company named North Star Consultants for a paltry $1.4 million. To audit one of the largest financial operations in U.S. history, the CPA had engaged the services of a firm so tiny that it operated out of a private home near San Diego![4] The entire CPA system, with an abysmal lack of financial controls, was ripe for systemic corruption. It did not take long for predatory contracting firms of every stripe operating in Baghdad to ascertain that nobody really knew where the money was going.

The last contributor was the one ingredient upon which all others depended. To finance nation building in Iraq was extraordinarily difficult in 2003, for Iraq had no central banking system to speak of, its currency was of dubious value, and it lacked the capacity for any type of electronic or computer-based financial transactions. So the United States turned to the oldest and most corrupting system on earth, *cash*. The numbers are breathtaking. According to the special inspector general for Iraq reconstruction,[5] "The Federal Reserve shipped $11,981,531,000 in U.S. currency to Iraq between May 2003 and June 2004, according to documents from the Federal Reserve Bank of New York.[6] The cash was drawn from the DFI (Development Fund Iraq) and TSPA (Treasury Special Account) accounts containing revenues from sales of Iraqi oil and frozen and seized assets of the former regime. The CPA also controlled $926,700,000 in U.S. currency seized within Iraq, mainly from the vaults of the former regime."[7]

According to a report by the Federal Reserve Bank of New York,

This currency was shipped to Iraq on pallets loaded into C-130 cargo planes. A standard pallet of US currency contains 40 "cashpacks" of 16,000 bills each and weighs 1,500 pounds. In the 13 months that the United States administered the DFI and TSPA, 484 pallets containing 19,360 cashpacks were shipped from New York to Iraq. These pallets held more than 281 million individual bills, weighing 363 tons. In total, the US shipped to Iraq more than 107 million $100 dollar bills.[8]

The last week prior to the CPA's turnover to the Iraqi government on June 28, 2004, witnessed the largest single payout of U.S. currency in Federal Reserve history. According to a congressional report: "Ultimately, the last-minute cash was sent to Iraq in two separate shipments: $2,401,600,000.00 on June 22, 2004, and $1,600,000,000.00 on June 25, 2004. The $2.4 billion delivered on these days replaced the December 2004 shipment as the largest pay out of U.S. currency in Fed history."[9]

The combination of loose accounting added to a war zone swimming in freshly minted greenbacks and predatory contractors equaled disaster for the U.S. taxpayer.

"Frank Willis, a former CPA official, provided a first-hand account of the vast amounts of cash flowing through Iraq and the lack of financial and physical controls over the funds," according to a Senate Democratic Policy Committee report.[10]

During the second half of 2003, Mr. Willis served in Iraq as Deputy Senior Advisor to the Ministry of Transportation and Communications and as the CPA's senior aviation official. Mr. Willis explained that under CPA control, a "wild west" atmosphere prevailed and the country was awash in brand new $100 bills.

According to Mr. Willis, when contractors needed to be paid by the CPA, they were told to "bring a big bag" for a cash payment. Mr. Willis personally witnessed a $2 million payment to contractor Custer Battles in shrink-wrapped stacks of $100 bills retrieved from a vault.[11]

Custer Battles was eventually investigated for fraud, and the company is now out of business. Custer Battles was one of the first PMCs into Iraq and promptly landed a $16.8 million CPA contract to guard Baghdad International Airport. Yet in 2002, the company was only able to produce documentation identifying $150,000 for reported income worldwide. The money trough that was Iraq for this pair represents a 112-fold increase in revenues in less than twelve months. Shortly thereafter, their total contracts were worth in excess of $100 *million*.

In a footnote to history, Mike Battles's wife, Jacqueline, was arrested in Germany in the summer of 2006 for money laundering, after moving some $2 million into accounts opened in her maiden name.[12] At the time, the company pleaded insufficient funds to pay off the fines that had been levied against them in court after being found guilty of fraud.

However, given the reigning conditions of Iraq during the fall of 2003 and early spring of 2004, before companies like Custer Battles were stealing everything not nailed down, there was no promise of PMC growth. It must be remembered that armed contractors were extremely rare during the first year of the American occupation. There was no need for them.

The reason is self-explanatory. Iraq was still enjoying relative peace while the populace waited for conditions to improve. No private security was required as nobody was dying. The U.S. military's figures for those killed in action (KIAs) for February 2004 stood at twelve dead, which is statistically insignificant for an occupying force some 150,000 strong.[13] Conventional wisdom dictated a scaling down, not a ramping up, of additional manpower.

Sadly, the lack of bloodshed was soon about to undergo a rapid and violent transformation. The reasons were twofold: a bungled reconstruction compliments of the White House and a relatively unknown Arab equivalent of CNN based in Qatar called Al Jazeera.

Fallujah and the Al Jazeera Effect

The future of PMCs was sealed once and for all in April 2004, and the decision was not made by either Washington or the Coalition Provisional Authority. Instead, it was decided by violent outbreaks of fighting, directed against Americans. The insurgency had finally arrived in force. Civilian reconstruction firms had been anticipating a supportive, or at worst, neutral civil populace during the years it would take to restore the country's infrastructure. Those plans had to be radically revised after the first insurgent's shots were fired in anger.

The killing of the four Blackwater security contractors in Fallujah in the closing days of March 2004 had an impact far beyond the deaths of the individuals involved. The video of the charred corpses hanging from the bridge stirred emotions around the world. For all too many Americans, the scene was eerily reminiscent of the fallen Rangers who were dragged through the streets in war-torn Somalia. Although there had been casualties in Iraq since the summer of 2003, it was the first time that such grisly footage had found its way into the American mainstream media. President Bush was outraged and ordered in the Marines.[14]

The regimental combat teams of the First Marine Division duly commenced the assault a week later and engaged in a brutal house-to-house street fight. Al Jazeera broadcast the fight live, from the point of view of those on the receiving end. Whereas CNN tended to focus on publicly palatable clips of wounded Americans, Al Jazeera likewise focused on images of burning homes and civilian corpses littering the streets. Arab channels were much less restrictive in their editing, and scenes of human butchery saturated Arab airwaves. Two wildly differing views were being disseminated into the United States and the Arab world, cultures already at odds with each other.

The "Al Jazeera effect" had as profound an impact upon Arab society as CNN's coverage had on the West a decade earlier during the Gulf War in 1991.[15] For the first time in history, the Arab world had a dedicated news service that appealed to all sectors of the population. Millions of Arabs were glued to the television during the fight in Fallujah just as Americans were addicted to CNN during the Persian Gulf War. To the pan Arab states, what was playing in their living rooms in no way resembled war against a civilized opponent but rather a methodical extermination of a major population center. To this day, the American public has little understanding of how visceral an impact the television feeds originating from Fallujah had upon Iraqi and Arab viewers. It really did resemble Armageddon to the viewing audience, and Al Jazeera was nowhere near as objective with its reporting back in 2004 as it is now.[16] The power of the Al Jazeera effect, coupled with the lack of reconstruction progress, struck a deep chord inside many an Iraqi heart and soul. The CPA, and to a lesser degree the army, were caught flat-footed.

It didn't take long for the populace to react to the broadcasts streaming out of Fallujah. Faced with what many Iraqis perceived as imminent genocide, a popular uprising began.[17] Several cities, Najaf among them, burst into open rebellion, and all of a sudden Iraq wasn't safe anymore. The news bulletins now dominating American living rooms were a far cry from civil reconstruction and building schools. For the viewing and voting public, it appeared as if the war had started anew.

Five days after the Marines went into Fallujah, the overall security situation continued to deteriorate. A KBR fuel convoy of nineteen trucks, along with no fewer than seven American military escort vehicles, was ambushed on the road just outside of Baghdad. The result was a massacre. KBR lost 70 percent of its vehicles and the entire force suffered a casualty rate of nearly 60 percent. This death toll was closer to what Marine combat units suffered attacking Japanese-held islands in the Pacific than was to be expected from a group of civilian truck drivers in a war that had already been declared over. Worse yet, the convoy had been attacked and shredded while under the umbrella of American Army protection.

Overnight, the security situation morphed from pseudo complacency to borderline panic. American companies scrambled for safe lodgings in the Green Zone, preferring a ratty trailer behind sandbagged gun emplacements to a luxurious villa in an upscale neighborhood with no protection. Other reconstruction companies evacuated all but the most critical workers, suspending operations until the appropriate security measures could be implemented. It was no longer an issue of moving freely while assisting the Iraqi populace. Instead, it had become a question of trying to avoid being shot or kidnapped while they rebuilt the country.

The reconstruction effort, now finally beginning to gear up a year late, was gutted. The timing could not have been worse. The Iraqis were scheduled to take over the helm of government in just a few months; meanwhile, the U.S. Army was ill prepared for asymmetrical war and was scrambling to adapt. The changed focus left a security vacuum for the reconstruction effort, which had finally begun to gain traction.

Eight chaotic weeks later, on June 28, 2004, the Iraqi Interim Government assumed the reins, albeit surrounded by a bevy of American "advisers" who still carried the big stick. The first order of business was security, both for the Iraqis and for American aid programs. The cost of that security was mind-boggling. The GAO, on a random sample of Iraq reconstruction projects, found that security consumed more than 15 percent of total billings on more than half of all projects. On a quarter of the projects, the security bill ate up more than 25 percent of total billings. The Congressional Budget Office estimated that between 2003 and 2007, U.S.-funded contractors spent between $3 billion to $6 billion to acquire security from commercial companies.[18] The day of the private military company had arrived.

So at the precise moment when the pendulum may finally have started to swing in favor of Iraq's reconstruction, the insurgency began and the security situation collapsed within a matter of days. The U.S. Army was up to its ears in a shooting war again and needed every soldier available. The engineering firms engaged in reconstruction needed to be protected, and the U.S. Army couldn't do it. There was only one viable option left, short of withdrawing from Iraq and writing the whole adventure off as a waste of blood and money: the private military companies, some already coping with an eightfold expansion in size in less than a year, were the obvious choice. The gold rush, with Baghdad playing the role of the Klondike, was on.

There was one last detail left, and it would have an enormous impact on the life and death of thousands of human beings. Paul Bremer signed Coalition Provisional Authority Order #17[19] on the day before the official handover to the Iraqi Interim Government. In the ensuing hubris of the changeover and the deteriorating security situation, the fine print of Order #17 escaped public and congressional examination. Doubtless its timing was chosen for a reason, similar in nature to a president signing controversial pardons the day before he leaves office.

CPA Order #17 granted immunity from prosecution to all private security companies employed in Iraq. Buried in the order under section 4, subparagraph 3, were the first eight words of a critical sentence: "Contractors shall be immune from Iraqi legal process. . . ." As was discussed in chapter 1, contractors then could not be held accountable for their actions, regardless. The last remaining legal recourse to intelligent oversight had been voluntarily sacrificed in return for nothing.

In hindsight, with the passage of time and the unfolding of events in Iraq since, it is perhaps time for a reexamination of Bremer's actions in that broiling summer of uncertainty and fear. Though no fan of the former ambassador, this author does forward the hypothesis that Bremer was at least partly the victim of circumstance, in terms of authorizing PMCs, and that history has perhaps judged him harshly.

In retrospect, the dissolution of the Baath Party and the disarming of the Iraqi Army and police forces proved to be an error of the first magnitude, but the blame for these decisions must be shared equally among the White House, Congress, the Departments of State and Defense, and the military. All were equally convinced of the need to remove the Baath Party from the trappings of power, but Bremer was the sacrificial lamb who actually signed the order. In no way should he be held *solely* responsible for the disaster as he had a lot of powerful but silent partners.

It is equally difficult to fault him for dipping into the Iraqi Development Fund.[20] With the American money hopelessly bogged down in red tape, it was the only funding venue for immediate fixes to the national infrastructure. Had the insurrection held off for a couple of months longer and had the impact of the spending spree trickled down more quickly to the Iraqi in the street, the whole thing might have actually worked. How close it came to success will never be known, but it was an eminently reasonable gamble at the time, especially when compared to the alternatives. It is interesting to speculate that had the timing been favorable by just a few weeks, Paul Bremer could well be regarded as the savior of Iraq.

On June 28, 2004, Paul Bremer was scheduled to hand over the reins of government to untested individuals lacking national political experience. This mixed bag of American appointees was about to inherit a country beginning to seethe with religious and tribal tensions. An armed insurrection, mostly Sunni in nature, was already under way against the occupying Americans. How it all would play out politically was anybody's guess.

The infrastructure, in terms of power and water, was below prewar standards. To top it off, the American Army was badly overstretched with a severe case of mission creep. With a budding insurgency fast approaching, the army had neither the inclination nor the manpower to babysit reconstruction engineers.

With Iraq being the pot, Paul Bremer was in a high-stakes poker game with the Four Horsemen of the Apocalypse and fate had dealt him a pair of deuces. His only long suit was the potential force multiplier of a rapidly rebuilt national infrastructure. If the Iraqi in the street saw life improving, he might just hold off from rebellion long enough to allow the reconstruction to continue. It could be speculated that by Bremer's calculations, every day the situation improved was one day closer to peace and prosperity. The key was the pace of reconstruction, and if any factor upset the timetable the country would continue to slide toward the abyss.

This author supposes that it is reasonable to assume Bremer was fully cognizant of the brutality with which a minority of PSCs operated. For example, Blackwater contractors were some of the most notorious cowboys in the industry. Blackwater also happened to be the company that won a no-bid contract worth just under $30 million—replete with thirty-six men, K-9 teams, and three helicopters—to provide security for him.[21] Unless the former ambassador was both blind and deaf, he could hardly be unaware of his own security detail's actions.

But there can equally be no doubt that he also knew the magnitude of the disaster that would befall the entire reconstruction effort should in two days' time, after the handover, hundreds of contractors found themselves in Iraqi court accused of murder. The instant the first Western private military contractor landed in jail, every security company would pull out the next day. The engineering firms, lacking protection, would go home the following day, and that would be the end of the freshly minted Republic of Iraq. It was the devil's alternative, and a case could be made that he had no real choice.

By signing the order he was condemning thousands of innocent people to death without legal recourse for their families. By not signing it he was potentially increasing the casualty rate a hundredfold should Iraq slide over the abyss into civil war. Civil war was something the Bush administration, the army, and the American people wanted to avoid at all costs.

For any normal human being it must certainly be morally repugnant to authorize immunity from prosecution for crimes that have not even occurred yet. CPA Order #17 provides both explicit permission and removal of effective deterrents, creating an environment ripe for the commitment of battlefield atrocities. It can only be hoped that Bremer pondered long and hard before signing the authorization. Perhaps he hoped that it would be a short-term fix, applicable only until the country became stable enough to revoke it after reconstruction. But as with all things in Iraq, actions have an ingenious capacity to founder and only contribute to the prolongation of strife. But for such a sweeping order, with enormous ramifications for millions of people and one that led directly to the deaths of thousands, the onetime head of the CPA does a magnificent job of downplaying it in his own memoirs. The closest one can find, based on the date the order was signed and compared to the chronology of events in Bremer's memoir, *My Year in Iraq*, is a single fragment from a solitary sentence. It reads, "As I was working my way through a stack of documents that night, Colonel Norwood brought disturbing news." That line is the sum total of his reflections pertaining to the granting of immunity to private contractors.[22]

Thus, Bremer's greatest legacy, in terms of blood spilled and treasure wasted, was reduced to a bureaucratic byline, a "stack of documents," written in faceless Coalition Provisional Authority legalese. Once again, Hannah Arendt provides the most moving insight of such behavior, drawn from her reflections on Adolf Eichmann in Jerusalem. Describing how faceless or morally weak bureaucrats survive, she wrote, "The chief qualification of a mass leader has become unending infallibility; he can never admit an error."[23] How much of that observation is applicable to Paul Bremer or even the Bush administration is up to the reader to decide.

In any case, he signed the order. And in so doing, he let fully slip the leash that up till then had restrained the dogs of war.

The result was anarchy.

Chapter Five
Anatomy of a Disaster

The Center for Advanced Security Studies (CASS) was founded in South America in the mid-1990s and eventually moved to the United States in 1998. Based upon a perceived need for a dramatic and necessary retooling of what the public calls bodyguards, the company was established to train entry-level protection officers to the highest possible level. It was the original brainchild of a pair of extremely high-ranking NCOs—one had a storied history with the British Special Air Service (SAS) while the other hailed from the ranks of the U.S. Army's Delta Force. This author was one of the initial intake of former SOF candidates and eventually assumed operational control of the company, founding its American location in Florida.

Existing in a niche market long before 9/11, it had sustained steady if slow growth. Its core specialty was a month-long training program to instruct neophyte students in the esoteric skills of bodyguarding. Later the industry-wide name would be changed to personal security details in an effort to escape the negative stereotype inherent to the word "bodyguard."

The center fared well and was able to employ recent graduates throughout the security arena in areas such as Bosnia, Kosovo, and swathes of South America. The foundation for success is based on exacting standards. With a graduation rate of less than 40 percent, those that do pass are highly sought after. It is the longest and most intense training of its type commercially available in the world.

In the summer of 2003 the facility began to receive both queries for training and requests for potential employees for operations in Iraq. One of the interested parties in hiring graduates for work in Iraq was a twenty-three-year-old Canadian named Joel. Initially the e-mails concerned the possibility of preparing a group for deployment to Iraq for security operations. However, as the need for trained personnel increased, the focus shifted to a bulk hiring of recent graduates. For this story, all names of CASS personnel are pseudonyms.

Tristan, a senior instructor and former U.S. Army Ranger of many years, was placed in charge of the project. He picks up the narrative.[1]

At first, it sounded rather straightforward. But with the passage of time a few of the warning bells began to ring. Joel began to talk of his time with the Canadian Special Forces prior to Iraq. The problem was that the Canadian Airborne Regiment was disbanded shortly after Somalia and at twenty-three Joel was too young to have served. So he was inflating his track record. This is not unusual in this industry as many positions are based on who you "were" as opposed to who you "are." Special Forces, Rangers, and the like are generally given first shot at the best jobs, so there is a lot of pressure for other guys to artificially inflate service records in order to be considered competitive for the slot.

At the time we had thirteen available graduates. Of those thirteen, only five had graduated the course with our endorsement for employment. The other eight had technically completed the course, but we subjectively felt not all of them were ready for armed personal security detail [PSD] missions overseas. These reasons can be as varied as not being able to work as part of a team to an overly aggressive mind-set. They were not necessarily bad people but rather required additional training in some area before they were competent enough to be employed on a top-tier team.

So I gathered up the files and all the staff drafted up a report, which ranked the thirteen, each with their strong and weak points that we then forwarded to Joel. By intelligent balancing he should be able to pair people up correctly and have a competent detail. We fired off the report and thought nothing more of it.

The plot thickened when we received word that Joel wished to hire the eight who had *failed* to receive our endorsement for employment. Of the top-five-rated individuals, he wanted none.

Immediately, we smelled a rat. In our experience, the only time an organization actively sought low-caliber individuals was when leadership was lacking and would therefore be intimidated by competent employees. All signs pointed to a company hierarchy of immature young men.

Due to the unusual request, CASS opted to fly Tristan over on a reconnaissance mission prior to releasing the contact details of the selected individuals.

I arrived in Kuwait City in November of 2003. It was just a few weeks before Saddam Hussein was finally captured.

It was bad. I mean, really bad. I was taken to Joel's very luxurious apartment in downtown Kuwait City. I was flabbergasted when I walked through the door. One entire wall was stockpiled with state-of-the-art Motorola radios, GPS's, and a lot of other toys, many of which were expensive but unnecessary. In his bedroom were a mass of MP-5 submachine guns and heavy assault rifles. I nearly had a heart attack as I knew the Kuwaiti officialdom took a rather dim view of foreign nationals sitting on stockpiles of automatic weapons in their country.

I asked for the Table of Equipment and Organization along with the Employee Manual and the Standard Operating Procedures. These are the bibles of the security industry, where all is written down so the organization is able to work as one homogenous element. I cannot overstate the importance of these documents. In this industry it is literally a matter of life and death. He didn't have any but rather asked if I could make some. It was the same story with the budget, payroll, and accounting process.

The PSD staff had all come from Joel's previous company in Kuwait, where he was employed patching tents that the army had damaged. Upon close questioning, none of the employees had any previous experience in combat arms.

Tristan discovered that Joel had simply walked into the dining facility of the company where he was employed repairing tents and asked all his friends if they would like to go to Baghdad as "PSD operators." Collectively, there was not a single individual with combat arms training or experience. Two women were also chosen, including the girlfriend of one of the male team members. It was nepotism at its worst and a recipe for disaster.

Joel, realizing the potential shortcomings, wanted to hire the eight worst graduates from CASS, because while these individuals were trained, Joel felt he could control them and hide his lack of experience from them. Tristan continues the narrative.

I couldn't stand it any longer and asked him how he had managed to acquire a multimillion-dollar security contract from the United States Air Force. His response shed a lot of light on the way things worked at the time.

He informed me that a friend of his in Baghdad had heard about a civil engineering company looking for security. They were due to start up in less than a month, and the tender was posted at CPA headquarters in Baghdad. Joel got a copy of the notice and realized it would require some capital to start up. He approached a wealthy Kuwaiti whom he knew had done previous logistics contract work for the American Air Force maintaining U.S. facilities in Kuwait.

The Kuwaiti took one look at the contract, ran the numbers for about five minutes, and made a phone call. According to Joel, the required million-dollar start-up was available within the hour. He sent the letter back to Baghdad, and the engineering company, with the blessing of the CPA, awarded the contract the very next day.

The Kuwaiti, an extremely astute businessman who held an MBA [master of business administration] from Harvard, wasted no time. He contacted the engineering company directly and promptly sold them a turnkey logistics package for trailers, food, trucks, and security. The only thing the American firm had to supply was the engineers. This also allowed him to perform some slick accounting moves. He was able to purchase the SUVs outright on the local market, then turn around and lease them back to the engineering company from the logistical side of the contract. If one of the vehicles was destroyed by the insurgents, the engineering company was responsible for paying off the cost of the vehicle and for replacing it with another. The lease recouped the value of the vehicle in just over a month and this was a twelve-month contract. I didn't know about this until much later. It was perfectly legal, though the engineering firm was taking a huge financial hit. But that was the norm back then as it was free money without a limit when it came to reconstruction.

Over the next couple of weeks I met about half the teams. There were a few competent individuals, but for the most part it was just kids with guns.

It was the only time in my life I saw women employed as PSD members. One in particular was hopeless. It was all she could do to lift up the AK-47.

During the interview for this book, Tristan was asked to evaluate the competency of the organization.

They were doing stuff that a competent team would have heart attacks over. Communications were nonexistent and the vehicle-mounted teams were reduced to texting each other via cell phones. All the expensive radios they had bought lacked the necessary range to effectively communicate. It was my professional opinion they were an accident waiting to happen, and the truth was I didn't want anything to do with them. But God, they were making a lot of money. To a man, they were a huge liability, and the only reason they were still alive was that they were facing an equally inept fighting force in the form of the Iraqis, who compose the worst soldiers in the world.

It was at that time that Tristan had to make a difficult moral decision, based upon what he had seen.

Before I left to go back to the States, I asked for an interview with the Kuwaiti owner. To his enduring credit he listened carefully, clearing aside his other issues for the day. We conversed for several hours. At the conclusion, he asked what needed to be done. I spent a day longer and drafted up a sixteen-page report and gave it to him and that was the end of it. I left for the U.S. the next day.

Upon return we contacted the eight in question and explained the situation fully. Of the eight, six wanted to go forward and did so, flying out shortly after I returned.

The Center wrote it off as a lost cause and focused its attention elsewhere. We never anticipated hearing from them again.

Tristan returned to operations and teaching, deploying to South America to guard a corporate CEO, and came back to teach another class of five students in the spring. He picks up the narrative again after an interlude of seven months.

It was just a few weeks after the Fallujah shoot-up with Blackwater. The KBR convoy massacre was still in the news when the Kuwaiti called me at home. He minced no words and asked me would I like to become the new security project manager? He also suggested I speak to a newly hired director of operations. I replied I would be pleased to speak with him.

The new director of operations, Mark,[2] was a rare find in those days, being both honest and competent. He had been brought in to overhaul parts of the company that showed signs of increasing instability, specifically the Iraqi security detail. A former U.S. Army captain, he had a deep understanding of both the military and the civilian contracting world. He had lived in Kuwait for nearly two decades and was possibly the most experienced contracting officer in that oil-rich republic.

Mark and I spoke for several hours. The core issue was that the private security contractor side of the company was running completely amok. Nothing was working, and the client was not happy. I asked the obvious question pertaining to the ability of the project manager in charge. Mark's answer was as straightforward as it gets.

"We have had to fire the last two in a row. Both have stolen tens of thousands of dollars in cash. As you are doubtless aware Iraq is a cash-only operating environment, and the sight of a hundred grand sitting in a safe was too much of a temptation, I suppose."

"You are saying that of the last two project managers, BOTH have stolen money?"

"Yes."

There wasn't much I could say in response to that.

Mark continued to pass on the bad news.

"We have no control from here in Kuwait, what with both managers gone. It's not just the managers, either. Do you know an individual called Nader?"

I did. He had finished dead last on our list, with a heavy endorsement that the Egyptian-born individual not be allowed to possess firearms on operational assignments. His one saving grace was that he spoke Arabic, which made him attractive for all the obvious reasons.

"Well, Mr. Nader was in a gunfight not so very long ago. His team got shot up, nothing too serious. The word I am getting from the team leader is that the Egyptian spent about five minutes cowering on the floor, long after the shooting had stopped."

"Mark, that's not unusual for a first time. Granted, get rid of him, but that sort of thing occurs more than most realize."

Mark then informed me that long after the exchange of gunfire Nader recovered himself sufficiently to get off the floor and initiated return fire on the nonexistent enemy. All he managed to do was to shoot a thirteen-year-old girl in the head. She died on the spot.

He explained to me, "That's murder in my book, but there isn't a damned thing I can do about it because the team didn't stop. They just left the kid bleeding on the sidewalk and drove away. I only found out about it by accident. So I'm stuck with an inept killer on my payroll. My fear is, how many others are there out there that I don't know about? We know they are lacking solid leadership and running out of control. I have only had the reins for a couple of weeks, but this needs to get fixed in a hurry."

"Anything else?"

"Yeah, I think the logistics guy in charge of the camp is cooking the books, but I need to see them. So I propose we all go up and get it sorted out for a few days and determine the lay of the land."

Due to other operational responsibilities, Tristan was unable to take over as project manager but would go over as a consultant to assist in overhauling the company. CASS tapped Rupert, a former member of Britain's elite Special Boat Service (SBS), as a project manager. Another graduate of the program, he brought an enormous wealth of experience and was a standout choice for the role. In a very sad footnote, years later he too was released due to suspected mishandling of company funds. But in June 2004 he was the perfect man for the job.

The consensus was that Mark, Tristan, and Rupert would all travel up for a week. Mark would audit the books, Tristan would play the role of the enforcer, and Rupert, who would remain behind to lead, would come across as the fair and competent new boss.

It was during the second half of June 2004, while the CPA was feverishly doling out money, that the three of them were sitting in Amman, Jordan. The flight to Baghdad was the very next day.

Tristan once again picks up the narrative.

Mark had forwarded my name, not Rupert's, as the new project manager. Some of the employees knew me as I had trained and evaluated some of them, so they knew exactly who was coming. So they opted for a revolt en masse. They called Mark and threatened to take the vehicles and sell them or set them on fire. The whole detail was going to quit in protest. They couldn't guarantee our safety, etc. It was quite vicious so the three of us knew well what was in store.

Somehow or other word had gotten out that I did not tolerate dreadlocks, Mohawks, earrings, nose rings, or any other highly abnormal variation of human dress or grooming. This was a security company, not a band of pirates. This made us extremely unpopular as at that time even the supposed top-end guys like Blackwater were pretty wild in their attire and personal grooming.

For our efforts we were told the entire team had given each other Mohawk haircuts, and they didn't think we had the balls to fire them.

I told Mark that was fine and that we had lots of replacements standing by to fly in. We didn't, but they didn't need to know that. So they could Mohawk away to their heart's content, but nobody would have a job on the morrow.

The three of us caught the short flight to Baghdad the next day on the Royal Jordanian charter, paying more for a one-hour hop into a war zone than most people pay to cross the Pacific Ocean. We arrived at BIAP and were greeted by one of the security teams sent to pick us up. The atmosphere was decidedly tense.

There were three vehicles, with us in the only armored one. They had provided us with small arms and body armor, which was fine.

It was during the drive from the airport that the funny business started. The team leader sitting in the front passenger seat promptly turned around and informed us that we were "under fire" and that bullets were striking the ground between our vehicles. Both Rupert and I, having been in the real thing before, took a hard look around. No gunshots, no panicked driving, no obvious pucker factor, and no return fire. Bullshit. They were lying to us, trying to scare us before we even got to our quarters. We would find out why later.

We pulled into camp well after dark. A number of trailers greeted us. Of the contractors, there were none. The whole compound was deserted, save for a few locked doors.

In front of the door of my trailer lay an enormous quantity of empty Corona bottles and large volumes of human hair. It looked like a Mohawk showdown was imminent.

Rupert and I took a quiet stroll of the premises, inspecting the quarters where the contractors lived. I could best describe it as something out of a Quentin Tarantino movie. We found weapons, loaded and operational, tucked into every nook and cranny imaginable. One room yielded a haul of Russian antitank rockets. Another had a heavy-caliber machine gun tucked into a corner. Grenades were everywhere, spoons unsecured. The rooms were physically a mess and resembled a frat house after a wild party more so than any sort of professional organization.

The only thing in greater abundance than bullets was alcohol. Scotch, gin, bourbon, beer, everything you could think of. As for choice of music, it was overwhelmingly heavy metal, with the likes of Metallica the most popular. If one envisioned a Harley gang taking over a National Guard Armory with a distillery attached, you have a close idea of what we found.

The three newcomers settled in, preparing for the next day. Their light napping was broken only by the sporadic firing of a 155mm howitzer conducting harassment and interdiction on some insurgent part of Baghdad.

Tristan recounts the stunning discoveries of the next morning.

It was something out of *Apocalypse Now.* Of the forty-odd employees, no less than eight had vanished overnight. They had packed their belongings, taken the weapons they wanted, and been driven to another company by friends. There were no time sheets. Mark discovered that one of the women had been paid every day for the last three weeks at four hundred dollars per day, even though she was partying in Dubai the whole time. Her fellow employee and boyfriend was also on the books at four hundred a day. He was also in Dubai. Neither had been physically present for almost a month, but both were getting paid. There was no property book in existence, which meant we could not determine what was owned by the company and what was owned by the individual. There was no weapons registry but rather an enormous tractor trailer CONEX [shipping container] stuffed to the roof with Iraqi weapons of every type imaginable. It did not take long to discover a number of contractors were moonlighting as amateur arms dealers. Weapons were arriving and disappearing with amazing frequency, and any form of control was nonexistent.

Trading with the army was rampant, especially for alcohol. Grenades, rocket launchers, anything not on an army property book could be gotten from some quartermaster if the quantity and type of booze were high enough. We had an AT-4 antitank rocket in the operations room that came from God alone knows where. The army couldn't get alcohol, but all we had to do was drive to BIAP to the duty free where we could buy as much as we wanted. The Russians just flew in more when the liquor store was emptied by contractors. I later found it was emptied on a daily basis. Sometimes twice daily.

We reviewed our scope of work in the makeshift operations room. There were several dozen building sites we had to escort the engineers to and from. All were located inside Baghdad proper. There were no maps, no routes, no photos of the sites, nothing. We were restricted by institutional knowledge in that only one or two people would know the actual way to the site. If they weren't working, the engineers couldn't get there.

The logistician whom Mark accused of cooking the books had a trailer full of Iraqi women, all young and very pretty. They were being "protected" against the militia by residing in his personal trailer. We didn't know whether they were hookers or whether he just had his own harem. Equally high on the options list was that they had been kidnapped or were even sex slaves. It wasn't as if they could just get up and walk away of their own free will.

Many of the employees were drinking themselves into a stupor. Vehicles were smashed while driving under the influence, and numberless missions were run on severe hangovers. It had been like this every day for months.

If the three who had been tasked to overhaul the situation were appalled at the physical conditions and paucity of accounting, the introduction to the employees was infinitely worse. Joel, the Canadian who had landed the contract, had long since departed along with the corrupt project managers. The teams, inexperienced and incompetent, had been left in the lurch.

Tristan again picks up the story.

I didn't know whether to shoot them all or feel sorry for them. More than anything they were totally lacking in adult supervision. Through incompetent leadership, they had been passively allowed to devolve into something more akin to an armed gang than a professional fighting force. They reminded me of surfers, bikers, or other fringe elements of society who are proud of their rebel status. They glorified it, and the more outrageous the conduct the higher the esteem in which the individual was held. Anything childish was supported while anything smacking of discipline was derided.

Tactically, they were clueless. They didn't even know how to fight back from an ambush. They were making super simple mistakes, like running without spare tires. They had no drill to recover downed vehicles. If you got a flat, you would have to toss a thermite grenade into the vehicle because there was no way to recover it. Your flat tire just became a forty-thousand-dollar write-off. This was considered acceptable as the forty-grand loss was simply passed off to the client who passed it off to the U.S. taxpayer. They had taken one fatality, a victim of a high-speed rollover vehicle crash. I was never able to determine if the individual was drunk when it occurred, but all indications point that way. In memoriam, a twelve-hundred-dollar piece of body armor was destroyed to create an impromptu memorial. I was not impressed.

Fire discipline was nonexistent. Rupert and I rode with them for several patrols, and every time we pulled out of camp it sounded like the outbreak of World War III. Invariably it was the same trigger-happy morons who were indiscriminately engaging civilian vehicles that they thought had come too close. Often the Iraqi civilian drivers had no choice as they were simply caught up in city traffic like the rest of us. A couple of times the volume of fire was so high I thought we had been legitimately ambushed and a full-scale firefight was in progress. Rupert, sickened by what he saw, actually ground his pistol into the ear of one shooter who had been happily lighting up vehicles and told him, "The next time you pull the trigger so do I."

We were killing an awful lot of people, and none of it was going on the books in the form of incident reports. We did indeed, in the literal sense of the word, have a license to kill.

During the fortnight or so I was there I averaged two patrols a day, spending hours and hours on the road in some of the most dangerous parts of town. I never heard a shot fired directly at us. This is not to say it wasn't dangerous, because it was and ambushes occurred frequently. But in those two weeks I heard hundreds, if not thousands of rounds fired, and all were outbound, fired by us. I would rather not think about the cost, in terms of blood shed by Iraqi civilians, as a by-product of our actions.

Tristan summed it up rather succinctly.

I have no doubt whatsoever that the overly aggressive actions displayed by some security contractors caused a huge loss of civilian life, which, in turn, further inspired many otherwise moderate Iraqis to join the insurgency. Many of us, through our indiscriminate and aggressive actions, directly contributed to the future loss of American life perpetrated by Iraqis who had lost loved ones at the hands of trigger-happy contractors.

What Cost the Profit Margin?

By the end of the initial inspection tour, at least one conclusion had been reached: many of the employees would have to be dismissed. They were immune from any type of legal prosecution, so the only option left to the company was dismissal. But even that action was not as straightforward as it sounded. Immunity from prosecution had radically altered the human equation in the drive for profits. Upon his return to Kuwait, Tristan was given a closed-door session with the top Kuwaiti manager of the entire company. The manager is Shia by birth. This aspect is important as most of those people we were shooting up were Sunnis.

During the review, Tristan came directly to the point and clearly stated that about a dozen men would need to be dismissed for lack of discipline, poor fire control, and overall substandard performance.

The Kuwaiti manager flat-out refused to dismiss them all.

"One or perhaps two at the most," was the official response.

Tristan was aghast and demanded to know why. The crisp retort from his manager, more than anything else, clearly identified what had gone so very wrong in the war as engaged in by PMCs.

The Kuwaiti explained his position to Tristan. "You are suggesting I fire a dozen men. These are twelve men I bill out to the client at about $1,200 per person per day. That costs me $14,400 in lost revenue per day. How long do you think it will take to replace these twelve men?"

Tristan suggested ten to fourteen days.

The manager continued. "Very well then. Let us suppose it is only twelve days. That means I have lost $172,800 in less than a fortnight. To those twelve who are dismissed I can also add $1,500 each to fly them all home and another $3,000 each to buy a round-trip ticket for their replacements. I must also house and feed them before I can get them to Baghdad for another $500 each. So that is another $60,000 of earned revenue already spent. So the total cost for me in lost revenue and money spent will be some $232,800, all on account of the fact that you don't like the way some of your employees are treating the local population."

Tristan nodded in affirmation.

"What is the going compensation to be paid for a dead Iraqi at the moment?"

Tristan, referring to a U.S. policy to compensate families of victims slain by Coalition forces in accidental shootings, commented that he believed it was about a $1,000.[3] PMCs rarely reported shootings, however, as to do so was to theoretically open an investigation by a U.S. review board. This action was something no PMC wished to have hanging over its head for one important reason. It looked bad on the company's record when bidding new jobs to have a large reported trail of dead Iraqis in the business portfolio. Additionally, owing to the fluid nature of the shootings, it was just too difficult to get the details. No civilian contractor wished to be halted on a street in insurgent-ridden Baghdad, trying to calm down a family after the rear gunner had just shot the son to pieces. The reality was that only a minuscule fraction of contractor shootings were ever reported and then usually only when Iraqi government officials, such as the police, were the victims.

The Kuwaiti manager, a shrewd businessman, was well aware of the PMCs' foot-dragging to report shootings. "So how many have been reported in the last month?"

Tristan responded that a single incident, where an Iraqi policeman had died, was reported to the U.S. authorities. Compensation had been paid to the family.

The manager summed it up succinctly, as Tristan recalled. "You would have to kill and report over ten dead civilians a month for the next two YEARS before I even came close to spending what you suggest I dispense with now. There is no financial justification in sending these men home. There are no criminal activities that they can engage in that I can possibly be held liable for as they are in fact immune from prosecution. The truth of the matter is that it costs less for me to allow your men to continue to allegedly kill Iraqis than it does to replace them with those who won't shoot everything in sight. A dead Iraqi has no monetary value to me, especially at the reported rate of one a month. I would like to remind you that we are fighting a war and that casualties such as what you purport to have seen are sadly inevitable. Besides, they are all probably insurgents anyway.

"Therefore, you may fire one or two at your discretion to provide an example, but only after their replacements are here in country. As for the rest I strongly suggest you check to see if you are tough enough to deal with the kind of situation we have here. This is a war and people die—even civilians."

Of course, that was the way it always ended for those brave enough to blow the whistle. They were told they lacked the intestinal fortitude required to finish the job or that they had become weak when confronted with the human collateral damage of war. This ploy was used repeatedly against any contractor who grew sick of the waste, fraud, and occasional murder he witnessed. The truth was that the CPA had given a horrible collection of human beings, along with many superb ones, a literal license to kill. This particular company refused to pull an undisciplined gang off the streets so it could add an extra $250,000 to the company coffers.

By June 2004, there were over a hundred private military companies operating in Iraq. This particular one, now defunct, was no better or worse than any other. That's just the way it was, and this dismissal of one contractor's concerns was by no means an isolated incident. It was the norm.

Chapter Six
Apocalypse Unleashed

"We had no time for contractors. We thought them nothing more than a bunch of sorry bags of ass who had no rules and no military bearing whatsoever. The truth be known my men felt the same way. They didn't envy them in any way or wish to join them. Rather, they despised them."

—*A first sergeant with the U.S. Army Long Range Surveillance Detachment, commenting on contractors both in Afghanistan and Iraq*

The year 2004 was the best and worst year ever for private military contractors. They had proven their worth and were confronting record growth. The bad news was there were more spaces available than competent personnel to fill them. The quality of operators noticeably deteriorated, and the resulting strain on the industry soon would become evident. It was an ominous forewarning that presaged phenomena to come. The days of winning hearts and minds of the populace were gone, as if they had never existed. In its place lay brute force, lower-caliber staff, and a newfound willingness to pull the trigger at the slightest pretext. The focus was shifting from winning over the populace to fighting for its own sake as the means became an end unto itself. All too often the occupiers were inadvertently fanning the flames of the very insurgency they were trying to quell.

Jon Tripp, the former Special Operations contractor, had lived freely and successfully among the populace in the Red Zone in 2003. He began to observe differences the following year.

By the spring of 2004 the Sheraton had too many Westerners. It was a mix of military, PSDs, businessmen, and a lot of press. Most of them were friendly enough, a little loud at dinner after a few drinks, but not too bad. However, some of them treated the local hotel staff as inferior. The waiter would make a mistake, and right out loud they would say something derogatory. I actually heard one Westerner say, "No wonder they can't run their own country. Hell, they can't even get a simple food order correct." Everybody at that table just started laughing. This upset the server greatly. The manager came over and said so to the individual, and all he said was, "Yeah, so?" This would happen on and off, but it was usually the private business people doing it, not the private security. The security people would talk about how much of an asshole their clients were but couldn't do anything about it. At this time the security people acted very professional at all times. I met some really good guys here, but there is no doubt the conqueror attitude by some of the Americans infuriated the Iraqis to the point where they began to pick up arms. We hated it, but there was nothing we could do about it. We were voices in the wilderness.

An American in his thirties with two children, working for a well-known, reputable company, recalls the contractual free-for-all that occurred during the last couple of months of the CPA's tenure. This time frame was May and June 2004, when the Project Office was trying to spend billions of the Iraqi Development Fund dollars prior to the handover.

By the middle of May, we started to have problems with private security firms "acquiring" the names and contract bids of other competitors and trying to outbid them. All it took was to know somebody in the CPA, where all sorts of contracting drug deals (slang at the time for corruption) were brokered on a daily basis. So for that, and because I despise the press, which lived en masse just a few doors down from me and could never get it right, I left the Sheraton and went to the Al Safeer.

The first cracks were also beginning to show in what had up until then been a solid if informal alliance between the military and private contractors, as Tripp recalls.

As stated before, I was going back and forth between the private security briefings and the military security briefings. One day I tried to get in and was told I was no longer authorized. The NCO told me that the lieutenant colonel was tired of me making him look bad in front of the others in the briefing. Seems he did not like the fact that I had some intel he didn't have access to. A couple days later two reps from Halliburton started showing up to the private security briefings, and then they would report back to the lieutenant colonel. Of course, we didn't try to shut them out because they were God and could do whatever they wanted, including shutting us down. Nobody messed with Halliburton because your ass would be in the frying pan at CPA headquarters and you would never even smell another contract.

With the opening of the financial floodgates and the degrading security situation, corruption became omnipresent. This contractor, a highly decorated paratrooper in his forties, heard here for the first time, recalls his introduction to it. He found it to be a depressing experience.

I would meet with heads of local businesses, such as the Bank of Iraq or what have you. The idea was to train locals in static security and personal bodyguards to be used in these local businesses. This is when I first became acquainted with the term "consultant fee." I was told they had learned the term from the civilian contractors working for the U.S. When you submitted a contract for consideration, you had to have a built-in consultant fee for whoever was to decide on which contractor would win the bid. The higher the fee, the better the chance you would win the bid. I had heard of this before from my initial in-country briefing by my predecessor. For the Iraqis the fee can be put right into the contract, but for the private contractors you had to have it as a separate bid. This was my first confirmation of it, though.

It was not only Baghdad where consultation fees were employed. This incident occurred in Kurdistan in June 2004. The same American featured in the last anecdote describes his next exposure to the reality of corruption, not only among the Iraqis.

While in Kurdistan, the supervisor and I went to a meeting with a civilian representative of the U.S. military. He was the one who submitted the bids of companies for contracts with the U.S. government. My supervisor and the rep walked off for a moment. I could see that whatever he was telling my supervisor was pissing him off. He came back and grabbed me and said, "We are leaving."

When we got to the vehicle, I asked what happened. He said that the civilian stated the fee was too low. I said, "What fee?" He said, "The consultation fee."

It finally dawned on me we were talking about kickbacks and bribes for the American civilian. I had seen it with the locals, but this was the first time with my fellow countrymen. My boss wouldn't play so the contract was awarded to another bidder.

Jon Tripp recalls an incident that also occurred in Kurdistan. An increasingly large gulf separated the Coalition from the Iraqis who worked with them toward a common cause.

USAID said we had to buy U.S. vehicles (they were shit, no spare parts in the area) instead of local ones (more suited to weather and terrain, cheaper, parts available) while they drove around in up-armored German Mercedes SUVs for each client and each team. So what applied to us didn't apparently apply to them. They came to our client's place of business one time for a meeting with the client and the local leaders/businesses in the area. They refused to let the local leaders and businessmen into the complex for the meeting. The locals had to park away from the building and walk to the complex with their bodyguards. At the gate the bodyguards were not allowed in. These Iraqi security officers were targeted by the enemy, just as we were, because they were doing business with Westerners. I said it was wrong to treat them this way and was promptly told to keep my mouth shut while USAID was there. Our client said after the meeting, that right or wrong, we do whatever USAID wanted, because if we pissed them off they would just pull the funding for the company.

As greenhorn security contractors flooded into the country, the quality of incoming personnel declined precipitously. Gone were the days of the quiet professionals as thugs and cowboys began to occupy an increasing percentage of the security contractor ranks.

The author remembers some of his own experiences.

There is one man I knew who on the surface appeared helpful and kind. Somewhat obese, he was forever giving out candies to the Iraqi kids near our camp. He was the original roly-poly Santa Claus type. A devout Christian, he carried a small Bible with him and prayed briefly every night. He seemed to be pretty solid.

One day we overtook an Iraqi vehicle. It was the typical rattletrap sedan, occupied by an adult couple with two grimy kids in the backseat. In other words, they were no threat. Insurgents do not bring their children along to wage war. It was obvious they hadn't seen us, which is not surprising as we were doing about 2.5 times their speed and were well in advance of the main convoy. We began to slow down, in preparation to indicate to the driver to move to the side of the road for the convoy behind us to pass.

Without warning, as our truck pulled abreast, Bob (I shall call him Bob) leaned out the passenger side window and speared the Iraqi with the muzzle of his rifle. No warning, no wave, nothing. Just harpooned him like a fish in a barrel. The driver of the sedan, eyes wide and blood pouring from his face, hit the brakes as his car swerved to the side of the road. As we pulled away, Bob fired two shots, one into the ground and the second squarely into the radiator of the vehicle. Steam began to erupt from the grill while a very panicked family cowered behind the dashboard.

Upon questioning, he simply stated that he had thought he had seen a threat and had acted accordingly. By the literal interpretation of the rule book, he was entitled to have done what he did. But we had a hard time buying his concept of what "threat" meant. But that was becoming the norm as opposed to the exception, and no action was taken.

That was not the only incident "Bob" was involved in, as the author recalls.

On another occasion he came across one of the tractor-trailer drivers speaking on a cell phone. Cell phones are banned with transport companies as using them increases the accident rate on closely bunched convoys. The standard procedure is to collect the cell phone and turn it over to the president of the trucking company, who has final authority.

Bob, of his own accord, grabbed the cell phone, smashed it on the ground, and stepped on it, effectively squashing it. He did this in public, in front of all the other drivers. Bob weighs about 240, stands 6'4," and wears about 60 pounds of armor and gear. The driver, a Bangladeshi, weighed about 80 pounds soaking wet. Bob makes about $400 a day. The Bangladeshi, driving the same route with the same risks, maybe $35. I thought that was rather shitty but didn't say anything at the time.

Bob proclaimed himself to be a former Special Operations Command soldier—from First Ranger Battalion, no less, which happens to be my alma matter. So, as old soldiers do, we conversed about the good old days. Only problem was Bob couldn't recall the name of his company commander, first sergeant, or even the name of the drop zone where we made about 80 percent of our parachute jumps. It quickly became evident that Bob was lying.

Far too many of the inbound contractors lied about their military experience. In the rush to get men to Iraq, rudimentary checks were superficial. Thousands slipped through the cracks with deplorable results.

There exists a standing joke among former members of elite units. They never knew there were so many other people in the unit at the same time! If all the Brits who said they were with the SAS or SBS were coupled with all the Americans who vouched a past history with Delta Force, SF, or the Rangers, those units would be the largest formations in each army. Sadly, it made for poor unit cohesion.

The author's observations here apply to all the "Bobs" in theater.

Bob was a bully—nothing more, nothing less. All he could talk about was combat, explosive devices, and threats. He was scared shitless and, because he was scared, vented his fear on the innocent. He had no right to be there, and yet there are thousands like him who consider the Arabs literally as "Unteurmenschen," meaning subhumans fit for the gas chamber. His laptop contained a huge collection of war porn portraying violent death. But he still gave candy to the kids on the other side of the wire, was perfectly jovial in the chow hall, and prayed to be a good person every night. He was far too quick on the trigger and always aimed to destroy the vehicle, knowing full well that it was all most Iraqis had. Why? Because the prick could get away with it. Here, he was king. For him to return home, he would at best be a shift manager at Burger King. I believe power can be utterly evil. When I look at him,

I am often reminded of how seemingly normal men became concentration camp guards. Pat one child on the head and then shoot his parents. Had he been born eighty years ago in Germany, doubtless he would have found his way to Auschwitz. Bob was eventually quietly released and has since returned to the U.S.

There is an epilogue to the story. "Bob" returned to Iraq, where he quickly gained employment with a different company. Shortly after, he was severely injured in a motor vehicle accident, having been thrown through the windshield, over the hood, and onto the highway. He was nearly scalped and suffered grievous wounds, including severe damage to his leg. He has gained significant weight since the accident as he is no longer able to move effectively without the aid of a walker. His medical condition for the future remains uncertain. He boasts of returning to Iraq, but we both knew the odds of it happening were remote.

It was not just at the bottom level where the contractors' moral qualities became a point of contention. The following two stories of incompetence and corruption both occurred in Kurdistan in the second half of 2004, while the industry was expanding exponentially.

This former Marine, already working for his third company in six months and pulling down $15,000 a month at the time, describes the real possibility of shooting up one's own side . . . on purpose.

Unfortunately the guy they hired as the AIC [agent in charge] of the contract should have never been in charge of anything. He may have been an OK PSD, but as a leader he was unsound. We would have everything going well, the running of the houses, the mission planning and execution, etc. He would just show up whenever and make last-minute changes to everything so we had to scramble to adjust. These changes weren't because the client changed the schedule for the day or anything like that; he would just decide he did not like it. No reasons. It didn't help the fact that every morning when he showed up you could see and smell that he had been recently drinking. I never knew a single time he did not smell like alcohol. We would tell the home office in Baghdad, and they kept saying, "He is the AIC, so deal with it and work it out." When one or two guys say something bad about the one in charge, it can be written off as a personality clash. However, when ten out of fifteen guys are saying the same thing about him, it is time to look for a new AIC.

One day the owner of the company and the project manager came up and said they were going to fix everything. They started firing the PSD guys who had complained about the AIC. We were informed that since the client got along with him, they would rather let all the team go and bring in new guys rather than upset the client. That sucked, so a few individuals were going to take things into their own hands. I knew of at least two of the PSDs who were aiming to set up a fake ambush on the AIC. They were serious and had planned it all out to make it look like the enemy did it. We were definitely going to have a very dead agent in charge if these two followed through. Cal and I were able to talk them out of it.

I was the go-between for the AIC and the PSDs. Half my days were spent trying to defend the AIC and calming the PSDs over the latest stupid thing the AIC did. I came to find out he had been talking shit about me behind my back to the owner. That was when owner decided to come up and check it out himself. The good thing is, he and I had been friends before all this. We sat down and had a long talk about what was going on.

I went home on leave, my first in almost a year. Before I left I told the owner that if he did not meet the obligations of the contract and get rid of the AIC, he would lose the contract. He said he would take care of everything. Three weeks into my leave, I found out the client had fired the company and hired someone else. I was now out of a job.

The second instance revolves around a highly venerated former member of Delta Force. One of his American employees recalls the incident in question. The rot, in the form of too much easy money, was setting in seemingly everywhere.

When we were first hired, a well-known PSD, and current representative of the company that was hiring us, brought us into Kurdistan for decent pay. Shortly after arriving that representative was fired. Turns out he was diverting about five thousand dollars per man per month to his own account. He was also using the company's assets and contacts to bid for contracts on the side that were for him, without the company knowing it. After being fired he then began to bad-mouth the company, saying that we did not like U.S. PSDs, especially the Special Forces community. Yet we had two former Special Forces guys in the operation, with a former Delta Force operator as the project manager. The more money was involved, the worse the backbiting and bitching were.

This same American contractor, with two years in country, recalls interviewing a new potential employee several months later. Just as so many whose company loyalty was questionable, this individual had been employed by no less than five firms in the previous year. Such was the demand that the individual contractor, should he not like the company he was working for, could literally be picked up by another within a day or two. Being in country also saved the recruiting company the airfare. The downside was that it made a mockery of any form of quality control as substandard operators could always find work with a questionable firm whose operating standards matched those of the individual. The hiring contractor, an extraordinary operator, reflects upon the interview.

I recall asking him how long he had been in Baghdad and how much ammunition he fired off on a weekly basis. My company at that time was getting into one or two serious fights a month so I had a good idea of what to expect as far as ammo expenditure went. I nearly fell off the chair when he told me, in all honesty, about a thousand rounds a week. That was more than what I had used up in the last four months, and I had been on the road nearly every day! I was dealing with somebody who enjoyed dropping the hammer, and that was a very bad sign.

I took a closer look at him. He was a black kid from Detroit, maybe twenty-four or twenty-five. Lots of gold. Former navy with an "other than honorable" discharge. He was also carrying three different Glock pistols on his body, in both .40-caliber and 9mm caliber. Two on his vest and one in a useless ankle holster. This was in addition to his custom AK-47 with a seventy-five-round drum magazine. In all my years in the Ranger regiment, I had never carried more than one weapon. I asked him why all the pistols.

"In case they get too close or I am out of ammunition," was his response.

"Why three?"

"In case one or two don't work," was what he told me.

I was pretty sure by then he was a gangbanger. Just a punk who could pull the trigger whenever he felt like it. If he did this shit back on the block in Detroit, he would be in jail. But over here he was some kind of fucking hero. The only people who carry a multitude of weapons are those who are scared shitless. Lack of confidence both in yourself and your weapon so you make up for it by carrying multiple backups. I had seen it before, but this case was extreme.

I asked him how many ambushes he had been in.

"Four and a half."

That was a new one for me. "How did you get in a 'half an ambush'?"

He replied that he had been in the vicinity when an army unit got the chop up the road so he figured he was entitled to say that he was in a "half an ambush."

We didn't take him and told him to go look for work somewhere else.

I only saw him one more time, a few months later, just off a big intersection on the way to BIAP. He was taking photos of a shot-up car full of dead Iraqis. Probably his own handiwork. I couldn't see any weapons on the bodies. But there was nothing I could do, so we just drove on.

Baghdad was also undergoing a physical transformation. Socializing with local Iraqis became more difficult. Unarmored vehicles were not such a good idea anymore. As interaction between occupiers and occupied decreased, suspicion and violence grew in equal proportion.

A New Zealander, a brilliant platoon sergeant with high-risk duty in the Balkans, East Timor, and the Solomon islands, recalls the subtle changes transforming the city landscape.

More and more people were going outside the Green Zones less and less. The guys in charge would never go outside. They tried to deter me and another PSD from going shopping or going out at all. The boss said we were reckless and thought we were hotshots. This same guy, when he first got to Iraq, would go up to the roof of the Sheraton and shoot off into the streets of Baghdad wherever he felt like. He would tell this story at the drop of a hat. He was very amused with himself.

Jon Tripp who arrived in 2003 recalls with regret the ease with which he was once able to move and broker deals in the city compared to a year and a half later.

Within eighteen months, all of the restaurants I used to go to would be attacked and blown up for serving Westerners. No one went down the streets shopping anymore or you were dead. The same people who once laughed and talked with me would look the other way or close the shop up if we were in the area. Any weapons or equipment you wanted still had to be purchased down backstreets at night, but now you had to send a local to make the deal. They didn't always come back. Later their body would be found in the streets someplace, or we had to pay an additional cost to get the body back.

The cycle of violence would continue to spiral downward. The army, preparing for unexpected fighting, was no longer as kind to or forgiving of the populace at large. A fresh wave of security contractors arrived with attitudes, guns, and a blanket immunity for all crimes committed. If anything, this influx strained relations with a well-disciplined army even more. Base commanders were having difficulty coping with freewheeling, cowboy PSD teams that recognized no military authority as legitimate. Gone were the days of close cooperation. It was also during this time (late 2004) that extremely unscrupulous contractors began to import third-country nationals (TCNs) in an attempt to drive down costs while still providing a human being who could occupy a seat as outlined in the contract. For the old hands, the quiet professionals who had been plying the trade for years, this scheme was a heart-rending blow and the nadir of their professional existence. Their industry would never be the same again and had changed in a direction that many intelligent, seasoned professionals began to despise.

A British operator reflects upon his last mission with a company he had been with for nearly two years.

The PSDs had changed considerably within eighteen months, too. Originally they were all professionals with extensive backgrounds and combat experience. They didn't shoot blindly or just spray the entire area during an attack. They stayed calm, worked together, and identified their targets before engaging. That changed. It was becoming too expensive to hire that caliber of individuals for an entire contract. So the quality of PSDs went way down. It seemed they were just hiring whoever they could that would take the money and show up. The last team I was on shot first and asked questions later. They constantly said they couldn't wait to shoot more Iraqis. They kept count of them. A commonly used tactic is to wave off a car that is getting too close to the convoy. If that doesn't work, you place a couple rounds into the pavement as a warning. If that doesn't work, you shoot into the cab. It is a good SOP [standard operating procedure]. Sometimes you can't go through each step, depending on the situation, but in general it is sound. I saw guys give no warnings, just shoot into the cabs without taking any time to ID the occupants, and then say, "Oops, my bad. I'll be more careful the next time."

During one mission I had a car getting too close to us on the road. I could see the occupants. A man and woman in the front arguing with two small children in the back with their faces against the window looking at us. I tried to wave them off, but the adults weren't paying attention. I stuck my entire upper body out the window and began waving my arms and yelling. The driver finally saw me, his eyes went wide, and he slammed the brakes and swerved away. I was yelled at in the vehicle as well as when I got back to the base for not shooting them. I quit the contract and went to work for a friend.

Jon Tripp recalls a car bomb aimed at the U.S. Army with significant casualties on both sides. The soldiers were becoming less sympathetic to the plight of Iraqi civilians in light of their own increasing losses. As for Mr. Tripp, it was the end of the road for him. Unbeknownst to Jon at the time, the blast partially severed his spinal cord, in addition to fracturing his nose and cheek. He was later classified as having a "permanent partial spinal cord injury" and was no longer deployable. Medically disabled, he lives with the result of his injuries to this day. He is now fifty-five pounds lighter than he was during his prime spent fighting in Iraq. Here then, is Jon's final contribution.

There was a VBIED [vehicle-born IED] that detonated behind the safe house I was in. It was trying to hit a U.S. convoy passing by and not us; they did not even know we were there. Neither my client nor anyone else in the house, other than myself, was injured in the blast. My back hurt like hell but I could still move. On the road it was a different story as two U.S. soldiers were killed, several more injured, and more than thirty Iraqis were killed with even more needing medical attention. The military locked the area down and wouldn't let the locals try to get their injured to hospitals.

Myself and several other PSDs grabbed our med bags and tried to give as much help to the locals as possible. It was horrible, and we all ran out of supplies trying to treat them. It was several hours before the lockdown was lifted. To this day I still think many of the locals may have been saved if they could have made it to the hospitals sooner. Most died from shock and lack of IV [intravenous] fluids.

Another American, with over a year in country, recalls his first brush with his company's quest to maximize profits, a sign of decreasing company stability.

I had been working nine months straight, fifteen hours a day on average, and had only four days off the whole time. I was told I was doing a hell of a job and all our clients felt very safe with the local security guards I had trained. I was also told that when my initial contracted ended I was to be hired full time. They sent me off for some rest up north. When I came back, they told me my position had been eliminated. They had taken my training material, cut it down from three weeks to five days, and had the interpreters I had used during the training teaching the course. They decided to use them because it was cheaper to hire three of them than to pay me, even though they had no experience in security. That was it. No thank you. No nothing. Just pack your bags. I hate to say it, but I found out later that this was the rule as opposed to the exception.

As the war dragged on, the rules continued to change. The American Army was placed under tighter rules of engagement while the private contractors were still under blanket immunity from prosecution. At the small unit level, where both parties knew each other, a strange symbiotic relationship occasionally formed.

The author witnessed the events described below.

We had an army unit beside us with whom we had a good working relationship, of which there weren't many left at that time. Unlike many PMCs we were military heavy in experience, and the two organizations got along really well. We really did feel like we were brothers in arms. One night their platoon commander came to us and asked for a favor. Apparently they had found what they believed to be a house full of insurgents, but under the new rules they couldn't just blow it up anymore without reasonable proof. They couldn't shoot unless they saw a direct threat, and the house was painfully innocent on the outside. However, we did not suffer from that, being immune to prosecution and all. So we made the plan and would execute it on the morrow.

About noon the following day, our civilian truck was in the lead of quite a column of tanks and Bradley fighting vehicles, full of American soldiery. They stopped just before the intersection, with the house maybe a hundred meters down the road. We dismounted, crept forward, found good cover, and started to shoot up the building in question with our rifles. Sure enough, after about a minute, we began to receive sporadic return fire, and we could see figures scrambling around up on the roof with RPG-7s that definitely make you a bad guy.

As soon as the army heard the first burst of AK-47 fire from the house, the Bradleys and tanks clattered up and promptly leveled the place, killing everybody in the process. They could officially say they had been engaged by the insurgents. We did that a few times over a period of about six months. Everybody was happy.

As the shooting war escalated, the mental stress upon both the military and the security contractors increased. When lethal violence becomes commonplace, the human being must adapt to the new environment. Any adaptation involves managing complex emotional and physical challenges that must be overcome if one is going to continue to be employed in a combat environment. The result is a set of operating protocols often at odds with life in the "normal" world.

The author, based upon personal experience in Iraq, reflects upon the casual acceptance of violence.

One gets used to the violence and it becomes a routine, if such a thing is possible. As long as nobody is shooting at you directly, it's somebody else's war. Even the chaos can be predicted to particular neighborhoods at certain times. Some things bother some people more than others.

I now tend to focus on what "is" while others focus on what "could be." We once passed a corpse lying on the side of the highway. Stray dogs were gorging on it, long coils of human intestine hanging from their jaws. That bothered me not in the least. Past history, and the owner of the body is gone, and therefore it doesn't pertain to me. Others look at the same picture frame and imagine themselves as the corpse. They freak out.

The flip side of the coin is that a mile later we can pass a group of children on the side of the highway, barefoot and in rags. Somebody tosses out an MRE [meal, ready to eat] or two. The children, ages six to eight, then proceed to beat the living snot out of each other. This goes on until the victor, in true Darwinian form, steps forward to claim the spoils of his application of violence against others. This distresses me greatly, watching a free-for-all with six-year-olds; while others say nothing, and some find it amusing and break out laughing. I no longer throw out food from vehicles unless I have such an overwhelming surplus that I am sure everybody is going to get something. Others fill MRE bags with rocks and deliberately target children. It is extremely rare, but it has occurred a couple of times.

This contractor, a former Force Reconnaissance Marine who was quoted several times earlier, had to be prodded by voluminous quantities of beer before he would recount the incident mentioned here. He began to weep as he narrated this story.

Just one simple macabre act more becomes the proverbial straw that broke the camel's back. Jeff was in charge this time, and there was a huge fireball a kilometer ahead in the Al Dora part of Baghdad, which means it is utterly routine as there are huge fireballs there practically on a daily basis.

It was a car bomb. Our team dismounted and moved forward to render aid. It was a really bad one. The stink of burnt flesh laid heavy, and the usual collection of innocent civilians lay moaning in pools of blood. A foot, complete with shoe, was lying detached some twenty meters from the nearest possible owner. I distinctly remember the laces were still neatly tied.

There was a car about thirty meters behind the point of explosion. It was small and had suffered grievously from the blast. A massive wave of fire had rolled over the hood, melting the windshield. Jeff, along with a very new man, had arrived first. Jeff turned to the new guy and told him very clearly, "Don't look inside," as he motioned for a poncho liner to place over the charred contents. Our new man, gung ho, for whatever reason, looked. He left a week later, never to return.

Inside that incinerated husk of a vehicle had been a family—husband, wife, and a baby. Perhaps they had been able to observe the fireball wash toward them or perhaps it all happened so fast it was over before they knew what hit them.

But they must have had some time to prepare, for the husband clearly had his wife's hand in his. And the mother, with her other arm, had brought the infant fully into her chest, trying to cover the baby with her head and shoulders. So they had at least a second to react.

That was how we found them. Only the blast had made them one, united in death. So hot was the fireball that their bodies had fused together into a single lump of carbon and incinerated meat. Still holding hands, you could see that from the way they melted. Only the craniums, which generally don't flash burn, identified them as human. The baby's skull was maybe the size of a softball, eggshell white, and would have easily fit inside my hand. Nobody spoke much for the rest of the day.

The Marine involved in this incident is undergoing counseling for posttraumatic stress disorder with the Veterans Administration. It is hoped he will make a full recovery, but he has not done so as of this writing.

Another American, also a former Marine, shares a similar experience.

It was late 2006, and the attack occurred south of Nasiriyah, which was unusual as we used to consider that relatively safe. We were all a bit jumpy as we knew the Iranians had started training the Shia militias in regards to explosively formed projectiles [EFPs], which were far more lethal than the simpler IEDs. But at the end of the day there is nothing you can do except hope not to get hit.

We didn't make it. One of the other gun trucks got hit. It was an uparmored F-350. The blast threw it over fifty meters off the highway, and it landed upside down. We drove over and arrived within thirty seconds. The Iraqi gunner in the back had been thrown clear and was dead from impact with the ground. The driver was decapitated. The guy in the back was hanging upside down from his seat belt, which was rare as hardly anybody ever used them. Seat belts make it too constricting to shoot out the window as it cuts down your maneuverability. However, it saved this guy's life. We managed to get the door open and cut the seat belt. He was unconsciousness. We dragged him out and got him on the stretcher. He was eventually to make a full recovery and has no recollection of what happened.

That left the guy in the front passenger seat who also happened to be one of my best friends. He was not wearing a seat belt. Somehow or other he had managed to get stuck. The engine block had partially come off its mountings, and Cameron (not his real name) was trapped underneath it. He was pretty fucked up but conscious and lucid. He knew what was going on. The gas tank was leaking and gas was pooling on the floor of the upside down vehicle, so everybody was pretty stressed. We had just topped up so there were maybe fifty gallons of gas in the truck when it had been hit. It was a miracle that it wasn't already burning.

We tried to get him out for nearly three quarters of an hour. We didn't have any heavy tools, only what we carried in the toolbox, and the vehicle was badly deformed. Jacking up the engine was soon abandoned as hopeless, so the only way to get him out was via the backseat. We didn't have any rescue equipment, and the gas kept leaking. We used whatever we could find to try and mop it up. We would get a towel saturated, run away for a bit, wring the gas out, and come back to do it again. Cameron was in great pain and thought his leg and maybe his pelvis were broken.

A medevac had been called in but was still about half an hour away. Apparently Joe was having a bad day too, and the medical helos were busy. The good news was that another element was inbound with the heavy equipment we would need to get him out.

To make a long story short, we didn't make it. There was either a spark or a hot wire. I don't think it was us. In about two seconds the gas caught, and the whole thing went up like a torch. One of the guys had about a second to get out and managed to singe most of his hair off. He was lucky.

My best friend in Iraq burned to death in front of me. I could hear him screaming. There was nothing we could do, and I really don't want to talk about it. I still have nightmares where my wife has to wake me up.

I went back to Baghdad and stayed shit-faced drunk for the better part of a week. It sucked. And I never want to hear another fucking civilian bitch about how tough life is back here in the United States. They don't know the meaning of the word.

Chapter Seven

SATMO: Doing It Right

Fort Bragg is the home of the 82nd Airborne Division, where thousands of young paratroopers are stationed amid the pine trees of North Carolina. This sprawling army post, the largest in the world, is also home to the Special Forces. The highly covert Combat Applications Group, formerly known as Delta Force, also calls Fort Bragg its home. So do many Special Operations training and support formations.

In a slightly more subdued corner of the post, adjacent to a chapel, stands an obscure building with the rather mundane title of United States Army Security Assistance Training Management Organization. Established in 1974, it falls under the administrative umbrella of the John F. Kennedy Special Warfare Center and School, which is often referred to as the university for the Special Operations Command. Both the dull-sounding title and the drab building are misleading. SATMO, as it is known, has deployed over a thousand training teams to more than a hundred countries since its inception. It is a present-day model of successful military-contractor integration and is currently the only type of its kind in existence. The ten men deployed to Kenya in chapter 1 were initially processed through the quiet building sitting astride Ardennes Avenue amid the bustle of Fort Bragg.

The mission of SATMO is simple in theory but challenging in execution. It provides foreign military assistance to friendly allied nations. These operations are as diverse as teaching Pathfinder techniques to Kenyan Rapid Deployment Battalions to advising the Philippine Navy on how to set up a maintenance plan for offshore patrol craft. A recent mission involved mentoring military medical teams in Nepal. Many, though not all, of the missions are armed.

For over three decades SATMO has served as a successful model, producing a viable methodology for integrating contractors, reserve soldiers, and full-time active duty troops into one working entity. It is unique in the world. During the author's time in SATMO, he was able to observe a two-man explosives ordnance team dispatched to Norway, a team of eight bound for the Philippines, and a half-dozen personnel destined to advise Colombian Special Forces. Another four were bound for East Africa on a Pathfinder training mission, a couple more were en route to Saudi Arabia, and the group of ten contractors mentioned earlier were preparing for Kenya. As a general rule, the size of the deploying elements is usually between two to thirty men, with the majority numbering less than a dozen. The aforementioned were all assembled together for a two-week collective train up.

The process begins when the host country requests training assistance through the U.S. regional security officer (RSO). An active duty military officer, the RSO works out of a U.S. Embassy or consulate. RSOs exist in nearly every embassy in the world, and their job is to liaise with the host nation's military. The RSO, coupled with the armed force requesting assistance, determines the actual tasking.

In Kenya's case, the government asked for assistance in training several infantry battalions to serve as a quick reaction force. The Kenyan request was forwarded from the U.S. Embassy in Nairobi through several agencies, including the State Department and the Department of Defense. Both federal entities determined the validity of the request and the strategic desirability of improving Kenya's capabilities. Approval of these requests is not automatic.

For example, between 2006–8, a training mission to the Democratic Republic of the Congo was delayed until the Congolese government could vet all the attending students. The United States, drawing upon its experience from the notorious School of the Americas, whose alumni include many Latin America dictators, has no desire to discover it has been training war criminals. (It may be of interest to readers to note that the army, pulling a page from the contractor textbook in terms of creating fuzzy titles, has renamed the School of the Americas. It now carries the rather blurry nomenclature of "Western Hemisphere Institute for Security Cooperation.")

Returning to the case at hand, the long-festering civil war in the eastern Congo, coupled with a lack of ministerial accountability, rendered it difficult for the Congolese to confirm that potential trainees were untainted by past human rights violations. Until they do, the training teams will stay at home.

The U.S. agencies decided that training the Kenyan Army was in the best interests of both the Kenyan and U.S. governments. Kenya's geographic location in the Horn of Africa, with Somalia to the northeast and the Sudan to the northwest, was not lost on the Pentagon.

The funding source for such exercises is either the host country or a pool of U.S. dollars specifically designed to train allied militaries. In this case it was paid for by a congressional supplement to support the war on terror, of which Kenya has proven to be a strong supporter.[1]

After gaining State Department and DOD approval, the request arrived in the SATMO office's inbox. The next segment of the process should be underscored for it is at this point that SATMO becomes extremely relevant to the military contracting environment.

SATMO, moving in tandem with the host country requesting training and the RSO, must make two determinations. The first is whether the host country making the request desires active duty army personnel or contractors. Active duty army is usually the requesting country's knee-jerk initial response because of the prestige associated with being trained by the U.S. military. Prior to 9/11 the Special Forces conducted many of the training missions themselves, and SATMO's operations were considered a top mission. However, with the advent of multiple shooting wars on far-flung continents, the priority to provide Green Berets to SATMO has plummeted. The U.S. Army, already stretched thin by real-world combat in Iraq and Afghanistan, just doesn't have enough highly qualified individuals who can disappear into the wilds of Kenya for a year or two. All personnel are needed in the combat theaters. This is not to imply the quality of individuals tapped by SATMO going overseas is anything less than stellar, for they are professionals to the core. However, the truth is far fewer of them are available, and it is much more difficult for SATMO to pry them away from various commands.

Lead time is the other factor that can discriminate against the uniformed services. It is not unusual for an interval of eighteen months to elapse between the host nation's request and the time the first set of active duty boots touch the ground. Such is the blinding speed of the U.S. federal bureaucracy. If a requesting nation is fighting a border war or faced with issues such as Kenya confronted in 2008, eighteen months is too long to wait for help.

Enter the contractor. Private training companies indeed lack the prestige of their active duty cousins; however, almost all contractors are former military and a high percentage hail from Special Operations units. Collectively, contract teams routinely have a higher combined number of years of service than their active duty counterparts, who are only partially through their careers. The average age for the contractor team deployed to Kenya was roughly forty-five. Most of the SATMO personnel who were active duty army and bound for other locales were twelve to fifteen years younger. For a host country to expect a dozen Special Forces or Army Rangers for six months is totally impossible. Meanwhile, the same number of contract personnel may have over a century's worth of combined time spent in those very units, thus bringing an enormous breadth of experience to the table.

Contractors have another great advantage, speed. Private industry, unhampered by most bureaucratic red tape, moves like lightning compared to the government's plodding pace. A fully qualified contractor team can be on the ground in less than sixty days compared to the year and a half for the "green suits" of the army.

The downside of engaging contractors is cost. A private military contractor may cost as much as 400 percent more than his active duty equivalent. That is not to say that the contractor makes 400 percent more in take-home pay. One must factor in the recruitment, training, and middlemen, not to mention a company's profit margin, all of which are not considered in the army's totals. There is no doubt that contractors are more expensive to the host nation than utilizing the regular army.

Perhaps surprisingly, the numbers in the last few years have swung heavily in favor of contractors. As recently as 2004, contractors were represented on only 10 percent of the foreign training missions under the SATMO umbrella. Today, contractors represent just over half of all those deploying on missions, and there is no reason to assume their pace of expansion will slow down. Several nations with long-term training plans have opted to continue with the PMCs for additional rotations regardless of the increased price tag.

The host country, the RSO, and SATMO determine which path will be followed, with the host country having the final say regarding active duty personnel or contractors. If the host country chooses the active duty option, SATMO has the power to levy troops from all sectors of the army except Special Operations soldiers. If contractors are chosen, SATMO contacts the handful of companies that provide the specialized service and puts the project out for tender. SATMO plays the role of intermediary, forwarding the proposals and résumés to the host nation. Unlike Iraq, where the client routinely has no control over who gets hired, every résumé and military qualification are reviewed by the host nation, which has the right to decline any given individual on the grounds of professional competence. Thankfully, objections are still an infrequent circumstance.

The next step is for SATMO, in collusion with the appropriate embassy staffer, to perform site surveys in advance and determine the logistical requirements of the incoming personnel. In-country billeting and transportation are arranged, and security arrangements are finalized. If a contractor is chosen, then a representative from the company will accompany the pre-deployment survey team. The advantage of this addition is that when the contract team arrives in Fort Bragg for the two-week workup prior to its overseas deployment, it will be passed real-world and real-time information from the officer who conducted the preliminary site survey. This resource has proven invaluable for it provides up-to-date intelligence and paints an accurate picture of exactly what the team can expect.

Several weeks before deployment, all outbound personnel arrive in Fort Bragg. Every soldier or contractor must pass through the doors of SATMO for a mandatory preparation phase. Civilian contractors bound for Kenya and other destinations are seated shoulder to shoulder with active duty advisers deploying elsewhere, say, to Colombia and Sierra Leone. All are processed in an identical manner. Both sides profit. The contractors work alongside the Special Forces tasked with running SATMO, and all parties interact with an easy informality. It can be a busy time.

Each outward-bound individual is provided with host country orientation, intelligence briefings, and weapons training if necessary, and the small mountain of necessary paperwork is completed under one roof. Classes are long, arduous, and intense.

The improvised explosive device class receives everyone's undivided attention. To reinforce the methodology being taught, the SF teams have access to military video not available to the media. It is viscerally repugnant to watch Americans blown apart by roadside IEDs, but the footage serves to drive home the point that assignments can be perilous. Car bombs, suicide vests, and kidnappings are all covered in exhaustive detail. Part of SATMO's underlying theme is to produce at least a bit of paranoia for all new personnel who have not previously been forward deployed. The goal is not to instill fear but rather a healthy awareness of the potential dangers the host environment may offer. In so doing, it keeps younger troops more alert, which in turn may help them evade attack.

The exhaustive intelligence briefings focus not only on potential terrorist attacks but also on other equally lethal activities such as violent crime, health issues, and disease. Fatal carjackings are a daily occurrence in Nairobi. The intelligence officer's opinion was that the Kenya-bound team stood a better chance of being gunned down in Nairobi in broad daylight for its SUV than it did of being blown up by al Qaeda.

A class on cross-cultural communication has been taught for years, as SATMO identified the need long before the army addressed the issue in Iraq. Other more esoteric topics include training blocks on hostage survival and detecting terrorist surveillance. For most of the former Special Operations Forces, which nearly all the contractors were, it is old hat. No eyebrows were raised when sensory deprivation or surveillance choke points were examined. Hostage survival cannot be discussed in this book as it is still a closed topic of instruction. The conventional unit soldiers who had never been part of this eclectic community bent forward and scribbled furiously in their notebooks.

To stimulate situational awareness and countersurveillance skills, all students are placed under hostile surveillance by former Special Forces turned contractors. In accordance with domestic surveillance laws, all students sign a waiver authorizing them to be placed under observation for the course.

For the next week, the "hostile" force attempts to keep surreptitious tabs on the trainees. The former Green Berets employ tactics similar to those used by the various terrorist groups operating in the particular country where the class is destined to go. The students utilize the necessary countersurveillance techniques they have been taught, and the covert war is on. Over the course of the week, a compendium of covert photos is taken, and on Friday the entire class conducts a debriefing with the hostile surveillance team. In this manner both the team's strengths and weaknesses are exposed. The outgoing personnel are better prepared to cope with the menace of surveillance, which invariably precedes any attack or kidnapping.

By far the most popular part of the program is the driving. Using SUVs, the students spend time at SATMO's own closed driving course. High-speed evasive maneuvers, threshold braking, and sweaty palms are the order of the day. The backseat of an SUV sliding through a skid at 50 mph is a bad place to be if one is prone to carsickness.

Just as all government institutions that specialize in placing men and women in dangerous positions overseas, both urban legends and factual stories abound in regard to operations undertaken in far-flung corners of the world. One particular legend centers on a naval adviser who was deployed to assist the Nicaraguan Navy.

This small Latin nation has a maritime force whose mission is similar to that of the U.S. Coast Guard. The Nicaraguans were attempting to interdict drug smuggling, thus the United States was happy to provide the naval adviser. The American naval officer was duly informed that he was strictly there as a noncombatant and under no circumstances was he to allow himself to become involved in actual counternarcotics operations.

Weeks into the training program, the adviser was participating in a routine exercise at sea when the radios began to squawk with alarming frequency. A major narcotics smuggling operation was under way, the cartels having launched it prior to the date provided by intelligence sources. Mexican and Guatemalan naval forces were also actively involved and recall orders were being dispatched to all available naval units, which included the one with the adviser aboard.

Operations justifiably take precedence over training in any military organization. Thus, the American found himself on the deck of a Latin American patrol boat whose sailors were opening the ammunition lockers for the cannon and machine guns mounted on the deck. The chase ran late into the night and moved farther out to sea while the naval forces coordinated maneuvers prior to the impending battle.

In the final lull before hostilities, the American finally cornered his Latin counterpart. The adviser, trying to keep to the letter of his status, politely informed the Nicaraguan captain that he was forbidden to partake in a naval action. The Nicaraguan, whose hands were equally tied by his headquarters in Managua, was most decidedly sailing into harm's way. The captain paused for a moment and blithely suggested the best resolution was to place the adviser in the small emergency lifeboat, cut him adrift, and return to pick him up after the battle on the following day.

The American pondered the combination of high seas, small boat, dark night, and no form of communication. He counteroffered by suggesting that perhaps all would be well and the letter of the law would not be broken if he could simply hide belowdecks for the duration of the action. It in fact transpired that way, and the adviser's most lingering memories are the "thuds" that the shell casings made as they clattered to the deck directly above his head.

As the following story patently displays, SATMO does not hesitate to point out the errors of others if it aids in training those preparing to deploy. Another more infamous incident concerns a member of a mobile training team in Pakistan whose safe house was located in the downtown area of a major city. Just across the road was a popular restaurant frequented by both Caucasians and members of the Pakistani government. For the team's protection, a pair of AK-47-equipped guards was assigned to the front of the safe house.

It was not long afterward that the predictable occurred, and the dining establishment was leveled by a suicide bomber, resulting in moderate loss of life. The safe house was clearly not the target although it too had suffered modest blast damage.

What was totally unpredictable was the action of a team member. The body parts had hardly been cleaned up when the American in question arrived in the wee hours of the night, just before dawn. He was attired in flip-flops, shorts, and a Disneyland sweatshirt. He flip-flopped up to the detonation point and began taking digital photos for the family scrapbook. What the Pakistani Special Police thought of this apparition arriving in the waning hours will never be known. Thankfully the rest of the team was cognizant enough to recognize the risk and promptly dragged him back under the muzzles of the friendly AK-47s in the safe house. There is no doubt that he would have at a minimum been carted off to a Pakistani police station for a lengthy interrogation had it not been for the quick-witted actions of his comrades.

Undeterred by his near miss with a Pakistani jail, the amateur photographer forwarded his digital snaps to SATMO with the caveat that the office could utilize these hard-won photos in future training classes. SATMO complied with his request, and every class since then has seen the same photo. The inscription reads, "This photo was taken by a flip-flopping DUMB ASS. DON'T PUT YOURSELF AT RISK TO ADD TO THE FAMILY SCRAPBOOK LEST YOU BECOME ITS FINAL ENTRY. DON'T DO THIS."

For the individuals headed to Kenya, the SATMO process was seamless. Ten strangers had come together in two weeks and been molded into a workable team. The Kenyan Army was going to get good value for its money.

The civilian contractors did suffer financial disputes and discord, but it was more a factor of the contract company's incompetence than a failing of the system as a whole and certainly had nothing to do with SATMO. The ten bound for Kenya bit their tongues on many occasions when faced with incompetent contracting company personnel who were clueless on how to run a training mission. However, that is a function of poor business practices as opposed to the breakdown of the training protocols developed in Fort Bragg.

For the team deployed to Kenya, there were some pronounced differences between the group and its contractor counterparts who were conducting similar operations in Iraq. Once again, SATMO is trail blazing the future for how things should be done versus how they are being done.

First of all, and most important, the contractors were accountable. They reported to a real military authority in the form of SATMO. The regional security officer of the U.S. Embassy, who maintained close communications with the Kenyan Ministry of Defense, inspected the team. Quality assurance reports would be funneled to the U.S. military. Although contractors, unlike their active duty counterparts, do not operate under the Uniform Code of Military Justice, their parent companies are held accountable to SATMO. This connection can have powerful ramifications for the individual in light of poor job performance, as was demonstrated on one occasion in Kenya.

A pair of contractors, who were not used to close scrutiny (which is an oxymoron in Iraq), opted to get exceedingly drunk every night. Between them they consumed an average of forty beers a day. One of them, while under the influence of alcohol, directed a few choice comments at the regional security officer during a visit. This is practically an everyday occurrence in Iraq, where accountability is completely absent and no bad deed goes punished.

Retribution for unprofessional conduct in Kenya was swift. SATMO gave a push, and both were sent home on an aircraft within a week. The individual with the disciplinary problem, hoping to sidestep accountability, put in for another training slot in Eastern Europe via the same shoddy contract company. The contract company failed to enforce any disciplinary action of its own as it was in no danger of losing the contract. Without a deterrent for dubious performance, the focus inevitably shifts toward cost rather than quality. If the company had fired him at its discretion it would have been responsible for the costs incurred of hiring a replacement. Thus, it is cheaper to keep the drunk on the payroll until the embassy steps in and orders him out. This shortsightedness is the bane of the industry and will never change until the government steps in with regulatory oversight. The RSO of the host country in Eastern Europe, however, noticed that a pending arrival had been dismissed in Kenya and sent an e-mail to the RSO in Nairobi. Upon learning of the incident in question, the Eastern European RSO promptly denied entrance to the drunken contractor. Two replacements were brought in whose personal conduct was without incident. Both proved to be solid performers.

For the first tour, 20 percent of the contractors were released for disciplinary problems. This total is worrisome when compared to the contractors' active duty counterparts, whose malfeasance rate is about 1 percent. Current high percentiles representing disciplinary action among contractors are hangovers from the early days in Iraq, where few serious attempts at quality control were ever implemented. The residual effect of this lack of foresight has spread to all four corners of the private security company world. A competent prescreening at the contractor company level would have identified the individuals who otherwise managed to sneak through SATMO. As per the industry norm, however, there were no background checks. Selection was based on unsupported résumés lacking official documentation. The one bright point was that a urinalysis was conducted, but even this process was flawed. The company was looking for the wrong form of substance abuse. While cocaine or marijuana use among contractors is nonexistent, steroids are rampant. The urinalysis tests administered do not check for steroids as this step costs more money. Private contractors realize this and abuse steroids instead of cocaine or pot. This selection process for individuals deploying to a war zone, which Kenya was, is pathetic.

At the time, Kenya was a very busy place. Elements of the National Guard had been called up to full-time status. They had a team in Isiolo running a preselection course for the American Army's much-vaunted Ranger school. A handful of Kenyans would be handpicked to fly to America to attend. Another contractor mobile training team was teaching Pathfinder operations in the vicinity of Nairobi. A regular army unit, normally based in the Washington, D.C., area but now calling Djibouti home, was teaching an infantry basic course. Special Forces were developing a Kenyan Special Operations Company, and in the midst of it all this contractor team trained a quick reaction battalion.

During tea breaks one could find Special Forces, regular army, National Guard, and civilian contractors all wearing the same uniform standing under one roof. It was a much more accurate cross section of America's current military than the public realizes.

The contractors deployed to Kenya did well. As with their counterparts in Iraq, 80 percent of them were never a problem to begin with and provided exceptional service in a professional manner. Meanwhile, the RSO nailed the two drunks.

The ripple effect of being held accountable for one's actions had several ramifications among the ten men described earlier. For those with long Iraq experience, it was the first time they had ever seen serious disciplinary action brokered against those who were patently deserving of correction or castigation. It came as a rude shock to one or two, and gave pause for reflection to several more.

In one circumstance, SATMO's indirect regulatory oversight on the contractors proved to be beneficial. The oldest and longest-serving former NCO adapted to the pseudomilitary environment. When faced with the immediate task of training soldiers, he fell into old patterns without further issue. The obvious deterrents, in the form of immediate firing and SATMO blacklisting, proved to be powerful. There was certainly no implied endorsement from higher authority regarding misuse of power, and his focus was to do the best job possible. When placed in a position of responsibility with clear boundaries, he provided high-quality training to the Kenyan Army, regardless of what his personal thoughts were. His ranting and political diatribes around the dinner table became shorter when he realized that he would be held accountable, unlike in Iraq. In short, he shut his mouth and toed the company line just as if he were back in the military. He would not be invited back, but he had bettered himself both personally and as a contractor. He departed Kenya a vastly improved human being with credit being due to mandated accountability.

It was only the youngest, a pure thug with just a few years' experience in the Marine Corps, who revolted in full. Intelligent, arrogant, and rude, he was astute enough to avoid disciplinary action and settled down to kill every bird and small mammal in sight with his slingshot. His sole aim was to get somewhere so he could "kill" again, and his tales of Iraq were never ending. However, as so many of society's derelicts, he was more talk than action. Strangely, as with all marginal individuals, he avoided job placements with a risk of heavy contact with the enemy but focused on positions with the most money and most control over those least likely to fight back. In short, he was a perfect case study of everything wrong with the contractor system in Iraq. His conduct in Kenya was kept in check by powerful deterrents emanating from above. He constantly complained and avoided those with significant combat time as it is hard to fool people who have really experienced it. He gained a suspicious amount of upper body weight and became both moody and aggressive, normally indicators of steroid use. He was the typical rogue contractor.

Upon completion of the first training cycle, he opted to return to Iraq. He applied and was accepted into a small company with an exceptionally bloody track record. It will be a perfect environment for him: low risk, lethal force authorized, and no oversight. It does not bode well for the Iraqis he will meet, undoubtedly through the gun sight.

Personalities aside, the Kenyan Army did well. The overall level of performance improved dramatically. Patrolling classes were taught in conjunction with raids, ambushes, and battle drills. The Kenyan Army is a well-disciplined force whose only real downfall is a shortage of quality equipment. That it would prove to be a powerful deterrent against Somali al Qaeda factions there is no doubt. Shortly after the contractor team completed the first rotation, D Company of the Kenyan Rifles was slated to head back for the border. It is a harsh land. Arid, snake infested, and covered with low scrub, it has proven to be tough terrain in which to deter Somali infiltration. However, the army's training at the hands of the contractors proved its worth as the quality of the individual fighting man improved dramatically. The military adviser program worked.

During the last three decades SATMO has created a clear precedent for the intelligent interaction of combined military-contractor teams. SATMO has also provided impetus for two associated themes central to the debate over private contractors. First, private contractors in an advisory role can continue to produce top-quality services for reasonable costs. The price tag for an advisory contractor who is a noncombatant, such as those in Kenya, is about half of what the bill rate is for those in combat roles in Iraq or Afghanistan. The Kenyan Army has been delighted, the soldiers have been proven to be motivated, and the skill level has unquestionably improved. Furthermore, a Special Forces assessment team forwarded a report stating that the tactics, techniques, and protocols as taught by the contracting team were in fact *superior* in scope and implementation to those of the active duty unit colocated with the contractors. Similar to the MPRI experience in Croatia discussed in chapter 3, in-depth evidence suggests the U.S. government receives excellent value for the money when it utilizes former servicemen to conduct training for allied forces in a structured environment. It must be remembered that trainers are considered noncombatants and do not engage in live operations.

The SATMO system has also proven that with the implementation of appropriate professional controls, contractors can be made to voluntarily hold themselves accountable for their conduct. In the microcosm of the Kenya exercise, SATMO did provide effective deterrents for unwarranted behavior. Tacit consent or implied endorsement for off-duty shenanigans such as alcohol abuse was not forthcoming. SATMO squelched unprofessional conduct, and the world did not end, contrary to the predictions of Iraq-based companies. With no less than 70 percent of the employees having PMC experience in Iraq, the Kenya sample proved to be an illustrative control group. After the first two were effectively disciplined for grossly inappropriate conduct, the regulatory adherence rate leaped to 90 percent, with only a single malcontent remaining. The last remaining "cowboy," now in a minority, opted to return to the only locale where he could still get away with such behavior—Iraq.

Based on internal recruiting, replacing the individuals who chose to leave for Iraq was no problem. Although too small a sample to provide broad analysis, this case does lend credence to the suggestion that the industry is beginning to auto-correct. More and more contractors are declining to return to Iraq. Whether that choice is based on moral common sense or whether it is because the malcontent 10 percent are now concentrated there is open to speculation.

What is known is that SATMO has clearly produced a successful model for future contractor operations. By blending military and civilians together into one all-encompassing team, the organization has shown the way forward from the current imbroglio in the Middle East. SATMO deserves to be recognized as a leader in the field of military-contractor interface.

Chapter Eight

Ten Minutes on Ambush Alley

Combat is an incredibly destructive undertaking. Those who engage in close quarters fighting are placed under the most severe psychological, physical, and emotional stress imaginable. The media has sometimes become victim to portraying a counterinsurgency as a "soft" war because casualties are a fraction of those derived from conventional conflicts. This supposition is a grave misnomer.

The following detailed account, drawn from interviews with the survivors, represents a ten-minute battle so insignificant it went completely unreported. However, it is a much more accurate portrayal of life as a private contractor in Baghdad in the summer of 2004 than the majority of what the media beamed into the living rooms of America.[1]

The Background

The firefight occurred in the vicinity of the much-touted "Ambush Alley," made infamous by television anchors. This roadway just off of "Route Irish" is well known and justifiably feared by personal security detail teams,[2] for attacks were a near-daily occurrence in the waning summer of 2004.

The two primary protagonists were Dan and George, both graduates of the Center for Advanced Security Studies and posted to Baghdad. Dan had already spent time in the Balkans with CASS and was a solid operator. It was George's first deployment. In his past life, he had been a cook in the Marine Corps but had done well with CASS and was thus granted his wish of working in Iraq as a PSD operator. Both had been in country for a little longer than a month and thus were well acclimated. This is their story.

Dan begins the tale.

We had already dropped off the clients and were heading home "clean," meaning just shooters and vehicles. Two gun trucks were rolling from west to east toward an elevated highway. We all dreaded this strip of pavement as it was nothing more than an elevated shooting gallery with us as the ducks. Like the army, private contractors were still using soft-skinned vehicles in 2004. To the north lay some forty meters of sandy median, the opposite two-lane highway, and perhaps thirty meters beyond there was a small, three-story shopping mall. A three-foot wall of sand had been graded alongside the road just off the shoulder, running in both directions. This berm was to play a critical role in the actions that followed. Directly to the south of the impact point was a four-story mosque, topped with the inevitable blue dome.

The gun trucks themselves were Chevy Tahoes; they were not outfitted with gun turrets, nor were they armored. Both had drivers in the normal positions and vehicle commanders who invariably sat in the front right passenger seat. The lead truck would usually have a single man armed with a rifle in the backseat who could shoot out of either window.

The trail vehicle was configured differently. As most attacks occur from the rear, the last vehicle drives with the rear cargo hatch open, and one man would maintain a belt-fed machine gun mounted on a post welded to the floor. Normally Dan had this slot as it was the most dangerous and required the greatest level of individual responsibility. Of course, Dan's field of fire is restricted to whichever way the aft end of the Tahoe is facing. This limited field of fire was to have a fatal impact upon more than one person as the fight progressed. A last note was that Dan did not carry a standard machine gun. His was operated on a solenoid switch and was without a conventional stock, rendering it ineffective for dismounted operations. In other words, Dan couldn't take his weapon with him if he had to leave the truck. If the team found itself on foot, Dan would have to rely only on his pistol, which was ineffective beyond thirty meters.

Seconds before the attack the trucks were weaving aggressively through light to moderate traffic, at a speed of just under 60 mph, while maintaining a separation of two car lengths. This was completely normal for Baghdad in 2004. They were headed home, just the pair of them, the clients having been successfully dropped off earlier. There were a total of six contractors, all combat effective, in two trucks.

The IED Blast

As has often been the case with this war, the attack was instantaneous and came out of nowhere. One second you are driving down a very familiar road close to home and all looks normal, and in the very next instant people are being blown apart, screaming, and you are taking fire from all sides.

The bomb detonated within meters of the lead vehicle. For once the insurgents had timed it perfectly. The massive blast hurled shrapnel, rocks, and debris over a hundred-meter area. The pressure wave was so strong it blew out windows within the same radius.

The lead vehicle disintegrated. The windshield shattered, a million spider webs of fracture lines appearing for a nanosecond before the whole pane blew inward. The engine was torn off its mount. Tires disappeared. The pressure wave buckled the left side inward from the back quarter panel all the way forward to the radiator. As a vehicle, it had ceased to exist, and now only a crumpled, smoking, hulk skidded onto the sandy median. The vehicle's carcass rotated some forty-five degrees to come to a rest with the front facing north toward the shopping center.

The occupants, by any calculations, should have been outright dead. But they were not, based more on dumb luck than anything else. There is a belief among many PSD crews that pressure waves from IEDs are best dealt with by leaving the windows down. Urban legend states this tactic allows the pressure wave to enter from one side and exit the other. As the windows were rolled down into the door panels when the bomb detonated, if nothing else, it reduced the opportunity for window glass to become shrapnel.

"Lucky" is a relative word in an IED attack and is best used when the other option is death. The driver was missing the top half of the calf of his left leg. The shock wave had caused the doors to buckle inward. The driver's door panel had imploded, and a large piece of door frame had blown itself through the passenger compartment, taking the piece of leg with it. The driver, although badly wounded, was lucky to be alive.

The Nepalese Gurkha, sitting in the front passenger seat, was paradoxically in better shape and in worse. He was in better shape as he had not sustained the immediate, potentially life-threatening trauma that the driver had. He was in a more precarious state because he was peppered with tiny shrapnel wounds covering practically his whole body save for portions covered by his body armor. Two of the most serious fragments had caught him in the stomach and thigh. He was in grave danger of bleeding out, meaning he would die through blood loss from the numerous tiny punctures in his body. This wound is difficult to treat in the field as it does not have one single, obvious hole that needs patching, like the injury sustained by the driver. There was also no way to ascertain how serious his internal injuries were. Lastly, any wound that penetrates the abdominal area is extremely painful, and morphine was not available. When the adrenaline and shock wore off, the Gurkha was going to be in agony.

The operator in the rear seat, for reasons known only to God, was relatively unscathed. But that was not to last as he was destined to be shot in the back within minutes.

All three were severely dazed from the concussion and pressure wave. No matter how dire the situation, a person requires several seconds to regain equilibrium after such a shock. The human body and brain lack the celerity to recoup faster. It is at times like these that many involved in critical incidents will recall that "time stopped and everything seemed to be happening in slow motion."

In a welter of smoke, blood, and screams, the lead vehicle slid to a stop on the median. For the next few seconds, the team was incapable of combat while recovering from concussion, pressure waves, and shock. The first bullet had not been fired, and the team already had two seriously wounded.

Dan's vehicle, trailing but fifteen meters behind, fared somewhat better. Shrapnel pierced the engine, cutting through many of the pipes and hoses. Radiator coolant, oil, and power steering fluid all begin to seep through hundreds of minuscule punctures onto the superheated asphalt. The driver, George, somehow managed to keep control of the vehicle and desperately swerved to avoid plowing into the smoking wreck the lead vehicle had become. This maneuver was all the more impressive for his Tahoe had both left tires blown out, another result of the lethal storm of metal tearing through that sweltering Baghdad afternoon.

Dan, sitting by the rear open hatch with the machine gun, was dazed, along with the other two. Hearing was nonexistent as they all had been temporarily deafened by the blast.

In the ensuing four or five seconds following the initial detonation, George was successfully able to regain control of the vehicle. He brought it to a halt some seventy-five meters past the first hulk, now lying like a beached whale on the median. Already, from underneath the inoperable Tahoe, faint tendrils of smoke were beginning to seep out, a terrifying preview of the inferno to follow. There was as of yet no movement, and the condition of those inside was not known but presumed to be gravely wounded or dead. The second vehicle was damaged and its occupants were momentarily combat ineffective.

Thus the stage was set for one of those savage, little cutthroat actions in the streets of Baghdad. In the next ten minutes, a desperate fight for survival would all boil down to tactics, marksmanship, morale, naked aggression, and luck. The winners would survive and the losers would die.

Dan recalled a favorite phrase of the time. It was a takeoff of one of Meatloaf's songs from the *Bat Out of Hell* album. The team had rewritten the lyrics to read, "Welcome to Baghdad/ Paradise by the dashboard lights."

It was a very garden-variety street fight. These occur many times a day in Iraq, the brutality of which is never effectively communicated to the public, who view only the sanitized aftermath of such "skirmishes" in the comfort of their living rooms. Dozens of men were about to die and it would not even make a footnote in the day's news; rather, it would be classified as a "routine contact" involving an IED and small arms fire (SAF). It was small, personal, ugly, and merciless but in no way spectacular, which is why the news media rarely report on these little blood fests, the foundation of all the dismounted combat occurring in that repulsive city.

For another three seconds all was quiet. George even remembers the hissing noise of air escaping the shredded tires as the gun truck began to list to port.

An instant later, to quote Dan, both vehicles were "engulfed in fire."

The Iraqis had initiated the second part of the ambush.

The Ambush

From all sides, a veritable hailstorm of incoming rounds pounded into the pair of vehicles. The initial volume was overwhelming. The insurgents had set up a machine gun and RPG in the tower of the mosque, and a half-dozen black-masked men were firing AK-47s at them from the roof of the shopping mall. Many more were engaging from the ground. The Iraqis possessed the double advantage of height. Not only did they have superior observation but also the ability to utilize plunging fire, which was already inundating the two immobile teams. Worse yet, being set up on both sides of the road and firing at a forty-five-degree angle, the Iraqis had successfully trapped the teams, especially the first one, in a lethal cross fire.

It will never be known how many times the lead vehicle was struck, for it was a total loss. The driver, attempting to staunch the flow of blood from his calf, recalls having the "steering wheel shudder" as bullets slammed into the column inches from his good leg. The remains of the hood began to sprout evil holes, magically appearing with that deadly "thunk" sound, matched only by the high-pitched scream of ricochets careening off the engine block. The vehicle shivered as bits of jagged metal mixed with insulation and wires fluttered down from the interior walls and ceiling. Bullets were tearing the Tahoe apart. Given the present circumstances, the first team had but seconds to live and they knew it.

Dan's truck fared a little better. The team was about two hundred meters from the shopping mall and one hundred meters from the mosque, which was double the distance of the unfortunate lead team. However, it didn't take long for the insurgents to find the range.

The Gurkha in the front seat recalls with startling clarity:

I remember the windshield starred within seconds, and the jagged holes in the safety glass were plainly visible where the bullets had punched through. Then there was a burst of fire that tore up the front quarter panel on my side. The next two or three rounds chewed up a section of hood just in front of the windshield, also on my side. I could see the metal twisting up from the impact and the rounds that bounced off the engine frame left holes the size of grapefruits when they ricocheted off the hood. I can recall thinking that the next one is the end of it as I am going to get hit. I was right. The last burst shot out the side rearview mirror and the post where the mirror attached to the chassis. Glass, metal, and bullets were flying everywhere, and some combination of that mangled my firing hand, punching a hole through the palm and nearly severing several fingers. That was almost the end of the fight, at least for me.

The account should have ended there, for the teams had no right to life for more than a handful of seconds.

The Iraqis had set up the ambush intelligently, and the two vehicles were immobilized inside the kill zone. One was a short hundred meters away, trapped on a median devoid of cover. Both were being shot to ribbons, and the contractors had yet to fire a round in self-defense.

It was here, on the verge of annihilating the contractors, that events began to imperceptibly go wrong for the insurgents.

Iraqi marksmanship has saved many a Western life. The Iraqis' competence in musketry is appalling. Most set their AK-47s on full automatic and blast away in long bursts. These long bursts are manna from heaven for the Coalition as the AK has such a recoil that only the first shot has any reasonable chance of hitting the target. Anything that follows that first round only goes up in the air unless the marksman compensates, and these men were not astute enough to make that all important correction. So although there was an enormous *volume* of fire hurtling downrange, the percentage of *effective* fire was only a tiny fraction of the total. In a straightforward shooting match, the Iraqi invariably comes off the loser.

Second, the insurgents, due to poor training, all tend to fire at the largest and easiest target. They thus score the highest chance of actually hitting something. In numerous ambushes, teams have evacuated their vehicles and returned effective fire, killing many of the attackers who continue to pound away at the much larger and now empty vehicle. For this reason, the standard drill with Western crews is to de-bus rapidly from the vehicle if bogged down. Vehicles are not called bullet magnets for nothing. The first team members in this ambush, finally coming to their senses, were already fumbling for door handles.

Last, in a grave breach of tactical common sense, Iraqis invariably shoot up the *closest* target available, as opposed to the *most dangerous*. This tendency is also a function of poor training and fire discipline. The first contractor team was the proverbial sitting duck, available for mopping up at a time of the insurgents' choosing. The most dangerous threat was no longer in the first vehicle. Instead, it came from the second vehicle's belt-fed machine gun, which held in Dan's capable hands even then was beginning to rotate and elevate toward the mosque. Any competent commander would have shifted fire to riddle Dan's vehicle and then return to finish off the first. The Iraqis failed to do so. Instead, Iraqi heavy weapons in the mosque continued to pound the mangled lead vehicle with rockets and rake it with machine-gun fire while the team inside began to exit. The volume of fire directed toward the second vehicle, though serious, was nothing compared to the firestorm that was engulfing the first. It should have been the other way around, especially with a machine gun sitting in clear view in the open rear door of the Tahoe. The ambushers had allowed Dan time to respond. The Iraqis were about to pay a heavy price in blood for their stupidity.

Dan yelled at George, "Don't move the truck for thirty seconds! Cover your side with the MP-5!"

George pulled out his submachine gun and settled down to wait. He was unable to engage as the enemy was beyond the effective range of his weapon. So all he could do was sit and watch staring in horrified fascination as the vehicle radio, located just inches from his right leg, was shot to rat shit before him. The radio from the first vehicle had not survived the initial blast. The teams were now trapped in a firefight with vehicles and communications equipment that didn't work.

Dan did not return fire for a few seconds while he gazed through the smoke and flame of battle. For just a moment, his eyes flickered over the battlefield, seeking the source of the RPG and heavy machine-gunfire wreaking such havoc. Observing the telltale back blast and muzzle flashes emanating from the top of the mosque, he made the corresponding corrections in traverse and elevation, ensured the belt of ammunition would feed cleanly, and settled down to work.

Myths abound about one person in the right place at the right time changing the course of battle or even history. Most are tall tales and best left for the bar where they belong. But it does happen, albeit rarely, and this firefight was one of those occasions.

Dan had scanned the area, seeking out the insurgents' most dangerous weapons, which they had placed side by side in the mosque. Military tacticians have a word for this emplacement, "stupid." It is the infantry equivalent of putting all your eggs in one basket. Dan's first burst was a long one, nearly thirty rounds of 7.62mm aimed with careful precision. The result was a series of hammer blows against the enemy. The RPG gunner, standing upright, was shredded and actually knocked off the fourth floor. His corpse plunged some four stories along with the valuable rocket launcher. Death befell the machine-gun team on the next burst, the heavy bullets punching right through the brick wall to pulverize the crew and weapon. Within twenty seconds a competent Western gunner had knocked out the two most lethal systems the insurgents had. This loss was more than a disaster for the Iraqis. Less than a minute into the fight, they were reduced to only AK-47s with correspondingly poor marksmanship skills. But far worse for the insurgents was that Dan was now the sole owner of a belt-fed machine gun, which is the queen of all infantry battles.

However, the first team was still in dire straits. Under fire from the mosque and the more distant shopping mall, the men had opted to bail out in plain view of the insurgents in the mall. This way they would at least have the dubious shelter of the Tahoe for cover from the machine-gun and RPG fire coming from the mosque. They didn't realize that Dan would eliminate that problem in a matter of seconds. Flopping to the ground, regardless of their wounds, the torn and bloodied survivors hoisted their heavy FN rifles to their shoulders and began to selectively engage individual targets a hundred meters away in the shopping mall.

Once again, fate conspired on the side of the PSD team. The FN rifle is an old-school weapon, entering NATO in 1952. It fires a heavy bullet easily to a range of nine hundred meters. It is highly accurate, kicks like a mule, and is utterly lethal in well-trained hands. The insurgents' ubiquitous AK-47 fires a lighter, less accurate round only out to some four hundred meters. The FNs, firing on semi-automatic, began to chew up individual insurgents who continued to blaze away from the rooftop. The PSD team was firing far fewer rounds but scoring many more hits. The Iraqis still had the highest *volume* of fire, but the PSD team had the most *effective* fire.

Technology also played its role, in the form of the laser sights and holographic imagery systems carried by the Western teams. These systems dramatically reduced the time necessary to acquire a target and improved the odds of a first-round kill. To a competent shooter equipped with these optics at a range of fifty to two hundred meters, it is akin to shooting fish in a barrel. The Iraqis were beginning to pay a dreadful price for their lack of high-tech equipment and their deplorable marks-manship. One by one, they were picked off. The insurgents taking cover behind brick walls were living in a fool's paradise. The brick and mortar may have provided protection against the M-16s the U.S. Army used, but the Iraqis may as well have been taking cover behind a sheet of paper when up against the much heavier rifles the PSD teams were employing. The contractors, if unable to acquire a clear head shot, simply aimed for where the upper body would be and fired right through the walls with appalling results.

Thus ended the first minute of battle.

For the Iraqis at ground level, especially on the south (mosque) side, all still seemed to be going extremely well. They had taken practically no return fire, and the occupants of the first vehicle had debussed on the north side of the vehicle, leaving the south side wide open for the insurgents to attack. Best of all, the young Iraqi males could taste victory as they knew they had a team on the ropes. Emotions came into play, and all wanted in on the impending kill, especially when it seemed that it was going to be an easy one.

The Iraqis launched their attack. A handful of vehicles began to advance from the west and up the same road the Tahoes had so recently driven. There was a pair of Chevrolet Caprices, some sort of sedan, and a little Fiat, each with a bareheaded insurgent hanging out the passenger window and using the rearview mirror to brace his weapon as he fired. The vehicles rolled forward and began to angle toward the Tahoe. Simultaneously, six or eight insurgents armed with AK-47s abandoned the cover of the mosque and began sprinting across the open ground toward the highway. Their intent was to cross the deserted artery and fall upon the trapped team from the three contractors' blind side while they were still fully occupied with the Iraqis in the mall. The insurgent vehicles were moving in the same direction, and all would arrive at the first team's location simultaneously.

As they surged forward toward the smoking vehicle on the median, the Iraqis began to bunch together. This normal human tendency allows for close proximity to one's fellow man, inspiring courage and confidence, and dates back at least as far as the British infantry squares of Waterloo. In the heat of battle, peripheral vision shrinks and many suffer from what is commonly called target fixation, resulting in a decreased awareness of their surroundings save for what is immediately in front of them. Western armies go to great pains to ensure their soldiers assault in a tactically sound manner, completely unlike the headstrong mob that was pounding across the highway. Simultaneously, several of their comrades in front of the shopping mall also began to aggressively advance, creating a two-pronged pincer attack on the lead team.

The crucial phase of the battle had arrived. Those charging toward the Tahoe across the highway were a mere ten seconds away from falling upon the hapless team from the rear.

Ten seconds later the insurgents were all dead or dying, lying in a welter of gore and disemboweled body parts on the scalding pavement. The wounded, covered in blood and suffering shattered limbs, could only scream in agony and wait for the inevitable end as the machine-gun bullets methodically worked up and down the line of fallen bodies, chewing up asphalt and flesh with equal disdain.

The military term for a group of the enemy running across your front at ninety degrees is "enfilading fire." The popular, if coarse, term PSD teams and soldiers used in Baghdad was "a machine gunner's wet dream." At a range of a hundred meters, the Iraqis had literally crossed under the muzzle of Dan's machine gun. They were chopped down in seconds.

Hollywood's depiction of violence, even in the goriest of films, is a feeble shadow of reality. Thankfully the vast majority of the general public will never see firsthand how poorly the human form is designed to repel high-velocity bullets. The result is shockingly rude. Limbs are shot off, men are physically lifted off the ground from the hammer blows of bullets, and brightly colored intestines coil on the tarmac beside their disemboweled but still-living owners. Young men do not die well, lacking both dignity and grace. The air is rent with howling more animal than human. Others weep and cry out for their mothers in Arabic, pleas bubbling from blood-frothed lips.

There is no mercy as both God and Allah have deserted the battlefield, leaving only men. The bullets continue to tear into flesh. One is hit in the jaw, and bone chips and brains fly off the crown of his head where the bullet exits. The pink jellied mass splatters the face of the insurgent directly behind him. He does not even have time to wipe the grisly mess away before he too falls, his chest raked with a half-dozen bullets. The stench is overwhelming. The odor of human feces is in the air as corpses soil themselves when sphincters relax in death. The road resembles an abattoir in human form, and within hours the sickly sweet smell of deathly decay, familiar to all that have seen combat, will permeate the air. Such is close combat. Should the majority of the public ever experience it, most wars would end tomorrow. So ruthless was the cull that not a single insurgent was able to fire back before being cut down. Dan then proceeded to methodically fire up and down the line of fallen, ensuring all were in fact dead. It was a catastrophic error for the Iraqis and broke the back of the ground assault from the mosque.

The insurgents in vehicles found themselves in equally precarious straits. For now, instead of driving up to join their comrades on foot and overwhelm the first team, they were confronting a hitherto unknown machine gun barely a hundred meters away. For a weapon that is designed to kill to nearly a kilometer, a hundred meters is child's play. Even now, having finished with their pedestrian compatriots, Dan was shifting direction ever so slightly. The gun's muzzle began to track on the first windshield.

The horrified drivers, comprehension dawning on their faces, panicked. Some stood on the brakes, preparing to abandon their vehicles. The smart one in the sedan stomped on the gas and headed for the median, aiming for the shopping mall. He correctly assumed that it was far better to take his chances with the first team on the ground than to be parked before that lethal system held in Dan's steady hands.

The passengers, desperate to the point of hysteria, leaned out the windows and tried to gun down the quiet former Marine from California, who was even now closing the feed tray cover on a fresh belt of ammunition.

If anything, this massacre was even easier than the last. There is nothing to describe. Dan simply pointed the weapon, squeezed the trigger, and walked the tracers from one vehicle to the next. The insurgents had zero chance and perished in their vehicles, torn apart by the flailing hail of bullets fired from point-blank range. Dan was firing at a rate of twelve bullets a second, with each vehicle receiving a four- to five-second burst. Every insurgent car was pulverized with about sixty rounds of large-caliber, high-velocity ammunition in a matter of five seconds. It is little wonder no one survived. In less than thirty seconds, every Iraqi was dead or wounded to the point of incapacitation.

By astute manipulation of the only belt-fed weapon on the battlefield, Dan had utterly defeated the southern attack. Though there were still insurgents in the mosque and several others continued to fire from the ground in front of it, there was no longer a significant danger from the south side. That threat had collapsed in the face of one well-placed machine gun manned by one competent gunner.

The battle had been raging for about four minutes.

The Iraqi attack from the north, in the vicinity of the shopping mall, was enjoying better success. The insurgents had been able to successfully advance to the sandy berm alongside the main highway and were engaging the first team at a range of some thirty-odd meters. Hand grenades were now lending their flat, explosive "crack" to the noise of battle. More Iraqis were using the same wall of sand for cover and were rapidly scuttling east, parallel to the highway. In so doing, they would soon be able to exit Dan's field of fire, which was still oriented to the west. Moving up and parallel to the parked Tahoe would enable the insurgents to engage Dan and his driver with ninety-degree fire, against which Dan was unable to respond. George would have to rotate the truck so the machine gun could be brought to bear. George, finally able to do something other than patiently sit and wait to get shot, began to fire short bursts in the direction of the berm. His intent was more to suppress than to kill. A temporary silence descended inside the Tahoe as Dan yanked more ammunition boxes from the ready rack and broke open the first one, accidentally spilling the contents. Long coils of belted rounds slithered onto the floor of the Tahoe, already an inch deep in scalding hot shell casings. George continued to suppress the advancing half-dozen insurgents while Dan single-handedly worked what is normally a three-man weapons system.

Concurrently, the lead vehicle team, now all wounded, continued to shoot in the direction of the shopping mall from the pathetic cover of the sandy ground. (The only unwounded individual had taken a ricochet, grazing him slightly.) For them, an already grave situation was slowly growing worse. Although the enemy fire was slackening, so was theirs. When they had bailed out of the Tahoe, they had neither the time nor the inclination to grab their "go bags." Go bags are small daypacks that carry additional magazines of ammunition, a grenade or two, first aid supplies, and water. Granted, they each had some 120 rounds on their body armor and tactical harness, which they wore all the time; but 120 bullets do not last long in a close-range shootout when confronted with a superior force. It was the one drawback of the FN rifles they were carrying: their weight and size meant the men had to lug less ammunition. Nobody was quite prepared to crawl back into the death trap of a truck to recover some of the go bags, so the lead team had to slack off on the volume of fire, which meant that the insurgents would soon increase theirs. The PSD team was about to lose fire superiority because it had to conserve ammunition.

Seconds later that option was forever barred. The lead vehicle, with a "whoomph," burst into flame. Oily black smoke began to gush into the sky, providing some concealment to the stranded men on the pavement. But concealment came with a price for they all knew that within a minute or two the go bags would start to cook off with live ammunition and possibly hand grenades as the superheated interior continued to burn.

The other critical factor for the stranded team was the physical condition of the wounded. The human body is capable of amazing feats when adrenaline courses through the veins and the fight is for life itself. But for every minute they had to lie there and slug it out, the odds of one of the wounded losing consciousness due to blood loss increased. They had had no time to treat their wounds as their priority had been to survive, which meant shooting, not providing medical attention. The driver especially needed a short respite to bandage the gaping hole in his leg. Beside him, the Gurkha's clothes were slowly becoming saturated with the blood that oozed out of all his tiny shrapnel wounds. Sooner or later, those two were going to go down, and every man who was no longer capable of pulling the trigger represented a 33 percent decrease in firepower for that team.

As both sides were adapting to the new situation on the ground, the clock passed five minutes.

It was George, still suppressing the insurgents behind the berm with his MP-5, who identified the next threat. The Gurkha with the hand wound sitting in the passenger seat grabbed his arm and gesticulated urgently through the remains of the windshield. Some two hundred meters distant, yet another group of insurgents could be seen piling into three cars. Already, the lead vehicle, complete with Arabs hanging out the windows with AKs, was beginning to accelerate down the access road that intersected the main highway some thirty meters in front of the team. It was an attack from a totally unexpected direction, and the team was defenseless to the front. There was nothing to stop them save the driver's submachine gun, and George was fully occupied, employing it against the enemy closing from behind the berm.

Urgently, in as few words as possible, George called to Dan in between bursts of fire and explained the situation. Dan never even hesitated.

"Spin it 180 degrees! NOW! And keep shooting!"

George dropped it into gear, cranked the wheel all the way over to the right, and stepped on the gas. Running on two flat tires on the left side and with a shot-up engine, the Tahoe sluggishly came round to the right (clockwise) as the impromptu insurgent armada approached.

At that precise instant, a number of events occurred simultaneously.

The dismounted Iraqis behind the north berm exposed themselves and all began to fire as fast as they could at the Tahoe. They were trying to kill George before the Tahoe pivoted far enough to allow Dan to bring that lethal machine gun to bear on them.

The Iraqi drivers approaching from the east floored their accelerators to close the distance between themselves and the Tahoe as fast as possible. They too were in a race to arrive and kill George before the Tahoe could turn 180 degrees and allow the machine gun to engage *them*.

George also had the accelerator floored while firing a whole magazine into the general area of the sandy berm, hardly bothering to check where the rounds had impacted. He was firing his MP-5 with one hand out the window while his other hand was wrestling with the bucking steering wheel. Next to him, in the passenger seat, sat the Gurkha, with his Glock pistol drawn in his nonshooting but unwounded hand. He was waiting to engage the dismounts with his peashooter, which was better than nothing. Dan could only sit and wait with the machine gun while the vehicle slowly lurched clockwise. It had to spin 90 degrees before he could engage the insurgents behind the berm and a full 180 degrees before he could engage the fast-approaching vehicles that were even now only some 150 meters away. Dan made use of the time to link another two hundred–round belt onto the fresh one in the gun, giving him some four hundred rounds to fire before he would have to stop and reload.

For three, perhaps four seconds, the PSD team was defenseless. George's weapon was empty. Dan could not bring his to bear, and the Gurkha had no angle from which to shoot. The left front tire was torn off. There was a profound jolt, a high-pitched squeal, and a lot of cursing as the vehicle continued to turn on the rim. Incoming Iraqi fire, though wildly inaccurate, was still causing damage as bullets struck the engine compartment and chassis. One was particularly close. A green tracer round caromed off the rear axle and ripped up through the bottom of the floor, coming to rest on the belt of linked ammo. Owing to the close range, the tracer phosphorous had not worn off, and the brilliant green flame hissed and sparkled obscenely on top of the glistening belt of bullets. Worried about an accidental cook-off, Dan swept it out the back with his gloved hand, where it continued to sputter on the pavement.

For another couple of seconds, the Iraqis poured everything they had at the wheezing Tahoe, the noise of the firing almost drowned out by all the revving engines as the other cars tried frantically to close the few remaining yards.

After what seemed like ages but was in fact no more than a few seconds, the berm began to appear in the right side of Dan's field of view. He did a final visual check of the sprawling belts of ammo to ensure he would have a clean feed. He bent over his weapon, squeezed the trigger, and held it there for a long, long time.

At most, the fire spitting from the rear of the Tahoe knocked down only a couple of insurgents. But more important, as Dan ripped out a continuous raking fire, it forced their heads down. With increasing rapidity the rear of the vehicle began to slew around as its tires and rims finally bit in, and the truck gathered momentum. It was a very close-run thing. By now the nearest insurgent vehicle was only fifty meters away. A pair was right behind the lead vehicle, strung out in a slight *V* formation.

Dan let off the trigger for just enough time to recover from the long burst into the berm. The gun's red-hot muzzle swung upward as he took instinctive aim at the onrushing Caprice. He depressed the solenoid switch again. Red tracers tore into the engine block and were walked into the passenger compartment. The driver took a one-second burst to the upper body and head and promptly disintegrated. The passengers followed an instant later.

The remaining two cars, caught short in the race, should have just kept going and would have been out of danger in seconds. For whatever reason, both drivers slammed on the brakes, squealing to a stop with the unexpected side effect of throwing their shooters wildly off balance. The passengers had to hang on to avoid being ejected from the vehicle and could not engage the Tahoe's occupants.

The next car, a tiny Fiat look-alike, shuddered to a halt directly in front of Dan. The passengers were still thrashing and trying to regain their balance when the driver looked up and straight into the barrel of the machine gun. His eyes met Dan's. For a split second, vanquished stared at victor as the brass casings were already vomiting onto the floor of the Tahoe and their rounds struck home. The machine gun hammered for three seconds, went quiet, and traversed to seek out the other vehicle, which had collided with the first one and now lay broadside some forty meters away. One insurgent was screaming and trying to climb out the window, abandoning his AK-47 in the process. That was how he died, the top half of his smashed body hanging from the window, hands extended to the ground, as if begging Allah for forgiveness. An ever-growing puddle of blood continued to pool on the ground beneath the corpse. A final burst of fire and it was all over.

A preternatural silence cloaked the road. A few moans and a single insurgent crawled to safety, one hand over his stomach, leaving a crimson trail behind him. The Gurkha, now operating George's MP-5 with his one functional hand, killed the survivor with a clean burst of three bullets to the head. Having bandaged and treated his shattered hand, he was now back in the fight and was looking to even the score. He hopped out and scampered over to the wrecks, short bursts of fire indicating the dispatching of the wounded insurgents to Allah. Looking in one vehicle and sensing movement, he unclipped a thermite grenade from his vest, awkwardly managed to pull the pin with his good hand, and lofted it in through a window. Thermite grenades burn at over two thousand degrees Fahrenheit, and for a few short seconds the hiss and sparkle of the incendiary device were overshadowed by the screaming of the wounded men still trapped inside. Wonderfully polite and sturdy, the Gurkhas make for most excellent killers and have held a highly revered place in the British Army for centuries. This one jogged back, smiling.

Awash on a burning bed of shell casings and with the acrid stench of gunpowder everywhere, Dan reached up for another couple of boxes from the ammo rack. Looking up, he realized with alacrity that only one was left. He was running out of ammunition. He would be able to engage the enemy for another two or three minutes at most. Clipping a last four hundred–round belt together and lifting the feed tray to reload, he asked George how it looked to the front.

"Front's fine, but the bastards behind the berm are still major drama." George had taken back his MP-5 and was firing it one handed out the back window while the Gurkha continued to plink away with his pistol at the bobbing targets who would pop up, fire, and duck back down.

Dan glanced over his shoulder back toward the mosque, the shopping mall, and the still-stranded team. As before, he did a slow count to ten, forcing himself to allow sufficient time to make an intelligent decision. Then in a conversational voice he stated, "Let's go pick them up. Move forward and pull a U-turn, placing the wreck between us and the shopping mall. Leave me enough room to shoot out the back. I don't have much ammunition left, and we need to get out of here."

Laying down his MP-5 on the glass- and casings-strewn seat, George dropped the tired Tahoe into second gear and depressed the accelerator. The vehicle wheezed forward, the odd spark flying from the missing tire's rim, and slowly crept to the isolated team. Dan had forgone the machine gun for the spare AK-47 that was kept in every truck and was laying suppressive fire out the side windows at anything that even remotely resembled a threat. The Gurkha was performing the same on his side while George drove. As he commenced his U-turn to pull up alongside the wrecked lead vehicle, *the clock just cleared the seven-minute mark.*

The battlefield was a very different landscape from just moments ago. A number of vehicles lay smoldering, beneath which pools of oil and blood welled. Perhaps two dozen men were dead or seriously hurt. Cries from the wounded could still be heard. Rifle fire had become sporadic, and the insurgents appeared to be catching their breath. What would they do next?

The battered Tahoe finally lurched to a halt. The Gurkha hopped out to help with the wounded while George sat behind the wheel, reloading magazines with the engine running. Dan continued to scan rooftops and was only a couple of seconds away from the machine gun if necessary. The first team was a shambles. Covered in blood, faces cut by flying glass, scared, and nearly out of ammunition, they resembled survivors of a train wreck. The shrapnel-wounded Gurkha was first off the ground and, along with his countryman, rendered aid to the incapacitated driver who still had not bandaged his left calf. By now he was hazy, gently slipping into shock and not doing well. The sole combat-effective man from the first team continued to provide cover, his rifle muzzle moving incessantly from window to rooftop to window. The Gurkhas each took an arm from the driver, and the three of them staggered to the Tahoe and collapsed into the backseat in a pile of bodies.

George had reloaded his final magazine and was shouting for the last man to hurry up and go, for the limping Tahoe was almost as much of a sitting duck as the first one had been. Besides, they still had to run a gauntlet of armed Iraqis to their front. Even now, the Iraqi survivors behind the berm were becoming more aggressive, demonstrated by a marked increase in the volume of incoming rounds snapping overhead. But even as the *clock neared the eight-minute mark,* other factors were coming in to play that could still turn the tables against the PSD team.

The one thing that even the rawest PSD recruit is taught in Baghdad is never let yourself become trapped. For as soon as you become stationary, every insurgent with a cell phone, which in fact means all of them, knows your exact location. A seemingly quiet street can be swarming with insurgents within minutes if they hear there is an easy kill of Westerners to be had. So the trick is to move and keep moving. By staying mobile you never provide that stationary location upon which the enemy can fixate.

In this ambush, phone calls had been made, and every insurgent within earshot could hear the clatter of AK-47 fire. But Iraqi ears, well accustomed to the sounds of war, discerned there was no M-16 fire, which meant the U.S. Army was absent. So for the contractors, it was only a matter of time until the insurgent reinforcements came pouring in, especially when notified that one PSD vehicle had been blown up and the other was in dire straits. Everyone wanted a piece of the kill.

The other factor tilting the playing field was an emotional one. No man likes to come within an ace of victory, then get trampled and see the wounded victors hobble away. The insurgents were so close. Just one more well-aimed or lucky shot could knock out either the machine gun or the vehicle proper, and final victory would be theirs. Then the Westerners would have no chance. And there they were, within a couple of hundred meters, loading their wounded onto a vehicle lacking even tires and hoping to escape. So close. Just as any human being would, the insurgents mounted a final effort to bring down the team that was now fleeing for its life. More cars full of armed young men began to assemble. It was time to kill the infidels, once and for all, before the U.S. Army arrived, at which point it would be the insurgents' turn to flee. The survivors and the newly arrived began to fire again at the contractors struggling to depart the field of battle.

Back on the median, it was high time for the PSD team to leave. From the front George was yelling for the last man to get on board. Already he was gently pressing down the accelerator to provide the Tahoe some initial momentum. As the final Western operator popped to his feet and began to sprint around the wreck to the beckoning door of the vehicle, Dan eyed the rooftops and hollered, "Let's go!" With a smile on his face, eyes wide, the operator threw his rifle into the backseat. He breathlessly blurted, "Thank fuck you guys made it!"

And with that, he took a last leap and propelled himself through the back door. For him it was the only way to get the hell out of there. His teammates watched in helpless horror as he was shot in the back and collapsed on top of the others in the rear seat. The increased Iraqi fire had just paid its first dividend.

George floored the gas pedal. The vehicle gained speed and began to pull away, its door hanging open while the moderately wounded tried to haul the body of the freshly shot man fully inside the battered truck. For perhaps twenty meters his unconscious form was hanging from the door, his feet dragging along the highway before he was fully pulled inside.

There was nothing for it now. The PSD team was in full flight and had turned its back to the enemy. Granted, whoever was capable of further resistance was firing out any window with whatever was at hand in a desperate attempt to suppress the remaining insurgents long enough to make good the escape. Dan had traversed the machine gun to its full right limit and was sending short bursts in the general direction of the shopping mall. Firing from a moving vehicle is an iffy proposition, so now the aim was to suppress rather than destroy. If he wanted to kill, the vehicle needed to be stationary. George was again blazing away with the last remaining rounds for the MP-5. He was firing out the window at the heads and torsos popping up and down from behind the berm, drawing nearer every second. It was a surreal case of jack-in-the-box, never knowing where the next one would leap up with an AK-47 aimed at your face. Both Gurkhas were banging away, one in each direction, with whatever rifle happened to be available. One of the insurgents, only twenty-five meters away, chose poorly and stood up at the wrong time. His AK-47 was zeroed in on the cab. One of the Gurkhas dropped him with the last round in his rifle. He reached for a fresh magazine. There weren't any more. He pulled his pistol and started to pop off rounds.

George, wanting to escape as badly as the rest, kept the gas pedal pinned to the floor. The Tahoe accelerated and promptly threw the left rear tire. The entire port side was now on rims, creating additional control problems. The speedometer slowly inched up to 20 mph, eased back to 15, and refused to budge. That was it. If they were going to escape, it was going to be at a maximum of 15 miles per hour. Miraculously surviving the last gauntlet of fire, the Tahoe squealed forward in the direction of Camp Taji, still several kilometers away. Finally the SUV, full of wounded and bloody PSD members, lumbered out of effective range of the AKs. Dan glanced at his watch. *Barely nine minutes had elapsed.*

Behind them, the Iraqis watched in frustration as their quarry slowly limped out of sight. Enraged at the sight of so many of their own dead and furious that their intended victims had escaped, an emotional few opted to give chase. Loading into yet another set of cars, armed insurgents bent on vengeance accelerated cleanly onto the highway, carefully avoiding the carnage and their comrades in arms who lay mangled on the road. The fight was not over by any means, and the insurgents were determined to bring death to the infidels. All things being equal, they would catch up to the smoking Tahoe within two or three minutes.

The contract team was in bad shape. Only two men, George and Dan, were still combat effective. One was driving and the other manned the gun, leaving room for little else. The next most capable PSD member was the one-handed Gurkha, although now that the initial shock was wearing off the pain was beginning to set in. The man with the calf wound was in a special kind of hell and had a difficult time refraining from screaming as the wounded began to administer first aid to each other. Bandages were wrapped around the missing calf, IVs were inserted, and the man shot in the back was found to be still alive but out cold. It was terribly cramped with three wounded in the backseat of the Tahoe. All the windows were down, and some two kilometers from the ambush site, the SUV, with sparks flying and smoke beginning to pour out from under the hood, was reentering "normal" Baghdad traffic. Mothers returning from market, fathers coming home from work, and families moving about all gaped at the shot-up vehicle plowing through their midst, emitting that horrible high-pitched squeal as the rims tore into the pavement.

As ten minutes passed, Dan took stock of the situation as the civilian drivers swerved out of the way of the rearward-facing machine gun. The contractors had maybe fifty rounds of ammunition, one thermite grenade, no communications gear, and four wounded men, of whom only one was truly mobile. The Gurkha with the shrapnel wounds was unconsciousness. Keeping his eyes peeled to the rear, Dan queried George how the vehicle was doing.

George, with a quick glance at the instrumentation, responded briskly, "We have a massive pull to the left, and I think the power steering fluid is leaking because it's getting harder and harder to hold it. The engine temp is up but not red-lined—yet—and no matter what I do, we can't go faster than fifteen mph. Something's smoking from under the hood, and it smells like oil's burning. Other than that, life is great."

In a very clear voice, Dan replied, "Can we make it to any Taji?" The base was about ten minutes away.

George sweat pouring down his face, thought for a second. "No. I don't think we are going to make it. No way, man, no way. "

Dan took another quick glance to the rear, ensured all was secure, and then turned around and yelled at the pile of bleeding, torn bodies. "Listen up. We stay with the vehicle as long as it is mobile. We have no radios. If the truck dies, we start moving on foot. If we stop, we die. Other option is to hijack a vehicle, which I will do if necessary. Does everybody under—"

CRACK! CRACK! CRACK! There was no escaping the first burst of AK rounds whipping over their heads. The vehicle was under attack from close range. Instantly, Dan resumed his position behind the machine gun. The solitary Gurkha stuck a rifle out the window and prepared to cover the right flank. George would have to drive and shoot again, as there was nobody else left. The wounded were silent and immobile in the backseat.

A second burst of AK fire whistled by, one round striking the Tahoe's front quarter panel. The insurgents had acquired a pickup truck and were standing in the rear, shooting over the cab and through the densely packed traffic at the team's vehicle. The civilian drivers were just beginning to understand they were in the middle of a gunfight.

Dan was confronted with a problem of enormous magnitude. He couldn't get a direct line of sight on the insurgent truck without shooting through several civilian cars. The intended target was four vehicles back and one lane over. So he did the next best thing, doubtless saving many innocent lives in the process.

Angling the muzzle of the weapon into the sky, he let loose with a long burst of fire over the heads of all nearby. The red tracer flamed and sparkled as it tore out of the barrel at over three thousand feet per second.

The civilian traffic, with the drivers finally comprehending they were in the midst of a rolling gun battle, went predictably amok. The drivers closest to Dan, eyes only for the machine gun, stood on the brakes. Those drivers behind slammed into them. Others bounced over curbs while those closest to the median pulled a hard left and tried to grind across. Finally, some simply stopped their cars where they were, dismounted, and took cover on the highway. Pandemonium reigned.

The insurgents were stuck in the middle of it and were rendered immobile in a sea of panicked drivers. They continued to fire, but as the Tahoe continued to pull away, the visibility improved. Dan was able to put a good burst in the near vicinity of the insurgents' truck, which kept them cowering until the Tahoe made good its escape.

All was silent for the last few minutes, save for the squealing of the rims and the moaning of the wounded. The driver with the leg wound was beginning to scream in protest at his missing calf. The man shot in the back simply didn't move, though he was still breathing. Nobody wanted to think about his condition.

The engine continued to overheat, and smoke billowed from under the hood. A great fatigue was cloaking all the men, and it became increasingly difficult to stay focused. Nobody spoke as the last few kilometers clicked by.

Finally the front gate, replete with armed American sentries, came into view. Only fifty meters to go.

The Tahoe finally ground to a halt. The engine died and would not restart. It was the end of the road.

The American sentries, meanwhile, braced for an attack. A smoking, bullet-riddled wreck rolling up on rims had expired in front of their primary entrance. All immediately thought, "Bomb!" They took cover, preparing to engage whoever was inside. It was only the occupants' highly effective use of the coarser parts of the English language that began to convince the sentries that they were indeed Americans. Dan hopped out the back, holding and waving an orange VS-17 panel marker and yelling in English for medics.[3] George also got out, and his large mass and fair skin instantly marked him as Caucasian. The first casualty the pair gently lifted out was the Western driver with the injured calf. The commander of the security force scurried forward, took one look at the scene before him, and quickly gave Dan's badge a once over. With that he reached for the handset of his radio.

To quote Dan, the American Army was simply "awesome."

Within two minutes, a quick reaction force had arrived and was already at work securing the area around the crippled SUV. Medics came running, the hospital was notified, and shortly thereafter a fully equipped Humvee ambulance rumbled up. The fallen were placed on stretchers and moved to what little shade was available. Here they received medical aid sufficient to stabilize them for transfer to the trauma ward. However, a final incident occurred, one of those bizarre vignettes seen only in war that are humorous afterward but regarded as anything but at the time.

The man with the calf wound began to scream. He was also a fairly good friend of Dan's. As all who have been there know, the noise given off by the wounded is a tremendous drain on the others' morale and is very stressful to all nearby. It is horrible to listen to friends screaming.

Dan, who was assisting the medics, told the driver to please stop screaming. They were doing everything they could for him, and the recently administered morphine would soon dull the pain.

In response, the driver screamed again, more loudly than before. Dan looked the driver straight in the eye and distinctly said, "You are going to be all right now. So stop screaming."

In response, another howl of pain.

"Stop screaming!"

The patient responded with yet another wail. He was probably unaware of what he was doing.

"STOP FUCKING SCREAMING!!!"

The patient had already begun again but was cut off in mid cry about two seconds later as Dan clocked him with his gauntleted fist.

The wounded man was knocked out cold on the stretcher. He was punched out at the aid post with medics in attendance. Maybe forty people were there, including officers. But nobody said a word. Everyone carried on as if nothing had happened. Later Dan would be the first to visit the wounded driver in the hospital, and to this day they remain the best of friends.

That unreported ambush affected the lives of many and the pocketbooks of a few. The financial cost of that meaningless skirmish ran into the hundreds of thousands of dollars. Medical treatment, the write-off of the vehicles, and compensation for the wounded—all contributed to the final tally of about $600,000. Had anyone been killed, the life insurance would have increased the price tag dramatically. As it was, the cost of combat breaks down to roughly a thousand dollars a *second* for that short encounter. It would have been much higher if the combatants had been American soldiers rather than contractors.

The one bright note featured the man who had been shot in the back. The bullet had actually penetrated his body armor but not his skin. He only suffered a small burn from the actual round and an impressive set of bruises. The momentum of the round had driven his head into the top of the door frame when he was boarding, knocking him unconscious. He awoke with the equivalent of a bad hangover. He stayed on for the rest of his contract but was never the same and declined the opportunity to extend. He never returned to Iraq.

The two Nepalese Gurkhas both completed their tours in another couple of months. There were no other incidents, but neither of them opted to renew their contracts. Both returned to Nepal, rich men by local standards, and they were never heard from again.

The driver with the calf wound returned to administrative duty some six weeks later. He stayed for a month and then returned to South Africa, where he too opted to follow a different path in life.

CASS picked up Dan shortly afterward for a different assignment in the Pacific, South Africa, and Zimbabwe. He returned to Iraq for one last tour in 2006 and finally departed for good. He had seen enough and was sickened by the activities of the contract company he worked for. He suffers badly from posttraumatic stress disorder, some of which was brought on by this incident. He killed an awful lot of people that day.

The saddest case was George, the driver who acted so courageously under Dan's competent leadership. George became very religious, finding God everywhere. He also became isolated and withdrawn. He spent his ample downtime in Thailand, seeking solace in the arms of others who loved him strictly on a cash basis. Tragically, upon his return, he continued to booze it up and pray. Eventually, he began to mutilate himself with knives and a straight razor. George suffered from a significant psychological disorder, and, of course, the company had no interest in helping pay for any treatment. It would be more cost-effective to fire him and hire another. All because of a no-notice, ten-minute gunfight. Shortly thereafter, though, he quit and has since fallen off the planet, never to be heard from again. He did not even stay in touch with his closest friends. Such is life. All who knew him wish him well, although we fear the worst.

Chapter Nine
Life Inside the Asylum

A common public misconception about war is that the fighting is nonstop and intense. This is not the case. Private contractors, like the military, still have daily lives to lead, regardless of the chaos. Birthdays are celebrated, calls are placed home, and the mortgage payments must still be made. Regular life still somehow manages to exist among the rubble.

War makes for strange bedfellows, where the absurd becomes part of the daily routine. Sometimes life in a combat zone is bizarre, totally lacking parallels to any type of social norm. These juxtapositions make it so difficult for the veteran to explain the day-to-day activities of life in Baghdad. To provide narratives of combat alone would overlook the other 90 percent of life in theater, which is in fact the vast majority of any contractor's daily existence. The accounts that follow attempt to provide a sense of what life is like in Iraq for a contractor. Because of the ever-changing legal and moral issues addressed, the majority of the individuals interviewed wished to remain anonymous. Those who were willing to provide their names are quoted directly. Some, who are still employed in the industry, would be fired tomorrow should their comments for this book ever be linked to them. An often-quoted line at the Central Intelligence Agency is, "The truth shall set you free." In this industry it should be, "The truth can get you fired."

As addressed earlier, the contractor experience is unique. Sometimes the bullets fly directly at you, and sometimes it's somebody else's war. The results of prolonged contractor deployments are not pretty. The psychological toll has been high with many individuals suffering from the mental and emotional stress of their chosen profession. Coping mechanisms, usually alcohol and women, are not always the best remedy. Nearly all veterans speak of challenges faced after they left Iraq and tried to reintegrate in "normal" society. These hidden price tags of contractor life are seldom discussed in recruiting pitches.

"If you haven't been there you will never understand it," is an oft-recited refrain from security contractors. Witness the author's description of returning to Baghdad after spending a couple of weeks at home.

The usual drill at the airport. In the car park one donned body armor and loaded weapons. The same frenetic scramble through midday traffic. Our driver, a former Coldstream Guard with four years in country, giving us the routine play-by-play of Baghdad gossip.

"Beware that apartment block on the right; taking a lot of small arms fire from there lately," he interjected as we wove in and out of traffic. Up ahead a car is being searched, the owners covered by AK-47-wielding police.

"This is the intersection where the car bomb that killed seventy university students went off. You can still see the blast effects," he continued, rambling on as if we were discussing the latest football scores.

"When did they do that?" I asked. I can still see the bloodstains on the ground.

"Day before yesterday. So how was Orlando? Were you able to get those gloves and DVDs I asked you to buy?"

"I sure did." I replied. "Orlando is still there. My family says hi. Mind the guy with the AK on the corner up there. He looks like a cop, but I can't be sure."

"I see him. No drama. Welcome back."

"Nice to be back."

The author, who lives in rural Florida and bicycles past cow pastures on his way to the YMCA, describes his living arrangements in Baghdad. To this day, he jokes about living a bizarre double life, commuting from one to the other.

I live in a very peaceful part of Baghdad. Well, peaceful for January of 2007, which was one of the most violent months of the whole war. The reason for the peace is the neighborhood is composed almost entirely of ethnic Kurds.

These are the same Kurds whose parents were gassed by Saddam Hussein, and who would readily enjoy the opportunity to carve up a few Shias or Sunnis. The other two tribes give the neighborhood a wide berth, and we are quite safe here. [Nouri] al-Maliki, the Iraqi prime minister, lives just over a few doors away. Another security company is behind us, and the Kurdish checkpoints are every few yards on every street corner. However, our most exotic neighbors are Hamas, as in the terrorist organization, also just a few doors down. In keeping with the policy that war makes for strange bedfellows, we wave to them and they return the greeting quite cordially. Although not friends to the point of borrowing a cup of sugar from each other, it would seem that both parties have adopted a "live and let live" policy. This continues to promote neighborly goodwill and peace in a city torn apart by war.

Our happy residential area has severely defined limits, however, the most obvious one being that of the what-was-to-be Australian Embassy. Nearly completed, it has since been car bombed so many times that all that remains is a very pretty shell of a building. When I think of the word "failure," the image of that bombed-out embassy comes to mind. Beyond that, one travels at one's own risk. To our rear is a major bridge connecting our part of town to bad people country. When returning from missions in January, it became the norm to witness hundreds of Iraqis, attired completely in black robes, dance down the street to the beat of a couple of drummers. Every one of them waved an AK-47 above his head. I think it was a religious ceremony of some type.

Our last boundary is defined by a brand-new children's playground, complete with teeter-totter and jungle gyms. The playground itself is surrounded by chain-link fence, blast barriers, and barbed wire. Nobody has ever seen a child there in living memory. The citizens of some small Midwestern town in the U.S. got shafted in their charity money to build a playground for the Iraqi kids.

That's my home away from home, where I reside and work in my other life.

A former British paratrooper on his second rotation had this recollection of his particular neighborhood around the same time frame.

My second night there we were all gathered, watching some bootleg movie, when the whole neighborhood erupted in gunfire. It was not concentrated in one area, as firefights tend to be, but rather short bursts practically everywhere. Nobody else seemed too concerned so I played it cool and continued to watch the movie. A half minute later somebody let go a long burst on automatic, not more than a hundred meters away. This was getting a bit close for comfort.

Paul, observing my growing concern, glanced at his watch and simply stated, "Oh, that's about right. Not to worry. This shit happens all the time."

"Why?" was my response.

They all laughed at that.

"Football. What the Yanks call soccer. The Iraqis are playing on the television tonight. Every time a goal is scored by the Iraqi team all the locals run outside and fire weapons in celebration. They say that Sadr City sounds like Stalingrad if it's a big match. Fear not, they do the same thing at weddings too. You just have to be careful not to shoot up the newlyweds or the sports fans by mistake when you are on patrol. God, you should have been here the night they hung Saddam."

The lifestyle has become highly addictive to more than a few. Witness this American who became bored with peacetime America and volunteered for the streets of Baghdad. A civilian, he had forsaken the easy life of the United States for the rough and tumble of Iraq. Much to his surprise, he found he relished the daily violence and chaos.

In a paradoxical fashion, war can be peaceful. One is not overly concerned with the administrative bullshit that confounds so much of our everyday life. The price of gas, who won the football game, or the horrific fact that you have let your automobile registration tag go out of date back home are consigned to the part of your mind where they belong: the wastepaper basket. I actually got a call from my dentist's office on my worldwide cellular asking to set a date for a checkup as bullets were cracking overhead. Nobody believes you if you tell them the truth, so I just said I would get back to them and hung up the phone. I mean, what am I going to say, "Sorry, in a firefight. Let me call you back in ten minutes if I'm alive?"

Here we focus only on our immediate needs and the welfare of those around us. Life is simpler. After living this life, I don't think I could ever make it as an accountant or manager with a nine-to-five existence, which is why the draw for Iraq is so, so strong for so many who have been exposed to it.

Another topic of conversation among contractors is "Joe," the commonly used term to describe the American Army. Although occasionally mocked and sometimes cursed for the odd angry shot directed toward contractors, none ever doubted the enormity of the challenge the Americans faced or their resolve to do the best job they could. Hamish Burling Claridge, the platoon sergeant with time in the Balkans, East Timor, and the Solomons, had the following to say about his counterparts in the American Army in the dark months before the "surge" of 2007.

They do the lion's share of the dirty work and are on the short end of every stick. Just like back in New Zealand. And now they die daily against an enemy they rarely see and cannot possibly hope to fight back against. When a reporter sticks a microphone in their face, they all toe the company line. They don't have much choice as they are under enormous pressure to put on the smiley face for the millions back home. So they can't quite hop up and down and proclaim the war to be stupid. But when listening in the chow hall, and when they know you won't report them, the tone has shifted. Nobody ever talks about "winning." Now it's about making it home in one piece. They don't discuss the "possibility" of civil war. They are in one, and it is plain for all of them to see as they are the ones tasked to police up the body parts.

Bumper sticker observed on the back of a U.S. Army Humvee patrolling Baghdad:
"God, please save me from your followers."

Graffiti scribbled on an overpass on MSR Tampa:
"Pete's Mom is HOT!"

One very old hand, a Brit who had been there from the very early days, recalls supplementing his income via one of the oldest ploys in the book: bootlegging liquor. Most contractors are extremely reticent to discuss this portion of the industry, and this individual, still employed in Iraq, has requested total anonymity.

We used to buy the booze at the duty free in BIAP. To begin with, it was Corona, Heineken, and Johnny Walker, but that didn't take long to change. Eventually there was everything imaginable there. Like most cottage industries, we started small, running over the Kuwaiti border with a few bottles stuck inside where the spare tire would normally go. The Kuwaiti guards were way too lazy to check.

But as time went by we got a bit more organized and worked on a larger scale. One of the administrative chaps in Kuwait City was in tight with one of the Kuwaiti royal family, of which there are many, meaning we didn't need to worry about getting nailed by the cops. This junior member of the royals was the buyer and mover, which kind of gave us yet another immunity from prosecution in addition to the one we already had in Iraq. We would take military flights with footlockers stuffed to the gills with booze. It was a solid investment. We would buy a bottle of vodka for maybe $20 and sell it in Kuwait for $140. At one point I was making more running liquor than I was carrying guns.

Time spent on the sharp end in Baghdad was difficult. Many contractors chose to escape to Dubai for a few days where two things were in abundant supply—alcohol and women. Thousands of prostitutes worked the hotels and clubs of Dubai, offering their services to the contractors who flooded the place. It was not a cheap pastime, with an hour's worth of physical pleasure running from $500 to $1,000. But for a contractor, it was less than a day's wages.

Many of the women, both young and pretty, hailed from the former Soviet Union. Some were forced and some signed up on their own. It was a bleak existence, and the girls were paid a tiny fraction of what the Mafia who ran them billed the client.

A French Canadian, hailing from Montreal and speaking here for the first time, recalls meeting one on a personal basis. The young lady and several of her coworkers had spent the night with several of the Canadian's comrades, all of whom were in Dubai for five days after losing some comrades in an ambush. His insights into the world's oldest profession resonate along a theme similar to that of the lives of contractors fighting in Baghdad.

He has arisen early and is having coffee on the balcony when he is joined by a Ukrainian call girl.

She was by far the smartest and utterly stunning in the physical sense with long blond hair and bright green eyes, all accentuated by a wicked sense of humor.

I finally got up the nerve to ask her how she had wound up here.

She said that she had two options. She could work on the local economy back in Ukraine and achieve no forward progress. Her family was poor and her job would be menial labor, foredooming her to poverty for life. Or she could knowingly sign the dotted line, where she would be paid to go fuck strangers for cash. She signed. So however demeaning and mentally debilitating her chosen profession, she clearly elucidated to me that it was better than rotting away in the middle of nowhere doing nothing.

"Why is this better?" I asked over a second cup of coffee. She was an early riser, and everybody else save the two of us was still in bed. In fact, everybody else was in the *same* bed, but what the hell, a bed is a bed.

Leaning back, freshly showered, she toyed with the ends of the white terry towel robe, doubtless stolen. I found it amusing how she could fuck somebody senseless the night before literally in front of your eyes but the next morning become as modest as everybody else. Maybe it makes a difference when you are engaged as a human being as opposed to a sex toy.

She gazed out at the sea, then turned, and replied in fractured English, "It's really quite simple. Right now I am sitting on a balcony in a fancy hotel, drinking coffee with a rich man from Canada. In Kiev, I have no hope. Here, though it can be very bad sometimes, I have hope. I hope that one day I can learn enough English to get a better job, a real one, and get a resident visa for here in Dubai. Then I would like to go to school, educate myself more, and try to move to America. I would like to go shopping at a mall with a credit card in my name, and one day I would like to have a family and a normal life. I do not have the luxury of debating whether I am being 'exploited' or not. I do know that I can send a lot of money back to the Ukraine, which has made a big difference to my family. They are now able to pay for goods and services otherwise unavailable to them. I know that the price of my dreams is that I have to perform certain actions that I don't like. I must turn off and become a robot and lie and smile and do what needs to be done for me to move forward. That much is simple and that I understand. I am willing to pay that price for the chance at a better life. Going back to Kiev is unthinkable; save for my family, Kiev is without hope.

"But the only skill that I have is that God has graced me with a body that men call attractive and pay a lot of money to have their way with me. And perhaps it will work and perhaps it won't, but I will never know if I don't try. Because bad though it is, I am still one step closer to my dreams. And the money that I make from 'bad' acts keeps my family going, and what I keep I save to go to America one day."

We had a few more conversations over the next day or two. I realized she was ultimately a victim of economic circumstance and was not unlike some of us who had volunteered for Iraq to escape the trailer park. Had she been born in the USA, she would be getting ready to graduate from a university. She would probably have her own apartment with her own automobile and credit card. But luck had destined her to be born in a shitty little village on the outskirts of nowhere whereas twenty-odd years earlier I was born in one of the most prosperous nations on earth. So it sucks to be her.

I feel it just confirms my belief that the overwhelming majority of the world is colored in various shades of gray. There are just a few percentage points of absolute black or absolute white at either end of the spectrum that is called humanity. It's just the luck of the draw as to whether you are born Iraqi with nothing or Canadian with everything. Simple chance.

The news media and private contractors maintain a relationship that is adversarial at best. Private security companies go out of their way to avoid the media lest video catch them in something that would prove difficult to explain. The few videos that have made the news have all been filmed by contractors themselves and leaked to the world via the Internet. It is not a happy relationship. But, as this account provides, sometimes the shoe is on the other foot. This incident occurred in the very early days of 2004, before the ranks of the professionals were overwhelmed by hordes of amateurs. An American who was on this particular detail recalls:

We were sitting around at a power generating station, one of several in the neighborhood. It was fairly quiet for that neighborhood for that time frame. Meaning nobody had shot at us yet. Not that we ever got far away from the guns or vehicles.

So we were just sitting, listening to the radio, and a couple of guys were in the back, reading the paper. Everything was cool.

Up rolls a few cars, low profile, and out pop a couple of guys with cameras and their local security team. Considering their job, it was a smart way to move. The only thing that really was out of place was the newsman himself. He had the mandatory blue body armor with a big PRESS logo, like that's really going to help when you are dressed in an orange jump suit. I think somebody snickered a bit.

He walks up and introduces himself. We don't move and have no desire to talk to him, but somebody is civil enough to greet him.

He wants to know about "contacts," which is the fancy term for a fire-fight. Jimmy tells him if he wants contacts, he just needs to keep driving around and pretty soon his wish will be granted. Guaranteed.

But he wanted us, so he offers us about $1,500 to stage a thirty-second firefight. Just shoot up some buildings and claim it was the insurgents. So he can get it all on film and make the news. You know, Mr. Clark Kent, stud-muffin-reporter type. Probably has a wall full of pictures of himself.

We declined. But I'm sure he got it somewhere. Everything was for sale. You name it, it was for sale. But it soured my opinion of the press a bit further, if that was possible. I wonder, now that I've left, about how much of it is crap. How much of the media is rigged. But I don't care anymore. I learned that there, too. Not to care. The first commandment of Baghdad is, "Thou shalt not care," because otherwise, "Thou shalt go crazy." I don't care. So be it.

Everything was indeed for sale. Some of the most aggressive capitalists were the new breed of Russians. Many of the leased supply aircraft were flown by Russian crews, who were used to seat-of-the-pants flying in the world's dingier corners. Some of the most fascinating reading to emerge from the Iraq War concerns the U.S. government's hiring of the world's most infamous arms dealer, Viktor Bout. A Russian believed to be of Tajik extraction, Bout was featured in the bestselling book Merchants of Death *in addition to the movie* The Lord of War. *That the world's most notorious name in an industry full of notorious names was actually on the U.S. payroll tasked to fly supplies (possibly including arms) into Iraq is totally surreal, save for the fact that it actually happened early in the war. (The reader might find it interesting to note that Viktor Bout was arrested in Thailand in 2008 by Americans posing as Colombian terrorists wishing to buy arms. At press time, Mr. Bout remains behind bars in Thailand.)*

But back in 2004, his Russian pilots were infected with the same laissez-faire attitude toward capitalism, as this anecdote by a British Special Forces type so eloquently confirms. Whether this flight used one of Bout's aircraft will never be known, though the contractor would prefer to believe that it was.

One of the lads needed to get to Dubai, which is a very short hop from Baghdad. The problem is that there were at the time no routine scheduled flights out of Baghdad save for Jordan, for which you pay dearly.

So Paul was at BIAP and needed a lift. Normally most of us can poach rides on Royal Air Force aircraft with the right ID. No such luck today as everything was full.

However, there was a Russian airline with a cargo jet parked on the pavement. A Russian airline in this case consisted of a couple of pilots, a crew chief, and a loadmaster along with the huge, rust bucket transport. That was the whole airline. Rumor at the time was that it was one of Viktor Bout's birds. We found out later we were right, or so we were told.

The crew had just walked into the terminal from their cargo plane and from eavesdropping it was evident they were flying to Dubai.

So Paul walked over and asked for a lift.

The pilot, dressed like all Russians in the mandatory brown leather jacket and blue jeans, continued to chain smoke in the terminal directly beneath a large No Smoking sign. The conversation went something like this:

Paul: Hi there. Are you going to Dubai?

Pilot: Yes.

Paul: Do you have room for another?

Pilot: You want go Dubai?

Paul: Yes.

Pilot: Yes.

Paul: How much?

Pilot (staring a little at Paul): How much you got?

Paul: How does two hundred dollars sound?

Pilot: OK.

Paul: When do you want me here?

Pilot: 1500.

Paul dutifully returned and waited for his ride. At ten minutes of, the pilot walked by, still chain smoking and still wearing the brown leather jacket. Just like the rest of the crew.

Paul: Hey, remember, I'm going to Dubai with you.

Pilot: You want go to Dubai?

Paul: Yes, we spoke earlier.

Pilot: Ah, yes, you Mr. Two Hundred Dollars.

Paul: Yes.

Pilot: Ok, Mr. Two Hundred Dollars, follow me.

And without any further formality, no customs, nothing, they simply walked over to the darkened Antonov transport in the afternoon sun. Upon entering the dark, steamy vault of the cargo hold, the conservation began again.

Paul: Where would you like me to sit?

Pilot: Where you want.

Paul: Anywhere?

Pilot: You want sit in door with feet hanging out, I don't care. You want sit up front with me, I don't care. Just pay me now, please, in case you fall out.

Paul: So I could take the copilot's seat?

Pilot: I don't care. Fine. Then copilot doesn't need to fly, and he can take break. He's drunk anyway. No problem. You sit in copilot seat. Two hundred dollars, please.

With that, Paul forked over the cash.

With surprising dispatch, the aircraft was soon ready. The pilot wasted no time. Paul strapped himself into the right-hand seat and was soon joined by the entire crew. Without any ceremony, a bottle of vodka was pulled from an ice chest, and pewter tumblers were passed around. Paul thought they were kidding. But he accepted the preferred shot glass nonetheless. Without a word, the loadmaster poured a round. The pilot hit the starter, and Engine #1 cranked and caught.

"Ching" went the shot glasses and the vodka disappeared. Paul slugged down his and was speechless when he realized they really were doing vodka shots in the cockpit. The happy copilot refilled the glasses.

Engine #2 started. "Ching."

Engine #3 and #4 cranked and spooled up. "Ching. Ching."

Without even a by-your-leave, the pilot assumed command, ensured the auxiliary power units were disconnected, and began to taxi. In less than a minute they had found an open runway, the crew took a good look around, the pilot spoke very briefly to the tower, and with that the throttles went forward and the huge Antonov began to lumber down the tarmac. Engines at full power, the massive machine finally cleared the runway and began to climb. With a "thunk" the landing gear retracted and the flight was airborne. "Ching."

A few minutes later the flight was climbing through 10,000 feet and hence immune to anything hateful coming up from the ground. "Ching."

A number of hours later the plane was cleared to land at Dubai. "Ching."

Paul was feeling no pain. The crew looked as if they had been drinking nothing stronger than water.

Somewhat the worse for wear, Paul observed from the right seat as the pilot made a beautiful landing in Dubai.

Western policy dictates that arriving crews clear customs, turn in paper-work, and so on. Not this group. They parked the Antonov on a quiet sector of the airport and just turned it off. They were about a mile from the arrivals hall and that entailed walking over a lot of active runway, which would give fits to Western security staff.

Paul, ever the diplomatic Brit, tendered the obvious: Umm, excuse me, but how do I get to the immigration building?

Pilot (a bit upset): Immigration? You no say nothing about immigration. You say you want to go to Dubai. Well, you in Dubai. Here you are. Dubai. Finish.

Paul: Well, yes, that was a brilliant flight. So, what's your name if I—

Pilot (more upset and interrupting Paul): My name? Why you need to know my name? I don't know your name. You, Mr. Two Hundred Dollars, who wanted to go to Dubai, you in Dubai. Why you need to know my name?

Paul smiled, thanked them all profusely, and began a long trek across open runways to the arrival hall. He illicitly entered a side door, and eventually managed to attach himself to a tour group of camera-toting Japanese tourists. He smiled, gestured, and got his passport stamped and was soon thereafter in Dubai legally.

A veteran of multiple conflicts described perhaps the most surreal incident. Dripping in cynicism and gallows humor, it is reflective of the mind-set of so many men who had spent long periods of time in Iraq. A slowly acquired lack of respect for the law and all things Arabic is plainly evident in this colorful passage. But beneath the droll writing lay serious warning signs. Cynicism, contempt for the law, alcohol abuse, and a mocking of Arabic culture clearly indicate it was time for him to take a break from the rigors of combat. His coping mechanism was plainly beginning to break down.

This fascinating episode begins about an hour after a shooting incident on MSR Tampa that also involved the author of this book.

A short thirty minutes later saw us safely to our camp at Safwan. The vehicles were downloaded, weapons cleaned and stored, and I returned all the explosives to the locker. The Tahoe was stripped of all things warlike, even down to removing brass shell casings and machine-gun links. We then stuffed every hidden nook and cranny with bottles of booze to smuggle into Kuwait. I made sure my precious gin was in a locale not likely to get broken. A half hour later we were just clearing customs on the Kuwaiti side of the border. A very strong sandstorm was causing significant drifting, partially obscuring the road. It was just past 0700 Kuwaiti time. Opting to bypass the border Burger King as it only serves Whoppers, albeit 24/7, we mashed the pedal to the floor, grossly exceeding the speed limit. However, the Kuwaiti Police do not bother with all things American. We made the 130 kilometers to Kuwait City in less than an hour, pulling into the parking lot of our favorite Parisian restaurant smartly at 0800. Our armored Tahoe, covered in dust, blood, and bullet holes, rested gently in a lot full of Mercedes, Porsches, and a Lamborghini in the corner. Still reeking of ammonia from sweat, wearing clothes from our sojourn in war, and sporting a four-day growth of beard, we were flawlessly escorted by a gorgeous Malaysian girl to a table replete with fine china. Around us dined rich and elegant Kuwaitis, who, having nothing else to do since so few of them actually work for a living, continued their idle gossip. They passed us only the occasional rude glance.

It was barely over two hours since I had been actively firing a heavy rifle with the intent to kill. Now a delicate omelet, replete with feta cheese and accompanied by a superb French press coffee, was presented before me. The cotton tablecloth was starched and of immaculate whiteness. CNN babbled on in the background, the anchor speaking of a "deteriorating" security situation in Iraq. No shit. With that, we returned to our meals, engaging in workplace gossip and the same topics that the world entire speaks of over morning coffee. What a strange nether existence we lead. What a strange war.

We returned to Nigel's villa, which has a beautiful view of the Gulf. We parked beside his Ferrari, his other vehicle after the armored gun truck. It is always easy to know whether Nigel is at work or at play. One only needs to see which vehicle is missing from the parking lot.

Nigel himself, a twenty-nine-year-old Scotsman, has done well in the last three years since he arrived in the Gulf. He is always the one of smiling face, good humor, and possesses irresistible charisma when he chooses to use it. Slightly roly-poly with a penchant for drama, he is well loved by all. This is a good thing as some of his antics, both on and off the battlefield, have landed him in hot water on more than one occasion. He is the perfect happy pirate, who would be lecherous enough to screw your wife while you sipped highballs in his living room. However, once the ground rules are laid out, he has invariably proven to be a solid operator. Nigel is a wonderful comrade, provided you keep your girlfriend locked up. His villa is spectacular, stuffed to the point of bursting with all things musical and electronic. His Ferrari is bright red, of course, and is one of his favorite toys. When he is not engaged in breaking things or people in Iraq, he can be seen with either one or the other of his second favorite toys, his girlfriends. One is Lebanese and gorgeous, the other Norwegian and gorgeous. Of course. He is careful to ascertain the whereabouts of one before he takes the other out for a drive. On his next vacation he will be flying (first class, of course) to Tanzania and Mozambique to look at oceanfront property he is considering purchasing.

As we enter the villa and I clump across the Italian marble floors, I discover he has called ahead and arranged for the Filipino maid, who is also gorgeous, of course, to run our baths. I am not much for bubble baths, but it does tend to relax one after the rigors of the road. Even more relaxing is when the same maid, who most assuredly is not difficult to look at in a terrycloth robe, quietly pads in. She gently places the world's finest gin and tonic, replete with lime of course, on a stand beside the scummy bubbles underneath which I am immersed. Naturally booze is illegal, but everyone has it, and besides, this isn't booze. It's Tanqueray and tonic. The great part is that one can never get busted for any type of alcoholic infringement, as no regulations are on the books as there is no alcohol in the first place! Before she leaves I have already indicated the need for another, though the first is untouched. The clock strikes nine chimes in the morning. Before the last "bong" resonates through the hallway, the tumbler is empty.

One gin leads to another. And another. We retire in terrycloth to the gabled terrace, in order to conduct a survey of Nigel's eminent domain. By noon we are rather lit. Nigel has his satellite phone out, calling everybody he knows everywhere in the world, regardless of local times, to chat.

Much later in the day, when one of his girlfriends has arrived, Nigel stumbles upon the unique idea of going skating. As in ice skating.

"Brilliant," was the best I could muster in response.

Some thirty minutes later I am seated with Nigel's girlfriend's girlfriend. She is from Beirut, volatile, gorgeous of course, and maniacally curses both the Israelis and Syrians in equal measure as we weave madly through the traffic in the red Ferrari at about 110 mph. She continues to babble on in a mix of French, Arabic, and English, but all I can fixate on are a pair of Angelina Jolie–class lips and breasts straining to burst out of the white shirt, which is way, way ridiculously too tight. Of course. Every time we hit a bump they gently sway up and down in harmony with the soft suspension. We should have taken the battlewagon, which practically has no suspension whatsoever. The view would doubtless have been even more enticing. We never get pulled over for our insane driving: they must assume we are locals. Nigel is not far behind in the armored truck.

Merely twenty minutes later I find myself on a skating rink, surrounded by hordes of Kuwaiti children in Western clothing. Their mothers and sisters, in the perfect surreal touch to cap this surreal day, are gently gliding about the rink in full ninja attire. All one can see are skates emerging from beneath the black robes and darting eyes behind the veils and black burka. Strange breed, that.

Shortly thereafter, the stress of the past few days, combined with alcohol, sets in and I am passed out cold by 8:00 p.m.

When the war is discussed among contractors, the topic of luck invariably comes up. It is sometimes difficult for Westerners to accept that they can be tactically brilliant, do everything right, and still be blown to bits by a twelve-year-old armed with a cell phone. For in the end, often it comes down to dumb luck. Being in the right or wrong place at the right or wrong time is the difference between living and dying. Eventually many come to accept that every day is simply another roll of the dice.

An anonymous contributor summarizes his opinion of armed conflict.

War is legalized insanity cosponsored by erratic randomness. The closer one gets to the front lines, the more valid the theorem. You can be perfectly secure and still die. The first time I was in Baghdad we had to police up two young men—one a private contractor and the other in the army. Their father, who had flown out some three hours earlier, had been killed on the military transport aircraft. How? Somebody with an AK-47 had taken a potshot at his plane, which was already over a mile high, moving at 130 mph and accelerating rapidly. Only three people were in the cargo hold, seated side by side. The golden bullet traveled upward over said mile, punched through the aluminum skin of the fuselage, and had neatly taken the top of the head off the man in the middle. The other two were completely untouched, save for being covered in blood and brains. The odds of a successful shot at that range? Zero. It can't be done. But the loadmaster was still hosing the blood and bone chips out of the transport and we were still driving through Baghdad in the middle of the night trying to get his boys to the airhead so they could fly home with the body.

A black British contractor who had previously served with the London Metropolitan Police ventures his thoughts. This same contractor, getting on in years, had also served in the Royal Marines in the Falklands fighting way back in 1982 and draws his first anecdote from the South Atlantic campaign.

Others can tap dance through the minefields buck naked for years on end and emerge without a scratch. Only to die choking on a hot dog back home. I remember, in the Falklands, I once turned my head to talk to someone. At that exact instant, the someone was shot in the face. Had I not turned my head I would have caught that round. Another time, near Baghdad a bullet came through the window of a truck moving at 95 mph and nicked the side of my head just enough for a trickle of blood to flow. I thought I had been stung by a wasp, not an AK-47 round. Literally an inch away from death. But it matters not because it missed, and it doesn't matter how close it came if it ultimately failed to impact the intended target.

A former U.S. Air Force sergeant cum contractor, reflects upon a life-changing circumstance, based on a larger-than-expected amount of paperwork one day in Baghdad. This is his only contribution to the book, though a powerful one.

One of my friends had been riding in the front right seat of an escort vehicle every single day for three months. On one obscure Tuesday he was pulled to conduct routine administrative chores, and another friend of mine took his place. The replacement never came back. He was killed. The survivor still carries enormous guilt though it was no fault of his own. The Arabs have a saying that roughly translates as "When it's your time, it's your time." Much older and wiser now, I tend to agree with them. Such is war.

Of course, by trusting to luck, one accepts a certain loss of control over one's life. For many contractors and soldiers, a loss of control equals an increase in fear. Fear is a very difficult challenge to overcome for many who have spent a prolonged period of time in Baghdad.

The author, in close contact with American combat forces, penned this at the height of the fighting as he observed the daily foot patrols of an adjacent army unit.

Fear is another demon that must be wrestled with and eventually overcome if one is to function in a combat zone. Surprisingly enough, fear is generally in remission when one is actually under fire. There is much to occupy the mind and focus on and fear is thus pushed to the far fringes of the consciousness. It is during the quiet times, especially before impending combat, that fear sallies forth from the dark corners and scales the ramparts of our mind. Intelligent people with active imaginations perhaps suffer worse, for it takes no effort to transpose their own face onto any one of the resident corpses whose sole remaining job is to play rotting extra on the stage of war. When one arrives and the unit has not taken casualties, it is easy to pretend and believe that skill is what has kept all alive until now. But the sheer randomness of violence ensures that sooner or later somebody gets hurt for war is still a great deal about luck. Fear runs riot in the quiet hours of the night, in the bright glare of the mind's eye, as the vision of a friend, torn and bloody, being loaded onto a helicopter plays across the imaginary screen. Stuck on permanent replay, such images are as caustic to the soul as battery acid is to the stomach. One begins to wonder, "How will I get hit? Is today the last day of my life? Who will come to my funeral?" Younger troops suffer more than older ones.

The author, drawing upon personal experience, also reminisces on the topic of every contractor's secret fear of being captured by the insurgents.

On the inside of the turret hatch, welded to the vehicle armor, was a little steel box with the open side facing me. Inside was a fragmentation grenade, and the only thing that secured it to the inside of that box was a piece of green tape. I timed it, and in about two seconds I could have that grenade in my hands with the pin pulled. Besides that, I carried a spare magazine for my pistol. The last three rounds were Black Talons, which is a super hot load on a really mean bullet. Like everybody else, I had seen videos on the Internet of the Orange Jump Suit crowd getting their heads cut off. I was not going to go out dressed as a Halloween pumpkin. Fuck that, and to be honest I think every other guy felt the same way, but we never really talked about it. If there was no hope it was going to be by my own hand via the grenade or pistol. I know that sounds very brave, my sitting here in my living room now as I write this, but the truth was we were all utterly terrified of being captured. Your odds of survival were zero, and I had no wish to be tortured to death while it was being broadcast live on the Internet. I really think I would have done it. We would have fought against impossible odds because the only alternative was to die screaming in agony.

I kind of think sometimes that the insurgents became their own worst enemy because it caused us to develop a "shoot to the second-last bullet" mind-set with the last one for ourselves. I am certain that it brutalized an already harsh insurgency even more. But it was what it was and you could always go home. Thankfully I never came close to having to test myself, and I don't regret that one bit!

As the contractors' role expanded, companies made every effort to reduce costs but still maintain the same astronomically high bill rate. One of the first ploys was the recruitment and importation of third country nationals, whose pay was a minute fraction of what a Westerner received. This American deployed straight from Iraq to Kathmandu, Nepal. His mission was to select some eighty Nepalese for PSD and static assignments in Iraq. He picks up with his arrival in Kathmandu, late in 2004.

I was picked up by Rudi, my Nepalese point of contact, and promptly deposited in the nicest hotel in town. It was a bit run down due to the Maoist insurgency currently tearing the country apart, but Kathmandu itself hadn't changed much since my last visit. The only thing on television was endless reruns of Fashion TV so all I did in that room was sleep.

Iraq is a good deal for the locals. The average Nepalese earns about $1,000 per annum. Other Nepalese were working for American multinationals in Afghanistan for $18 a week, and they were ecstatic. We were offering jobs at $80 per day, so I knew the turnout would be huge. The client gets billed at $1,200 per day, which is the same rate as Westerners. Ten dollars per head per day goes to the recruiter. Another ten goes to the guy who ships them from Nepal to Iraq and pays for visas, etc. We pay them $80, which was outrageously high at the time. They receive no medical coverage, no life insurance save for a one-time payout of $1,000 if killed in the line of duty, and substandard equipment. They are packed twenty to a room versus four Westerners to the same area and do not have dining privileges. So they cook their own food, paid from their $80 per day. The profit margin on a Nepalese is about $1,100 of the $1,200 daily bill rate. The profit margin for Westerners is about $500–$600 per day, so the use of TCNs effectively doubles the bottom line. The only guy who really loses is the client who gets shafted twice. The first time is getting hit with an astronomical bill rate predicated on an all Western team. The second is because when you have a Caucasian team leader, Fijians for drivers, Nepalese for operators, Ugandans for gunners, and Iraqis as guides, it doesn't work well in combat. You are reduced to using hand signals when the shooting starts as nobody can speak each other's language.

If you suffer from compassion, TCN recruiting is tough. Rudi, my supplier of people in Kathmandu, has to post the notice some two weeks in advance. This allows time for the villagers in the outlying areas to walk in as there are no cars in the mountainous portions of Nepal, which is practically all of it.

We arrived at the office the next morning at 0800, and there were already hundreds of people in line. Hundreds more were packed like sardines in the courtyard waiting to get into the line. Many had slept rough the night before to keep their place in the queue. It took ten minutes to elbow our way through the throng and get upstairs to the interview office. There were nearly twenty-five hundred applicants already, and we would get another five hundred per day for the four days I was there.

I interviewed at the flat rate of thirty an hour, which equated to under two minutes per applicant. I would ask, "Why should you be selected to go to Iraq where you can make a year's wages in thirteen days?" They had ninety seconds to sell their soul. That was it. If you stammered, just stood there, or otherwise did nothing, you were dismissed before you had a chance to speak. Harsh but effective.

Some of the young aggressive guys who spoke good English did well. They piled right in and started speaking military experience, weapon systems, etc. Of course, this was exactly what I was looking for, and they got hired.

Others would pass over tattered service record books from their Indian and Nepalese Army days with faded photos decades old. Then they would come to attention, ramrod straight, shoes shined as best they could, and wait. I could hardly look them in the eye when they were turned down.

I remember two in particular. One character gave exemplary answers to every question in fluent English until I asked him what part of Nepal he was from. He stumbled for a bit and then responded with a perfect recital of weapons characteristics in flawless BBC English. It finally dawned on me that he didn't speak a word of it, but had rather spent hours memorizing paragraph-length answers to fifteen questions he thought I might ask. The question of where he was from wasn't on the list so he got nailed.

Through the interpreter I got him to cough out the truth. The reality was he had arrived in Kathmandu ten days previously and had tracked down a local English teacher. He had spent about half of everything he owned paying for the teacher to help him word the answers correctly and check his pronunciation.

We looked at each other, and he didn't budge. Nor did he ask for mercy. He was caught and he knew it. He stood at attention, fingers along the seams of his trousers, and stared at a spot on the wall behind me.

I told him to fork over his notes with the questions. It was about four pages long. I asked him each question in turn. He replied with a word-perfect response. He never mispronounced a word nor did he ever get a syllable out of sequence. Every fucking time.

I hired him. I figured what he did took initiative, brains, and balls, all of which I was seeking. He did very well during his eighteen months in Iraq and has since returned to run a business somewhere in the Annapurnas, a very rich man by Nepalese standards.

I also hired a sixty-five-year-old former sergeant major who had so much command presence it practically oozed out of him. He also acquitted himself in an exemplary manner, shooting up a number of Iraqis in an ambush.

We closed up the office, usually around seven or eight o'clock at night. It was hard on those who had waited for hours only to have the door shut when

they were maybe three or four away from being interviewed. I know many
of them spent the night sleeping in front of the door or on the stairwell. The
toughest times were walking across the courtyard to the car to take me back
to the hotel. Invariably I would be surrounded by very polite men, all desperate for work. Often you would see a father and son, the old man pushing his
kid forward, volunteering him for war as that was a way for the family to
climb out of grinding poverty. Sometimes this all occurred by candlelight as
the electricity wasn't always a sure thing. So it was rather spooky and exotic
at the same time.

*This contractor, a Brit who appeared in chapter 2, sums up his feelings for the Nepalese
who so willingly volunteered to fight another man's war.*

Not all of them came back, you know. Some are still there, buried. I hope it
was worth it, but by God, they were all keen to go. I have immense respect
for them, to do what they did. Sometimes I feel I have more in common with
them than I do with Americans. When I hear people bitch over stupid stuff
here, I feel we in the West are very spoiled. We don't understand how it is in
the rest of the world. I am now much more grateful for what I have. Iraq and
Nepal both taught me that.

*One of the ugly side effects of contract work in Iraq is a lack of medical coverage. Regular
army soldiers have a raft of counseling services to cope with the horrors of war. Private
security contractors have none. The result, as described by this American, is not pretty.
The rage and displaced anger are self-evident. So are the obvious intelligence and
thought-provoking hypotheses of the person who penned it.*

A very dark by-product of our lifestyle is the extraordinarily difficult time
the vast majority of us have in maintaining any type of long-term, intimate
relationship with women.

There are a few, some of whom I know personally, who are simply gone.
When I say "gone," I mean that they have spent too long in remote corners of
the world viewing the landscape over the muzzle of a rifle. They have become
cold, indifferent, and callous. They only live for the moment and view women
as a means of sexual release. These are the guys who go to Thailand every

vacation to indulge in an orgy of physical pleasure, then return to combat. Some will never really return to the United States, for they fully comprehend that they are far enough gone that to return home is nothing more than a fast track to jail. They realize this, and therefore keep their trips home super short. All are excellent operators as they have nothing else to live for. There are a few friends—and I mean no ill when I say this—that I sometimes secretly hope will take a bullet the day before the war ends, as it would be construed as a mercy killing. For them to return home after enduring their time in the combat zone is nothing more than a slow, lingering death. They are utterly unable to cope in a "normal" society.

On the other hand, some of those who were married before their tour are able to maintain that relationship, building on past structure. For them the war is about making a mortgage payment, nothing more. They are probably a little over half of the total.

For the rest of us solo warriors, returning home to the United States is an excruciatingly miserable experience. We are complete strangers in a land called home. We no longer have any commonalities with anybody who has not undergone the same collective experience we have. Our social code is completely rewired, at odds with the norm of society. I suffer gravely from this, and mine is a mild case. Let me explain.

Combat strips one bare. There is no room for prejudice or preconceived notions. Everything is subjugated to the one end: survival. It does not matter that the man beside you is black or Hispanic or rich or fat or good looking. Nor is it important what type of car he drives. What *is* important is his ability to shoot, move, and communicate. One gets to know one's comrades far better than one knows lifelong friends or even family. Infantry combat is a white hot furnace that bonds men for life because the price of failure is death. And so it goes.

Then, without any decompression time, we get on airplanes (exactly like the leave rotation used by the armed forces in Iraq) and some twenty-four hours later are dumped in Orlando, Omaha, or Edinburgh, alone in a vast sea of faces that have never known the fear we have faced daily.

War does different things to different people. Some become remote while others party as hard as they can. I have found that I actually have become much more compassionate, generous, and overall more caring. I stop to feed the squirrels and tend to seek intelligent, intimate relationships as opposed to having a revolving door on my bedroom.

What a lost cause.

We have become a nation (or perhaps we always were and I just never caught it) of fat voyeurs vicariously living out their childish fantasies by viewing inane and idiotic reality television shows. We equate material consumption and wealth directly to happiness, which is a colossal error as the two are completely separate entities. We focus on the superficial—the types of cars, breast enhancements, hair removal, the newest technical gadget—all meaningless. I am not even remotely materialistic anymore.

At least that is how I feel when I return. The first couple of days are wonderful. Real food, real sheets, cooler weather, and the color *green*. Everything is brighter and the colors more luminescent upon return. I get my haircut from the same barber who opened the place in 1946 and get to work out in a real gym.

And the longer I stay at home the more I realize the less I have in common with everybody else. For it is not society that has changed, it is I.

When one returns from far-flung fields of horror, a couple of changes occur. The first is that I am overwhelmingly grateful for what I have and the lifestyle I am able to lead, with life, liberty, and the pursuit of happiness as the first three chapters. When one undergoes serious travail, the meaningless barbs of everyday life are pushed to the margins of importance.

But it is the second one that causes angst. For in learning gratitude and appreciation for life, we become intolerant in the ways of a society that takes it for granted. It is both the bane and boon of great democratic civilizations: our forefathers have striven mightily to construct the foundations of just and free societies, only to have their grandchildren grow up to take them for granted and thus lose focus of the important (which was bled for), for the children are rich and fat enough to become consumed with the trivial and inane.

After a week I become withdrawn and closed, rarely venturing out of the house. The Jack and Cokes are consumed earlier each day, and every morning the fuzziness is a little bit worse between the ears.

Late that night, deep inside the whiskey bottle, the sorry truth arrives. I am not going to fit in anytime soon. Not without serious support. And that support is in Iraq, or Afghanistan, or Colombia, where all my friends are. For there I was not judged and was accepted for who I was, and the feeling of camaraderie I had with them was far better than I could ever expect to see in the real world.

So I live in a big house by myself, rarely venturing to go out, alone in a sea of thousands, which makes it all the more lonely still.

The hardest part is having to forgive society. I cannot judge you for you do not know. How can you possibly be expected to have more emotional depth when the most traumatic thing that has ever happened to you is having the air conditioner break for an afternoon?

I must forgive America for her being obsessed with the trivial, the mundane, and the idiotic. It frightens me that so few of you have ever had to fight for it, to viciously engage in mortal combat with those whose sole desire is to eliminate you from the face of the earth. You may hear my words, but they do not register for you have no scale upon which to measure the reality of them. I must forgive you because you do not understand. And I am glad you do not understand because that means you will hopefully never gaze upon a small boy trying to rearrange his internal organs that lay spread on the ground all around him. I do not wish for you to see that, ergo I must forgive your ignorance.

Which makes me even lonelier, the mournful wolf padding softly through the snowy forest under a full moon, while the rest of the world sleeps. With a bottle of whiskey. I love you all. Now fuck off and leave me alone.

This American deployed to Iraq, made a great deal of money, and came home to use those dollars to start his own business. He does well, living a modest version of the American dream. Though on occasion he misses the action and camaraderie, he has taken to passing judgment on the war by using a different yardstick to measure it.

In the stairwell to my office dwell the plaques of my friends who have died in Iraq. I only honor the dead. If I put up plaques for the merely maimed, I would need a bigger stairwell. One was an especially close friend, a former British paratrooper who worked as a ski instructor for disabled children. His girlfriend, an incredible gal, was also partially handicapped and blind.

We worked together on an extraordinary high-risk job in Colorado, which thankfully turned out well, thanks to him. He left for Iraq shortly thereafter. Mike has been dead over seven years now. He died fighting to the end, trapped, alone, and surrounded. He killed six and wounded nine before we could recover the body. I wasn't there so my last memory of him is not of a bullet-shattered corpse.

Mike died in vain, and for me that, more than anything else, personifies the war in Iraq.

Another American contractor shares a similar view of Iraq.

What a waste. So in the end, we do not fight for flag, for political or religious belief, not even for country. We fight for the man to the left or right of us because my team came from all over the world. We fight for each other. We fight for the team. It always has and it always will be, regardless of what the politicians say. Iraq brought a lot of laughs and a lot of money to my life. But it brought more pain than it did joy and, in the end, was the biggest waste of blood, money, and national prestige I have ever seen. It is the biggest God-awful waste on the planet. What a fucking mess.

A third American, with a different opinion, disagrees with the above.

We should have done it a long time ago. And we should flatten Iran and North Korea. Fuck it. Nuke them till the sand turns to glass. I hated them when I went over, and I hate them now, and the faster we kill every last one of those dirty ragheads, commies, and terrorists, the safer the world will be for those of us who deserve to live in it. My only regret is that I didn't kill enough of them while I was there.

The thirty-two-year-old Korean American who deployed to Kenya summarizes his feelings.

It's a shame the U.S. put controls on us. We were doing the world a favor, wiping out useless Iraqis who only breed and kill Americans. I am proud of my service; proud of the numbers that I killed, which wasn't enough; and proud to say I smoked a lot of Iraqis on behalf of our government. We need more like us, not less. And if I make $150K a year doing it, then more power to me for having the balls to step forward. I can't wait to get to the Sudan to do it all over again. They are all just useless mouths anyway.

Chapter Ten

The Big Fix

Private military companies, in at least two of three configurations, are here to stay. They are now too heavily entrenched in the system to facilitate easy removal. The positive news is that when correctly implemented with adequate controls, PMCs are a valuable, cost-effective asset to the government. However, in view of the fiasco that is Iraq, they are badly in need of corrective action designed to improve performance standards in future conflicts.

An interesting comparison of standards pits the PMC industry against the Professional Association of Dive Instructors (PADI). The association is responsible for the certification process involved in teaching novice scuba divers. Faced with a disconcerting number of fatalities in the sport's early years, the industry managed to self-regulate by adopting a strict set of professional standards. Today students must follow a highly regimented program of training modules before being certified as basic scuba divers. Student must satisfactorily complete reviews, practical exercises, and written exams long before they roll over the side of a boat. Understanding that the sport can be fatal if an individual is poorly taught, PADI puts entry-level instructor candidates through a grueling multiweek training program where the washout rate is high. Instructor candidates must be graduates of four previous courses pertaining to their professional development and have completed a specific number of dives to qualify. After all this preparation, the failure rate can still approach 50 percent in portions of the qualifying examinations.

PADI's process does not end with the issuance of a license. Instructors caught teaching outside the parameters of established guidelines face disbarment and loss of their licenses. They may also be found criminally liable in civil court, and PADI will not represent them.

PADI's efforts to overhaul a previously dangerous recreational activity have been wildly successful. Instructors are now covered by professional liability insurance, and rare indeed is the occasion that PADI loses a lawsuit if the instructor has been acting within the regulatory guidelines. The results are also seen beyond the courtroom. Scuba fatalities have plummeted over the last two decades while the numbers of participants have increased dramatically. The key to this success was the industry's ability to identify a potential problem and to self-regulate before the government stepped in.

To apply as a security contractor, meanwhile, one must send in an application, which may or may not be fact checked. Many companies have no prerequisites and offer no formal training for the most part. Without further ado, one is issued a high-velocity assault rifle and has the power to terminate life. Welcome to the hunting club. That is the best a multibillion-dollar industry with stupendous profit margins has been able to concoct in terms of organizing its profession.

Private military companies have proven beyond any reasonable doubt that they lack the ability to self-regulate. That leaves few options on the table if the industry is to be saved from itself. By comparison, a group of civilian part-time dive instructors have come up with a better system than the best the much-vaunted PMC industry has to offer. Yet it is the PMCs who carry automatic weapons and must make life-and-death decisions in combat zones in the midst of large numbers of noncombatants. PADI prosecutes rogue instructors and prints the names of those disbarred in its trade publication. PMCs simply send them back to the head office for "consultations" before they reappear somewhere else. If PMCs bought out the diving industry, we'd all drown.

Private military companies operate without any form of oversight or industry-wide performance standards. Tactics, techniques, and protocols differ wildly from one firm to the next. Commonality of weapons, uniforms, or communication systems is nonexistent. It is a completely unregulated environment and lacks the capacity to inflict punitive actions against the most egregious breach of common sense.

The linchpin to any intelligent overhaul of the existing system *must* be federally mandated. Private military companies have every reason, in the form of profits, to vehemently protest any change to the status quo.

The truth is that it takes little talent to rant and throw rocks at existing PMC protocols. Any fool can do that, as has been proven by far too many of the ill-informed talking heads who are of the "fire them all" crowd. The real challenge is in designing intelligent formulas for future success while still maintaining a realistic view of the industry as a whole. The author and his peer group gave serious thought to how things should be done, and herein are the answers we believe will improve the profession.

Following are the issues that need to be addressed, complete with solutions, when overhauling the PMC industry. They are formatted into two options.

I. Option Stream A:
>   Specific Task Augmentation Readiness Training (START)
>   Army Contract Liaison Officers
>   Third-Country Nationals
>   Military Authority over Private Military Companies
>   Specific Operational Recommendations Pertaining to Types of
>   Contracting Companies
>   Specific Legal Recommendations Pertaining to Types of Contractor

II. Option Stream B:
>   Contractor Army of the State Department
>   A. Advantages

Option Stream A

Program A is designed around a multiweek course that *every* contractor must attend, to ensure the creation of universal standards, standard operating procedures, and effective interaction with uniformed members of the armed forces. I have chosen to call it Specific Task Augmentation Readiness Training (START).

Specific Task Augmentation Readiness Training (START)

The START program is nothing more than government-mandated basic training for all entering the private military company career field. The program aims to ensure that every contractor carrying a weapon on behalf of the U.S. government is certified to the minimum standard necessary based on the job description. The hypothesis is identical to that of the U.S. Army's pre-deployment workups where disciplined training beforehand pays off with improved combat performance. The START program is also designed to de-conflict the battlefield by removing many of the gray areas—such as the type of weapons issued, military-contractor relationships, and so on—in which PMCs currently operate.

The START program runs twenty-five to thirty-five days in length. Every security contractor must attend, regardless of rank, nationality, or previous experience. Those currently in the industry will have twenty-four months to become "certified" to the new standards as the industry is too new to permit grandfather clauses. Similar to the Security Industry Authority (SIA) standard of training recently enacted by the United Kingdom, that provides a specific set of core skills that all PMC employees must learn, the START program provides a balanced time line so that at the end of two years, all working contractors will have the necessary qualifications. The federal government will thus be able to impose a quality control process that has so far been conspicuous only by its total absence. In so doing, a selective filtering can be implemented, permitting only the best-performing individuals to graduate. Upon successful completion of the program, each contractor will be awarded an individual "license," which, in order to be eligible for any contracting job, he must maintain through continual training, proof of further learning, and refresher training for those whose credentials have expired. The setup is identical to that practiced by the emergency services and medical professions.

An independent service provider with direct input from the Departments of Defense and State should run the START program. Private military companies should not be allowed to run their own programs owing to the obvious conflict of interest with profit trumping quality. The service provider will include the following elements in the START program.

Drug Testing, Background Check, and Physical Fitness Test

Some insiders believe fully that half of the private contractors currently employed would not pass a background check when coupled with physical fitness and urinalysis tests. The impact is already being felt in the industry, where the more astute companies are demanding that personnel have a minimum of a secret clearance, regardless of need. It is in fact a clever contractor sidestep as the U.S. taxpayer picks up the tab to confirm the bona fides of the applicants. The company is then assured that no felons linger in the ranks while the American public winds up paying the bill.

A better system is to have every individual processed upon arrival with instant disqualifiers for drug use and certain felony convictions. Volunteers seeking more lucrative contracts can then submit their background check paperwork upon arrival for the processing of future security clearances. Just as in SATMO, the administrative tail needs to be kept under one roof.

The Army Physical Fitness Test (APFT) minimum standards according to age are also administered. Potential employees who wish to operate in hostile environments while wearing body armor and so forth need to be in sufficient physical shape so they can carry out their mission. Failure to pass the APFT is an automatic ticket home.

Mandatory drug testing, including the use of steroids, needs to be incorporated with random spot checking in the field. A positive urinalysis is an instant and permanent disqualifier. Guns and drugs do not mix, and the use of recreational narcotics or steroids is an unforgivable offense.

By pooling background checks and the results of physical fitness and urinalysis tests, the industry would establish a minimum baseline from which to springboard to a higher level of professionalism. By implementing just this initial screening process, however, those industry experts interviewed believe that 90 percent of the problem individuals would not clear this first hurdle to obtain employment.

Weapons Training and Qualification

The incredibly diverse array of weaponry currently in use is substandard. Some PMCs use only American-issued small arms while others utilize only former Eastern Bloc patterns. This system is not functional by any sane standard. Issuing a contractor the same weapon that the insurgents employ defies all tactical logic, especially when one considers the confusion created for American troops who may be in the area. Every time an AK-47 is discharged, the American GI must ask himself, "Is this enemy or contractor fire?" The distraction only increases the risk of "friendly fire" casualties. The procurement system is already a tangled web, and many PMCs opt for Eastern Bloc weaponry because they are easy to acquire at reduced costs.

All legitimate PMCs should instead be equipped with American government–issued weapons identical to those currently in use by the armed forces. They should be assigned complete with chain of custody forms and individual hand receipts. This system voids the issue of loose accountability and of determining friend from foe on the battlefield. It also eliminates the opportunity for black market arms dealing as there is no longer a reason to have any nonissue weapons in the weapons lockup.

The next logical step is to ensure that all contractors, regardless of their anticipated position, are qualified in the use of all U.S. and enemy small arms that may be found in the battle area. Cross training and familiarization should be mandated so that in an emergency any contractor can operate any given weapon system. Marksmanship must also be stressed and taught to those individuals found lacking. Doing so further reduces the risk of collateral damage in the form of dead and wounded civilians. Finally, contractors must qualify on all weapons systems ranging from M-4 carbines to the 240G machine gun. The individual must be competent with iron sights in addition to the array of optics now available. Failure to qualify results is a ticket home. No organization authorized to use deadly force should keep an employee who can't shoot straight.

Standardized Battle Drills

The current practice of employing multinational teams with a heavy concentration of third-country nationals produces a wide disparity of tactics, techniques, and protocols. Although situation-specific battle drills can be left to the individual PMC, a broad-based core set of skills needs to be mandatory for all employees. By standardizing the basic tactics per the U.S. Army's example, it allows interoperability among all elements in the battle area. Standardization will save both lives and money. The forced abandonment of a fifty thousand–dollar SUV because a group lacks the standardized towing apparatus is a case in point. Dealing with ambushes, IEDs, and calling in emergency air medevacs are all skills that everyone on the PSD team needs to learn regardless of their level in the hierarchy. Failure to implement such measures results in situations where a small handful of experienced individuals retain all the institutional knowledge. Should they become casualties, the remaining men are unable to cope with the resultant loss of life and matériel. By pushing responsibility forward and down to the lowest operator level, we improve the performance of the collective whole. This process will see fewer injuries and reduced operational costs.

Medical Training

Every man, regardless of position, needs to be certified as an emergency first responder with the additional skill sets involving the use of intravenous kits, oxygen, defibrillator kits, and specialty training in trauma. By raising everyone's skills, loss of life is reduced as are the medical costs that PMCs incur. This lapse is by far the most obvious in contractors' training, and correcting it will pay the greatest dividends in the shortest amount of time. Currently only a handful of companies have the foresight to include this preparation in their already-too-short training curriculums.

COMMUNICATIONS

All outsourced U.S. contracts should include a predetermined communications package. This equipment, in the form of personnel and vehicular radios, should be compatible with current military issue. It is critical that PMCs and the U.S. Army have the capability to effectively communicate in real time. Sound communications will reduce the chances of battlefield fratricide and speed the arrival of reinforcements if a unit is in trouble. A comprehensive standardization of communications represents the single biggest fix in Iraq today.

UNIFORM CODE OF MILITARY JUSTICE, USE OF FORCE, AND RULES OF ENGAGEMENT

Every graduate of the START program undergoes classes in the Uniform Code of Military Justice that explain the legal procedures applicable to contractors engaged in combat operations. American civil law is also reviewed for noncombatant contractors. Additionally, classes detailing the use of force and the rules of engagement are taught to those bound for combat zones. Such instruction ensures that every contractor in the theater of operations acquires a precise understanding of what he can and cannot do. It clearly underscores the appropriate manner in which to conduct operations pursuant to the established policies of the time. This practice eliminates the "I didn't know the rules" excuse, which has been so prevalent in Iraq, albeit with some legitimacy.

UNIFORMS

Uniforms have been in use since the era of the Roman legions as a means of identifying friend from foe on the battlefield. Uniforms provide an "official" presence, the theory being that a uniformed individual is an official representative of his country of origin. Specialized attire is also prestigious. One only needs to see the American public's esteem for the servicemen and women in uniform to understand that premise.

Some type of uniform for contractors is necessary, if only to separate friend from foe on the battlefield. Though adopting the Army Combat Uniform is acceptable for contractors in advisory roles, it would only create confusion between contractors and active duty personnel. Clothing that clearly identifies the individual as a contractor, however, is badly needed. Uniforms bring PMCs closer in line to complying with the Geneva Conventions while minimizing confusion in highly complex battle spaces.

Additionally uniforms provide the legitimacy necessary to demonstrate that the wearer is representing the interests of the United States. Although the medium may be a PMC, the final truth is that the wearer of the uniform supports the doctrine of the U.S. government instead of the freelance mercenary-outlaw-surfer gang too many companies now represent. Good-bye, bones woven into braided hair down to the waist. Hello, professional attire and grooming.

Finally, uniforms show "command presence" and lend an aura of respectability to the organization, especially in third world nations. The example of the advisory firm training the Kenyan Army is a case in point. The respect the Kenyans had for the instructors in sterile combat fatigues was far greater than if the same training team had arrived in civilian clothes. The Iraqis think the same way. Having sharp-looking uniforms is so important to Iraqi security guards because they are symbols of status in their society.

To illustrate, the reader should imagine driving up to the first of two checkpoints. Regular army troops with well-established protocols man the first one. They are armed and dressed alike and operate under specific procedures.

Irregulars attired in every form of civilian and military clothing imaginable run the second checkpoint. They are armed with a wide variety of weapons and are generally much quicker to use them. The man who examines your papers has a beard down to his stomach and more closely resembles a mujahideen fighter than a member of the Coalition. The individual pulling security is barechested under his body armor and sports sunglasses, death's head tattoos, and a shaved skull. Yet he is being paid more, and is therefore theoretically more valuable, than his professional military counterpart at the other checkpoint is.

Which checkpoint do you respect more? Which one do you fear?

Regardless of how the process is evaluated, at the end of the day an individual working on behalf of the State Department or the Department of Defense is an informal ambassador of the United States of America.[1] The security contractor in a faraway land may be all that the indigenous population has to go on when evaluating what an "American" is. Some PMCs have permitted their employees to resemble a gang of motorcycle thugs, and this example of an "American" is not how the U.S. taxpayer wants to be represented.

Just as members of any niche element who pride themselves on being "rebels," the security-contracting world has developed its own secret language and fashion. Fu Manchu mustaches, dreadlocks, body piercings, tattoos, beards, goatees, and hair dyed orange and red are the current vogue. For many companies, any attempts at personal hygiene are regarded with disapproval. As for clothing, the more disheveled the better. There are thousands of men who would be arrested as loitering vagabonds in the United States who are in fact making well into six figures a year in Iraq. It is precisely this "cowboy" image that draws so many underperforming individuals to the PMCs in the first place.

PMCs are designed to provide specific support to the U.S. military. They should not be hangouts for every rebel without a cause or havens of sloppy personal deportment. Nor should they be making fashion statements. It is the author's strong personal belief that if an individual is dissuaded by grooming standards similar to the U.S. military's, then that individual lacks the professional balance necessary to be entrusted with firearms and the power to terminate life. There should be no place in our national security system for those enamored with the outward trappings of a dysfunctional social code.

Cultural Awareness Training

The military's role is to win wars. In a secondary mission, it is occasionally called upon to occupy a foreign state, as is the case today in Iraq and Afghanistan. To that end, every soldier deployed to the occupied country has the personal ability to promote peace or violence. The human condition across cultures, regardless of religion or cultural codes, is similar enough for soldiers to understand extending compassion as opposed to brutality. Insurgencies end when the occupied cease to hate the occupier. The vast majority of Iraqis are not religious zealots, members of al Qaeda, or rabidly anti-American. They wish for the same thing the vast majority of their American occupiers do—that is, a quick return to peace and the opportunity to live their lives without the omnipresent chance of violence.

Although not always an easy task, soldiers and PMCs need to treat civilians with dignity and respect. When civilians are derided, abused, or wantonly killed, the cycle of violence is perpetuated. Cultural awareness training in the START program, therefore, is mandatory. Dehumanizing the enemy is a necessary tool when preparing young men for mortal combat, but the same condition inhibits overtures for peace when employed after hostilities cease. By understanding foreign cultures we are better able to move toward mutual coexistence, which translates to bringing more soldiers home faster.

The U.S. Army itself has finally recognized this correlation, and the counterinsurgency field manual reflects this forward-looking policy.[2] Winning the war is not enough if the army cannot maintain the peace. The manual is drawn from the years of experience of occupying Afghanistan and Iraq. The identical doctrine should apply to PMCs.

Cross Training with the Army

If one is tasked to support the U.S. Army, then logic dictates that one should understand how the army works. Cross training with the military is essential to the successful integration of contractors working in close proximity to the fighting men in a battle space lacking front lines.

Both the army and PMCs have similar needs, including the requirement for rapid medical evacuations, the prevention of friendly fire incidents, and the deconfliction of the battle area.

Instructing security contractors who have just arrived in country on the armed forces' policies is not sufficient. This technique relies far too heavily on improvisation, faulty institutional knowledge, and an ad hoc approach to ensure a successful interface with the armed services. Instead, the START program brings in a military officer with recent combat time in theater to brief all inbound contracting personnel. This class offers a comprehensive review of all pertinent army policies pertaining to PMCs. In far too many cases one side has opened fire on the other because of the former's ignorance of the other organization's protocols. A continued inability to effectively communicate and coordinate between PMCs and the military represents a possible needless loss of life on both sides.

This problem is one of the easiest to resolve, and that limited corrective action has been taken thus far could be judged as criminal neglect. By mandating an intensive overview of U.S. Army policies, to include a manual for contract personnel, every man arriving in theater will understand precisely the protocols necessary to ensure maximum survivability on the battlefield while operating in the vicinity of combat troops.

Army Contract Liaison Officers

To further assist in the successful execution of the PMCs' duties, each private military company should be assigned an active duty, combat arms army liaison officer (ACLO). This officer's mission is to ensure seamless interaction between civilian and military operations. Furthermore, the army officer has the responsibility of guaranteeing the company's compliance with all the rules of engagement, use of force, and other protocols as determined by the appropriate authority. This officer serves as a first line of review of any shooting incident and confirms to the board whether the contract company was in compliance with official U.S. policy. As an active duty military officer, he can provide the best possible interface with the military, which must deal with the increased presence of contractors on a day-to-day basis.

Third-Country Nationals

A common ploy among companies conducting logistics and operational work is to hire third world nationals at a fraction of what they pay Americans.

Uganda is not a member of the allied Coalition. The American public might be surprised to learn, however, that Swahili, the lingua franca of Uganda, can often be heard in Fallujah. Even more surprising, the Ugandans were once billed out in a manner identical to that of the Americans.

In 2003 and early 2004, security teams were composed of Westerners only. The only "pure" American teams were those on State Department contracts, where a security clearance was required. By the middle of 2004 the race for cheaper labor was on, and it was by no means unusual to have a half-dozen different nationalities from four continents on the same crew. The common thread was the ability to theoretically converse in English.

As the industry exploded into unregulated growth, the willing number of first-class, competent Western volunteers began to thin out. Contracting companies with an eye to maximizing profits, such as the fraudulent Custer Battles, began to quietly pad the battle roster with third world imports. Nepalese, Fijians, and other former Commonwealth soldiers who could speak English appeared in the ranks. Iraqis were still generally considered too unreliable; however, in later years, even though they were considered no more trustworthy than before, Iraqis were employed in order to optimize the bottom line. The details for the PMCs were found in the contracts' fine print. Only State Department contracts specifically dictated the composition of the teams. For the PMCs, it was a small but extremely lucrative loophole. Why pay an American $400 per day and bill him out at $1,200 per day, when you can pay a Nepalese Army Gurkha $80 per day for the same job? The daily $320 difference equates to $116,800 per annum, per man in additional profit.

The disparity does not end with income. Housing conditions are substandard for TCNs, and the quality of their equipment is vastly inferior. The TCNs are hardly in a position to complain: they can always go home to absolute poverty as opposed to relative poverty. Further, cold mathematics dictates that it is cheaper to replace the $500 initial investment in a Nepalese contractor than it is to spend $1,500 on the proper helmet and body armor to outfit him. If the company only loses two men killed per set of body armor over the course of the year, it is still in the black. Third-country nationals are at the absolute bottom of the medical evacuation plan, are often banned from sleeping in Coalition facilities, and routinely have their passports confiscated by unscrupulous contractors to prevent them from jumping ship for another company. Further, they receive no medical insurance.

Today, all non–State Department teams comprise multiple nationalities. No team leader can be expected to control his men in a firefight when they speak up to four different languages but are not fluent in English. Even the rare TCN who does speak English will invariably revert to his native tongue when the bullets begin to fly.

The solution is simple. All contracts are instead written with an eye to the exact composition of the team. If 80 percent of the team are third-country nationals, then the wage structure reflects that makeup. That means if the PMC opts to pay its TCNs less, then by law it is not be allowed to charge "Western" rates for the team's service. If the PMC opts to pay all members equally, then it has the right to bill at a flat rate for its service. What all parties must avoid is billing out TCNs at "American" rates, which is wrong for the TCN on the firing line, the company, and the American taxpayer footing the bill. Further, equipment, along with medical and insurance benefits, is standardized for the whole team. This arrangement goes a long way toward eliminating the vilest form of racism, where a man is placed in a more dangerous role with lesser-quality equipment and compensation based solely on his place of birth.

Military Authority over Private Military Companies

This recommendation is the most controversial and has engendered nothing but anger on the part of PMCs interviewed by the author. This recommendation states that when the U.S. Army and contractors are sharing the same battle space, the army has the right of way. It does *not* imply the military has the right to press-gang contractors into the line or that the military has any tactical control over PMCs. This suggestion simply allows the U.S. Army to enforce a code of conduct with PMCs in the exact same manner it does with its own troops.

Thus, PMCs must adhere to military standards when on military property and risk being turfed out should they violate those standards. The recommendation also means that the army has the right to intervene when it witnesses egregious conduct on the part of the PMCs. The big related question here really concerns those contractor privileges that are denied the army. Contractors have always had legal access to alcohol. Women are also a point of contention, but most contractors go out of the country if they desire sex. The eight hundred–pound gorilla then is alcohol.

There is a reason the post-Vietnam army has opted to go to war sans alcohol. In shorthand the formula states that Army + Guns + Alcohol = Trouble. Any experienced contractor has also witnessed catastrophes firsthand when guns and booze are mixed in a war zone. The issue of alcohol consumption is less controversial in logistical and advisory companies but not by much. The Kenyan training team, for instance, dumped 20 percent of its initial roster after arriving in country because of alcohol-related issues, and these men were engaged as *non*combatants, where the stress is much less than that suffered in combat units.

Operational units need to be dry, just as the military formations encamped beside them are. This dictate is not a case of punishing the 98 percent who are able to drink responsibly because the minority 2 percent lack control. Instead, it is a case of preventing that 2 percent from having access to devices that are designed strictly to kill people while they are out of control. When one factors in the emotional stress of combat and the daily horror show that occurs in Baghdad or Helmand Province, few individuals have the ability to "drink responsibly." In terms of unnecessary carnage that is self-inflicted in war zones, alcohol has no equal.

As an NCO in the Persian Gulf War, the author protested bitterly over the lack of libations. Maturity, hindsight, and firsthand experience after cleaning up the havoc of alcohol-related incidents have removed all doubt regarding the intelligence of keeping liquor in any form as far away from the battlefield as possible. The cost of booze, in terms of lives cut short, smashed equipment, and crushing hangovers when carrying rifles the next day, is far in excess of its value as a temporary numbing device.

In this program, the ACLO has the responsibility of ensuring the contract company remains dry while on an operational footing. Should the military have issues with the PMC, it only need contact the ACLO.

By including army liaison officers with the contracting company, a direct communication link is provided within the chain to effectively resolve contractor-army disputes. The goal is not for the military to babysit the PMCs but rather to ensure that all elements are working collectively toward the successful execution of U.S. foreign policy. ACLOs are a modest investment with the potential to yield great returns and should be implemented immediately.

Specific Operational Recommendations Pertaining to Types of Contracting Companies

LOGISTICS

The early experience of Brown & Root with the Logistics Civil Augmentation Program clearly illustrated the capability of the program. Its effort in Somalia was a decided success, along with that in the Balkans.[3] The truth is that the quality of service has not suffered significant degradation. According to one government insider who requested anonymity, "Very rarely is the problem to be found with the individual worker. Rather it is one of systemic fraudulent accounting and inflation of profits through the 'cost plus' form of compensation."

The reader should remember that this statement refers to logistical operations as opposed to combat-type PMCs. A precipitous drop in the quality of combat PMCs is far more lethal to the civilian population with whom they interact.

The reality is simple. The problem is not a function of LOGCAP, of cost plus policies, or of substandard performance. Instead, the root of the trouble is based on corporate greed. Halliburton; its former subsidiary, KBR; and other big names have repetitively been in the crosshairs of the Government Accountability Office for inflated charges on services that were never rendered or were provided in numerically smaller quantity than what was billed to the taxpayers.

This malfeasance is not a military problem. It is, in fact, a civil issue and nothing more than white-collar crime on an enormous scale. It is commonly termed "racketeering" when perpetrated by the Mafia, and the two are indeed identical.

The reasons such profiteering readily occur are twofold: opportunity and lack of deterrence. Corporations like Halliburton gouge the public time and again because they have zero incentive not to do so. Furthermore, why would any for-profit entity change its ways and stop propagating enormous profits when there is no viable deterrent for it to do otherwise? Halliburton and KBR have both been in the dock repeatedly for fraud involving hundreds of millions of dollars.[4] The result? Halliburton then promptly wins the next no-bid contract valued in the billions. The private sector has repeatedly demonstrated it is incapable of professional conduct when faced with an open trough awash in money. The only course of action more asinine is when the client, in this case the U.S. government, permits itself to be repeatedly fleeced at the hands of such carpetbaggers.

The classic definition of insanity is "a repetition of identical actions with the expectation of a different result," which aptly describes aspects of what Eisenhower termed "the military-industrial complex." The only loser in the equation is the American taxpayer, which means you and me.

Here is one solution based on the theory in the military that the general in charge is fully empowered to run the fighting unit as he sees fit. In times of victory, he is a hero, but if the army suffers defeat, then the responsibility falls on its commander. So it should be with LOGCAP fraud. There is little value in prosecuting the small fish when the entire ocean is polluted.

If the federal government prosecutes a civilian company for systemic fraud, then the audit trail of responsibility clearly runs to the board of directors. These all-powerful individuals will then have precisely the same legal rights as Mafia dons, who are prosecuted under the same criminal statutes. Racketeering, regardless of whether it is perpetrated by the Gambino family or a logistics firm, is still organized crime. The federal government should therefore apply the same statutes to Halliburton as they do to the Mafia. After the first few distinguished gentlemen spend some time behind bars, the message will be successfully conveyed that the U.S. government will not condone fraud regardless of the board of directors' political connections.

The second solution is to have penalty clauses included in the contract if a company is convicted of fraud in a courtroom. The penalties need to be both massive and immediate. When the fines are sufficiently enormous to give PMCs serious pause before trying to outmaneuver GAO auditors, the risk of fraud is dramatically reduced.

Gen. Norman Schwarzkopf, Jr., attained the laurels of victory in the Persian Gulf War. Gen. William Westmoreland and the late Robert McNamara will forever be associated with the fiasco of Vietnam. All three men were in charge and were thus directly responsible for their places in the history books, with one at the top and two in the dungeons. The same should hold true for large companies involved in LOGCAP. Honest brokers will have nothing to fear while scammers can expect swift justice. When the federal government finds the intestinal fortitude to toe the line with rogue companies, the results will be a dramatic turn for the better. As long as the federal government allows itself to be ripped off, the results are dismally predictable. What was that definition of insanity again?

ADVISORY COMPANIES

Of the three types of service providers—logistical, advisory, and operational—this one has best escaped the stigma of abuse. From the early MPRI experience in Croatia to present-day Kenya, the advisory firms have delivered quantifiable results with minimum fuss. This result stems primarily from the professionalism of those who work for these noncombatant organizations. What is required is an expansion of the SATMO-style program with cleaner interaction among the State Department, DOD, the military, and private contractors. As it stands right now, SATMO is only utilized when the host nation requests training from the United States. The SATMO model should be included for all contractors deploying overseas regardless of location or function. SATMO stands at the cutting edge, and its model should be expanded. This system has repeatedly produced the best results. Its success is based on superior communications and a single standard of collective training provided to both military personnel and contractors before their deployment overseas. The START program covered earlier is based on the SATMO format. Though it has its problems, as evidenced by contractor incompetence, SATMO continues to be a sign of progress for the realistic coexistence between private contractors and the military for the wars of the future. Advisory companies have proven to be the dark horse of the contracting world, rendering excellent value and a highly professional service for the money. If any area of the industry is due for an intelligent, controlled expansion, it is the private military's advisory companies.

OPERATIONAL COMPANIES

Operational companies have the greatest responsibility in terms of life-or-death decision making. They therefore require the most discerning attention to ensure a fair balance between justifiable self-defense and unnecessary brutality. Based on personal experience and hundreds of interviews, the author believes the following steps will contribute to improved performance with reduced civilian casualties. These recommendations are in addition to the pre-deployment training utilizing the START program. It also assumes that operational companies are alcohol-free, as described earlier.

Vehicle-Mounted Cameras
All operational vehicles should have both front- and rear-facing cameras. The rear view is especially important as it is where the bulk of the shootings occur. Cameras provide a nonnegotiable visible transcript of what transpires. Honest operators have nothing to fear; meanwhile, a major deterrent will be imposed on those who prefer to pull the trigger first and then ask the corpse questions. All videos will become the property of the U.S. State Department and DOD and not of the contractor company.

Quality Control Auditors
All operational companies, as part of their contract, should be eligible to receive an unannounced quality control (QC) audit at any time from government QC auditors. These auditors should have complete access to the entire operation and be empowered with a no-holds-barred authority to review anything at anytime. Their aim will be to ensure the private contractor is maintaining the appropriate levels of overall professionalism as prescribed by the State Department and DOD. Auditors will examine ongoing use of force policies, review videotapes of shootings, and conduct health and welfare inspections. Each auditor should have the power to impose arbitrary urinalysis checks, to include looking for the use of steroids. A company falling short of the prescribed standards will be given thirty days to improve to the standard necessary or face losing its contract. TCNs would be inspected under the same regulations.

Incident Reports
Every time a trigger is pulled, an incident report should be filed. Its purpose is to provide documentation of the incident with regard to actions, outcomes, and lessons learned for future operations. Both the army and PMCs have long included incident reports in the "should report" category for any shootings. The army diligently files the paperwork every time. All private contractors, however, have been just as diligent in not submitting them. This abnegation of responsibility is unacceptable.

Incident reports provide real-time intelligence in terms of enemy trends and are a valuable source of information to Coalition planners. Additionally, incident reports will eventually identify employees who may require further training on use of force policies or face expulsion from the company.

Specific Legal Recommendations Pertaining to Types of Contractor

The blanket immunity Paul Bremer and the Coalition Provisional Authority provided was a de facto license to kill.[5] No other single provision has done so much to smear the professional reputation of thousands of contractors who have tried hard to do the right thing under trying circumstances.

The solution is self-evident. The first step is to ensure that all contractors, *regardless of nationality*, fall under American jurisprudence while deployed under the auspices of an American firm. This same legal status should apply for foreign companies working on U.S. contracts. This stipulation means that if a South African working for a British company based in the Cayman Islands under contract to a U.S. firm murders an Iraqi civilian, the contractor falls under the American legal umbrella. Critics will oppose this provision based on legal precedents of trying foreigners from a third country. The author's riposte is that if the U.S. government is willing to hire foreigners to carry arms on its behalf, then it has both the right and the moral obligation to police those individuals.

The industry retorts by claiming that this theorem is predicated on the contractors formally working for the U.S. government, and that issue has not been addressed so far. The position of bottom-level gunslingers is that the U.S. government has not hired them; instead, they are hired by private firms working for the U.S. government. Even the dumbest bear in Yosemite can correctly interpret the weakness of that argument.

The legal status of all contractors can be further broken down: it is based on the *type of contracting work* versus the *nationality* of the individual engaged in it.

LOGISTICS

Those contractors whose *primary* duty is logistical support, such as the truck drivers of KBR, should fall under American civil law. These contractors are clearly noncombatants and depend on either the military or security companies for protection. However, the rule of civil law must still be maintained. The recent situation in which KBR employees raped an American female contractor in the Middle East is a classic case.[6] Because the female was assaulted in theater, the U.S. Department of Justice declined to prosecute, stating that it lacked jurisdiction. The bottom line should be that if a civilian contractor who is classified as a noncombatant and is directly or indirectly working for the United States, he or she falls under American civil jurisprudence. The appalling failure to prosecute in the rape case only underscores the necessity for rapid overhaul.

ADVISORY

Contractors working in an advisory capacity are considered noncombatants and are thus unarmed. American civil law should take precedence in the same way it does for logistical personnel as described above. As advisers are employed in an unarmed capacity, they need not be covered under the UCMJ, regardless of whether they are wearing a uniform. As civilians hired in what is essentially a teaching capacity, they have similar characteristics to their logistical counterparts and thus should be treated for precisely what they are, civilians.

OPERATIONAL

Contractor personnel whose *primary* mission is combat oriented, either in an offensive or defensive capacity, should be considered combatants. They therefore fall under the jurisdiction of the UCMJ. *The nationality of the individual is irrelevant.*

There is a precedent for this precept. Thousands of active duty servicemen are actually resident aliens and are *not* American citizens.[7] While in the service of the American military, they fall under the UCMJ. It doesn't matter that they are Mexican, Filipino, or European by birth. While they serve in the regular army, they have signed on to the rule of UCMJ simply by enlisting. The same analogy can be applied to foreign national contractors. By signing on as contractors, they automatically forfeit certain rights and are willing to come under the legal process as outlined by the UCMJ. Their other option is not to sign up and thus maintain the legal rights of their nation of birth. The notion that one is immune from prosecution based on citizenship and the location of the alleged crime is preposterous. If one has both the authority and responsibility to utilize lethal force in a war zone, then there is an equally pressing obligation to ensure these life-taking powers are invoked in the most professional manner possible.

Critics of the scheme will voice concern over the haphazard recruiting policies that arm men without proper indoctrination, thus exposing them to the "perils" of the UCMJ without their being aware. The logical response is that "ignorance of the law is not an excuse" as pertains to American law. If a START-type training program is instituted, every graduate would be firmly grounded in the UCMJ, rules of engagement, and all policies regarding the use of lethal force long before he is ever in a position to apply it.

The vaguely worded existing guidelines also need to be stiffened regarding the use of firearms and lethal force. If any noncombatant, regardless of whether he is a logistical or advisory, engages in open conflict with weapons, the ensuing investigation is under the UCMJ protocols. In 99.9 percent of the cases, the reason for using force is self-evident. No court in the land would ever dream of prosecuting the survivors of the massacred KBR convoy who picked up the rifles of fallen soldiers to defend themselves. The right to self-defense is plainly clear. However, the latent awareness that a possible criminal offense would be judged under the harsher light of military law should give pause for reflection before pulling the trigger.

The legal remedies described above are not harsh. Active duty military personnel operate under far stiffer penalties for wrongdoing. It should be the goal of the contracting industry to enforce the highest possible standards of conduct if the industry is to survive. At worst, an errant contractor would be judged in an identical manner as a private soldier of the U.S. Army who works beside him. The UCMJ system has been in force since 1951 and is uniquely designed and flexible enough to compensate for the fog of war. As a general policy, only egregious breaches of the rules of war are aggressively prosecuted, which is exactly how it should be.

The last point in favor of the UCMJ is one of opportunity. Creating an organized and disciplined forum for resolving alleged combat atrocities will act as an instant deterrent. An infantryman is always aware that he is accountable every time he pulls the trigger. For years in Iraq, the contractor was beholden to none. With the imposition of the UCMJ on armed contractors, the situation will change, and the contractor will be held accountable. This is not to say the individual in question will hesitate to pull the trigger if necessary, but rather he will be as sure as possible before doing so. This subtle change in mind-set will reduce the number of dead Iraqis and Afghanis by the simple expedient of introducing accountability where there was none previously. No human should have immunity from the indiscrimi-

nate slaying of others. All PMCs who support such a rabid stance are only displaying their own incompetence and lack of respect for human life. A truly professional
organization should not be deterred in the least by operating under the UCMJ and
should consider it business as usual. Those who protest vehemently usually have the
most to hide and the most to lose as they are most likely to be abusing the system
in the first place.

Option B: Contractor Army of the State Department

There is another viable solution, albeit radical in concept, to overhauling the PMC
industry. The State Department currently has its own security division, which is
tasked with guarding State Department officials. Its employees are federal agents.
The Bureau of Diplomatic Security (DS) personnel who accompanied Blackwater
to ensure the civilian contractors adhere to the rule of law while conducting operations in Baghdad. The premise of this option is simple: eliminate these civilian
operational-type contractors by creating an in-house security force.

Its table of organization and equipment would be based on that of the National
Guard, where only a handful of selected individuals are employed on a full-time
basis. The regular guardsmen train for a couple of weekends a month and several
weeks in the summer. If and when the guardsmen are needed, the units are acti-
vated and undergo pre-deployment training to ensure their highest possible level
of competence. The unit then deploys and assumes an active duty status until the
mission is complete. Upon returning to their home of record, the troops are released
until the next routine training cycle commences.

The government wins financially as many of the guardsmen are former active
duty military, and the relative cost of keeping them trained is low as they are only
part-time soldiers. When the active duty call-up is finished and the guardsmen return to citizen-soldier status, many of the guard's benefits stop.

An intelligent plan by the State Department would create a similar force. Using a START-style program, it would create a pool of eligible contractors. These
contractors, as employees of the State Department, would have to undergo annual
refresher training just as the National Guard does to ensure their professional pro-
ficiency.

Should a situation like Iraq arise and contractors' services are needed, an acti-
vation notice would be sent out, and any certified candidate could volunteer. The

unit would then be trained to the necessary standard and deploy according to the department's dictates.

Advantages

Contractors, as employees of the State Department, would become part of the federal government. This change would, in one wave of a magic wand, eliminate 90 percent of the conflict currently occurring between private and government formations. Rules of engagement, uniforms, and military justice would all be consolidated according to the provisions that apply to the regular armed forces.

STREAMLINED LOGISTICS

With one stroke of the pen, the logistics nightmare would disappear. Weapons and vehicles would be standardized as they would all be State Department property. The department would regulate individual hand receipts return and controlled items in a manner identical to the U.S. Army. Overnight the need for arms trafficking via "back alley" deals, as described in chapter 6, would be gone. Furthermore, feeding and arranging accommodations for the personnel could also be brought under one LOGCAP-type contract, thus reducing costs even further.

LOWER OVERHEAD

Anytime a service provider is subcontracted, the bill reflects the risks of doing business. If a PMC anticipates losing two vehicles a month owing to enemy action, then one can rest assured that the anticipated replacement costs for those vehicles is factored into the bill. However, should the company have a good month and sustain no equipment losses, then the money set against the assumption of two lost SUVs is moved into the profit column. In other words, the money is not returned to the payee. The next month will see another duplicate billing in order to offset the anticipated loss of two SUVs the next month and so on. This practice has resulted in millions of dollars of profit for the PMCs. However, the contracting companies' defense of this cost of business implies that this policy is an acceptable form of managing risk.

The financially sane way to do business, however, is to replace vehicles as they are destroyed by enemy action. If the State Department had its own vehicle fleet, the savings created by not having to underwrite the PMCs' risk management fees would be astronomical. These savings would more than pay for the modest cost associated with both servicing the fleet and providing food and lodging for the mechanic teams.

The same policy can also be applied to the contractors themselves.

No PMC keeps inactive men on the payroll. Instead, PMCs maintain a large database of potential employees and simply call them up when work becomes available. The full-time organization (just like the National Guard) is only a small proportion of the company.

The State Department could operate in an identical manner. All contractors completing the START course would remain registered with the State Department. When required, the contractor would simply be notified of potential employment in much the same way as the National Guard does. Pre-deployment training would be conducted and the unit then shipped as a collective whole to its place of work.

The next consideration is wages. Federally employed contractors could expect to be paid 40 percent less than current rates. That means an individual who currently earns $550 per day, including paid vacation time, with Blackwater (now known as XE) would clear "only" approximately $350 per day, or $127,750 per annum; but food, lodging, and medical care would be provided. As the individual would be working overseas, the first $75,000 earned would also be tax free.

The manner in which the State Department would conduct operations is identical to the way the PMCs currently run their daily routines with one colossal difference. As the State Department is not a for-profit entity, the profit margin can be eliminated, which will reduce the total cost of the mission *by up to 50 percent.*

The individual contractor, therefore, would still be very well compensated but to a lesser degree than they enjoyed in the Wild West days of 2006. In return for his 40 percent wage cut, the contractor would fall under the umbrella of the federal government and accrue all the benefits this placement entails. When the deployment is complete, the individual would return home to await the next assignment.

The PMCs contend that this practice is an ineffective way to do business and that the for-profit entity's business model is actually more efficient. This assertion is not true as the State Department is utilizing exactly the same tactics, techniques, and protocols as the PMCs.

The reality is that the State Department's security detail would become much more efficient and could actually outperform PMCs because it would not have any demand for the profit margin. In this case, the government could actually retool along PMC lines and do a better job.

The Bottom Line and Last Word

The conclusion is self-evident. Either of the variations is a giant leap forward in comparison to current practices. The longer we wait to overhaul the system, the longer the list of American casualties grows. It's as simple as that.

Epilogue

A phrase commonly overheard in Iraq:
"I wouldn't take a million dollars for all the experiences I have had,
but nor would I pay a penny to repeat them."

The mist continued to drift down, drizzling on the grave. The Honor Guard was as silent as those they had come to bury. Drops of moisture sibilantly plummeted to collective death, falling in despair from the brims of the black peaked hats.

Silence.

I gazed at his family, who hailed from Duluth, Minnesota. Simple farmers attired in the cheapest best they could afford for this most solemn and forever of ceremonies.

Once during the interment, I heard his mother, a strong woman of Scandinavian stock, turn to her husband, weep gently, and proclaim, "I will just never understand."

After my friend had been transformed into a rough-hewn chunk of wet sod with a white cross impaled through it, I began to retire through the rows of headstones. I wondered how I would explain it all if somebody asked me what war was like. How does it feel? What would I say? What is this thing named war that morphs youth and enthusiasm into ashes and dust? Pausing in front of the grave of a teenaged Marine who perished on Iwo Jima, I began to phrase my answer to the disconsolate mothers everywhere. I realized I had nothing to say they could possibly understand. I moved on.

I mentally snapped out of my reverie. Nearby, a caisson rolled by, with its jet-black horses, severe young men in perfect blue uniforms, Old Glory so very brilliant and colorful against the highly polished mahogany casket. But it is always the entourage slowly plodding behind the gleaming horses on this final journey that catches my eye. The mourners are unable to relish the pomp and ceremony sponsored by the majestic republic in whose defense their sons and daughters have fallen. Invariably the soldiers, sailors, airmen, and Marines in the caskets are in reality not known for what was only their day job. The deceased's real occupations were as husbands, sons, brothers, and fathers, or wives, daughters, sisters, and mothers. Their names are no longer linked with specialist, petty officer, or staff sergeant; rather, their uninspired, not-very-glorious titles are Frank and Bill and Susan and Tom. Quite often they hail from places such as Oak Bluffs, Fargo, and Cusetta. And most of those who follow the caskets shop at Walmart as opposed to Macy's.

The caisson passed. The mourners plodded, mourning. The weepers wept, and the children didn't understand what was happening. They never do.

The procession gently rolled into the distance. I again padded toward the entrance. The next procession was already forming up. I gazed upon more severe men in blue, jet-black horses, weepers, and mourners. They all found their spot on the nation's stage for the pain-ridden farewells that make for such busy times in places like this cemetery nowadays. I continued to walk, my Burberry trench coat slick with the spring rain. It was not my first time here. Living in the company of so many dead always is a prelude to self-study with me. Again, my thoughts turned to those who are no longer here among the living.

I have a last confession to make, one that I have never admitted to anybody before. Every now and then, most frequently when I travel to foreign locales, I visit what I consider places of higher learning. Usually I go alone, and I never tell anyone where am I going. Often I tread upon the sacred grounds at either sunrise or sunset. They are places both for reflection and studied learning, and some would say places for a higher power. Invariably, they are well tended and quiet, and voices are muted.

Of course, as the reader doubtless knows, I speak of military cemeteries. They are the one place on earth where the ascending curve of youth, optimism, and idealism perfectly bisects the graph of foreign policy formulated by old men in conservative suits in the quest for national self-interest. Here we see the evidence of how often in history the children are asked to die for their grandparents' political failures, all in the name of glory, of course.

Some plots are breathtaking. Normandy is truly overwhelming, with its long rows of white crosses, smartly at the position of attention, from which the raindrops trickle off and water the immaculate lawn. Imperial and majestic could best describe this monument to the Greatest Generation's great crusade in Europe. The Canadians have one at Dieppe, not so very far away, but it has a cozier feel to it. The British, longtime masters of the craft, have a number of elegantly forlorn squares of interred war dead spattered around the globe, each one forevermore a small piece of distant Empire.

And then there is Arlington. Where I am now, here, today, no American can fail to be emotionally stirred when visiting this place. Beneath the silent sod of Virginia slumber, the finest sons and daughters of a great republic founded foursquare before the altar of freedom. As I tread between the ethereally white crosses, I take quiet solace from the youth interred here. That America's children are capable of such great enthusiasm and of flirting with eternity in the execution of their country's national policies is a source of deep and abiding comfort for me. I sleep better at night, knowing that I am safe from foreign oppression.

The clouds part and the sun shines down; the wind softly rustles the leaves above the rolling green, grassy glory that is Arlington. Bravery seeps from the ground, heroism lies thickly upon the grass, and sacrifice sits serenely inside every spring raindrop that flutters down to anoint the sleeping faces of the glorious dead, gazing upward to receive the bereaved, misty atonement of the heavens where they now dwell in peace.

It is what it is.

Glossary

AK-47: Avtomat Kalashnikov (AK) is the technical term, and 1947 is the year it entered service as the standard assault rifle of the Soviet Union. Along with the rocket-propelled grenade, it is the weapon of choice for both Iraqi and Afghan insurgents. While extremely rugged, simple to operate, and packing a considerable punch, the weapon's downsides include inaccuracy and weight. It also has an appalling tendency to "climb" when fired on full automatic, rendering all shots after the first couple harmless as the muzzle climbs skyward. Thankfully, both the Afghans and Iraqis prefer the full automatic setting, with dismal results in terms of marksmanship. Their lack of musketry skills has saved many a Western life, including the author's.

CPA: Coalition Provisional Authority, the entity that formed the interim government of Iraq until the end of June 2004. It was headed by L. Paul Bremer.

EFP: Explosive formed projectile. Far more lethal than an improvised explosive device, an EFP, though also generally homemade, used the shape of the charge to better pierce the armor used by the Coalition. EFPs eventually became so sophisticated that they were, upon occasion, able to defeat main battle tanks. It was an unwritten (and thus nonverifiable rule) that if an EFP-toting insurgent was discovered, he was shot on sight.

FN: Fabrique Nationale is a Belgian manufacturer that, even today, supplies many of the small arms to the U.S. military. The FN Self Loading Rifle alluded to in this volume is a 7.62mm rifle used by the North Atlantic Treaty Organization (NATO) forces and was brought into service shortly after the Second World War. It is the equivalent of the American M-14.

Green Zone: The heavily fortified section of Baghdad in which the headquarters for the U.S. Army and auxiliary U.S. entities, such as the U.S. Agency for International Development (USAID), were located.

IED: Improvised explosive device, or homemade bomb.

Joe: The all-encompassing term for the U.S. Army.

M-14: Although heavier and more awkward to wield in combat compared to the M-4, its destructive power and accuracy made it an extraordinarily potent rifle for Iraq. It had the range to engage far out into the open desert and the punching power to shoot right through the walls of most Iraqi structures.

PMC: Private military company.

PSD: Personal security detail, or the classic "bodyguard" teams of the movies.

RPG: Rocket-propelled grenade. A weapon designed in the Soviet era, an RPG is a shoulder-fired, reloadable rocket launcher. Though no longer capable of defeating Western main battle tanks, it can wreak havoc upon lightly armored or soft-skinned vehicles. It is the standard weapon for both Iraqi and Afghan insurgents.

VBIED: Vehicle-borne improvised explosive device, or in other words, a car bomb driven by a suicide driver. These weapons were the absolute bane of the Iraq experience and were the terror of the Coalition as they were indiscriminate and near impossible to deter.

Notes

Chapter 1. The Dogs of War

1. Michael Hoare, *Congo Mercenary* (London: Robert Hale Ltd., 1967).
2. Eeben Barlow, *Executive Outcomes: Against All Odds* (Alberton, South Africa: Galago Press, 1999).
3. Drawn from personal experience or interviews with the author from 2004 to 2009.
4. U.S. House of Representatives, Committee on Oversight and Government Reform, memorandum to committee members from the majority staff, "Additional Information about Blackwater USA," October 1, 2007, http://graphics8.nytimes.com/packages/pdf/national/20071001121609.pdf.
5. United States Department of Justice, "Five Blackwater Employees Indicted on Manslaughter and Weapons Charges for Fatal Nisur Square Shooting in Iraq," press release, December 8, 2008, http://www.justice.gov/opa/pr/2008/December/08-nsd-1068.html.
6. Timothy Williams, "Iraqis Angered as Blackwater Charges Are Dropped," *New York Times*, January 2, 2010.
7. Renae Merle, "Census Counts 100,000 Contractors in Iraq," *Washington Post*, December 5, 2006.
8. See the Coalition Provisional Authority, "Order #17: Status of the Coalition Provisional Authority, MNF-Iraq, Certain Missions and Personnel in Iraq," June 27, 2004, http://www.cpa-iraq.org/regulations/20040627_CPAORD_17_Status_of_Coalition__Rev__with_Annex_A.pdf. The critical text is on page 3, subhead 1, section 2. The actual quotation is, "Unless provided otherwise herein, the MNF, the CPA, Foreign Liaison Missions, their Personnel, property, funds and assets, and all International Consultants shall be immune from Iraqi legal process."
9. James Glanz, "Contractors Outnumber U.S. Troops in Afghanistan," *Military World*, September 2, 2009, http://www.military-world.net/Afghanistan/2376.html.
10. David Isenberg, "PMCs in Iraq," in *A Fistful of Contractors: The Case for a Pragmatic Assessment of Private military Companies in Iraq*, Research Report 2004.4 (British American Security Information Council [BASIC], September 2004), http://www.basicint.org/pubs/Research/2004PMC2iii.pdf.
11. See Coalition Provisional Authority, "Order #17."

12. "Full Text: Bush Speech Aboard the USS *Abraham Lincoln*," *Washington Post*, May 1, 2003, http://www.washingtonpost.com/ac2/wp-dyn/A2627-2003May1.

13. Jijo Jacob and David Cutler, "Timeline: Kenya in Crisis after Elections," *Reuters UK*, December 31, 2007, http://uk.reuters.com/article/idUKL3033036120071231.

14. Personal (or personnel) security details (PSD) are the classic "bodyguard" roles in the public's eye.

15. Brian Williams, "Looking back after Heading West," *Daily Nightly blog*, November 2, 2009, http://dailynightly.msnbc.msn.com/_nv/more/section/archive?year=200 9&month=11&ct=a&pc=25&sp=25#November%202009%20archive.

16. See endnote 8 for the link.

17. Hannah Arendt, *The Life of the Mind: The Groundbreaking Investigation on How We Think* (New York: Harcourt, Inc., 1978).

18. Hannah Arendt, *Eichmann in Jerusalem: A Report on the Banality of Evil* (New York: Viking Press, 1963).

19. For a complete list of those convicted of crimes pertaining to Abu Ghraib, see the chart accompanying the article by Eric Schmitt, "Iraq Abuse Trial Is Again Limited to Lower Ranks," *New York Times*, March 23, 2006, http://query.nytimes.com/gst/fullpage.html?res=9404E6D71630F930A15750C0A9609C8B63.

20. See the United Nations International Criminal Tribunal for the Former Yugoslavia, Trial Chambers, *The Prosecutor v. Stanislav Galic*, Case no. IT-98-29-T, "Judgment and Opinion," December 5, 2003, http://secnet069.un.org/x/file/Legal%20Library/jud_supplement/supp46-e/galic.htm; and Michelle Oliver, "Memorandum for the Iraqi Special Tribunal," Case Western Reserve University School of Law International War Crimes Research Lab, Spring 2007, http://law.case.edu/War-Crimes-Research-Portal/memoranda/oliver_michelle2.pdf.

21. See UN General Assembly Security Council, "Report of the International Tribunal for the Prosecution of Persons Responsible for Serious Violations of International Humanitarian Law Committed in the Territory of the Former Yugoslavia since 1991, Note by the Secretary-General," July 31, 2009, http://www.icty.org/x/file/About/Reports%20and%20Publications/AnnualReports/annual_report_2009_en.pdf. See also the tribunal's homepage http://secnet069.un.org/.

22. U.S. House Committee on Oversight and Government Reform, memorandum. See also "Statement of Erik D. Prince, Chairman and CEO, Blackwater, for the House Committee on Oversight and Government Reform, October 2, 2007," http://iraqslogger .powweb.com/downloads/statement.of.erik.d.prince.pdf?PHPSESSID=5428def 7b492ec4ccdf478fdbf6aaff9.

23. Based upon the author's personal experiences in Iraq.

24. U.S. House of Representatives, Committee on Oversight and Government Reform, "Private Military Contractors in Iraq: An Examination of Blackwater's Actions in Fallujah," September 2007, http://abcnews.go.com/images/Blackwater_Fallujah_Waxman_Report_070926.pdf. This report, with exhaustive research, also provides fascinating background for what the reality on the ground in Iraq was in early 2004 versus the official version emanating from 1600 Pennsylvania Avenue.

25. Mike Mount, "Army: Suicide Rate among Soldiers Continues on Record Pace," *CNN.com*, June 11, 2009, http://www.cnn.com/2009/US/06/11/us.army.suicides/.

26. John McCain, John Warner, and Lindsey Graham to Michael B. Mukasey, October 31, 2007, http://mccain.senate.gov/public/index.cfm?FuseAction=Files. View&FileStore_id=2ff245f8-ec97-466e-a24e-144415abc000.

27. See Colin Powell to John McCain, September 13, 2006, http://msnbcmedia.msn.com/i/msnbc/sections/news/060914_Powell.pdf, in this which Powell used the famous quote.

Chapter 2. The Contractor Experience: Iraq

1. Steve Fainaru, "Iraq Contractors Face Growing Parallel War; as Security Work Increases, So Do Casualties," *Washington Post*, June 16, 2007.
2. James Stephenson, *Losing the Golden Hour: An Insider's View of Iraq's Reconstruction* (Washington, DC: Potomac Books, Inc., 2007), 16.
3. Interviews were conducted in the period 2006–9 both in theater and in the United States. Several were done in Europe. Interviews were in person where events permitted and by telephone when a face-to-face meeting was not possible. It should be noted that I served personally with many of the men involved; otherwise, they would never have considered being so frank during interviews. The individuals in this volume, though using pseudonyms, deserve enormous credit for their willingness to step forward and speak the truth. The majority are still employed in the industry, and if their real identities were ever revealed, they would be fired on the spot. I salute their attempt to contribute positive change, via their stories cited here, to an industry that badly needs it. It has been a distinct honor for me to be lucky enough to stand alongside many (but not all) of them in times of danger. To these forward-looking souls go my sincere thanks.

Chapter 3. A History of Violence

1. Matthew L. Wald, "U.S. Lawyers Knew about Legal Pitfalls in Blackwater Case," *New York Times*, January 1, 2010, http://www.nytimes.com/2010/01/02/us/02legal.html?ref=us.
2. Pauline Jelinek, "For an American Soldier, Gear Now Costs 100 Times More Than in WWII," Associated Press, October 3, 2007.
3. T. Christian Miller, "Contractors Outnumber Troops in Iraq," *Los Angeles Times*, July 4, 2007, http://articles.latimes.com/2007/jul/04/nation/na-private4.
4. James M. Carter, *Inventing Vietnam: The United States and State Building, 1954–1968* (New York: Cambridge University Press, 2008), 181–203; and interview with James M. Carter, "U.S. Military Escalation, Private Contractors, and the War in Vietnam," BBC Vietnamese Edition, December 2, 2008.
5. Comptroller General of the United States, *Report to the Congress of the United States: Survey of Internal Audits and Inspections Relating to United States Activities in Viet Nam* (Washington, DC: General Accounting Office, July 18, 1966), http://archive.gao.gov/otherpdf1/087467.pdf.
6. Drew Pearson and Jack Anderson, "On the Washington Merry-Go-Round," August 26, 1966, Bell-McLure Syndicate, American University Library, Special Collections, Washington, DC, http://dspace.wrlc.org/doc/bitstream/2041/52862/b19f17-0826zdisplay.pdf.
7. Statement of Senator Byron Dorgan, Democratic Policy Committee Hearing on Iraq Contracting Practices, February 13, 2004, http://dpc.senate.gov/hearings/hearing12/dorgan.pdf.
8. "Logistics Civil Augmentation Program LOGCAP," *GlobalSecurity.org*, http://www.globalsecurity.org/military/agency/army/logcap.htm.
9. According to a CBS–Associated Press report (September 26, 2003), "A report by the

Congressional Research Service undermines Vice President Dick Cheney's denial of a continuing relationship with Halliburton Co., the energy company he once led, Sen. Frank Lautenberg said Thursday. . . . An analysis released by a Democratic senator found that Vice President Dick Cheney's Halliburton stock options have risen 3,281 percent in the last year. Sen. Frank Lautenberg (D-NJ) asserts that Cheney's options—worth $241,498 a year ago—are now valued at more than $8 million."

10. P. W. Singer, *Corporate Warriors: The Rise of the Privatized Military Industry* (Ithaca, NY: Cornell University Press, 2003), 143.

11. Contractor fraud cases are legion. The following samples highlight only a few and display a systemic disregard for any type of formal accounting system: Christine Lagorio, "Contractor Fraud Unchecked in Iraq," CBS News, January 5, 2007, http://www.cbsnews.com/stories/2007/01/05/cbsnews_investigates/main2334784. shtml; Dana Hedgpeth, "Spending on Iraq Poorly Tracked: Audit Faults Accounting for $15 Billion in Work," *Washington Post*, May 23, 2008, http://www.washingtonpost.com/wp-dyn/content/article/2008/05/22/AR2008052203751.html; and Global Policy Forum, "Corruption, Fraud, and Gross Malfeasance," in *War and Occupation in Iraq*, June 2007, http://www.globalpolicy.org/component/content/article/168/37153.html.

12. See Uppsala Conflict Data Program, "Washington Agreement," March 1, 1994, http://www.pcr.uu.se/gpdatabase/peace/BoH%2019940301.pdf.

13. Deborah D. Avant, *The Market for Force: The Consequences of Privatizing Security* (New York: Cambridge University Press, 2005), 101–6.

14. Ibid.

15. Ibid.

16. Department of the Army, Headquarters, "Deep Operations," in *Field Manual 100-5: Operations* (Washington, DC: Department of the Army, June 1993).

17. U.S. Department of State, "Summary of the Dayton Peace Agreement," fact sheet, December 11, 1995, http://www.state.gov/www/regions/eur/bosnia/dayton.html.

18. Ken Silverstein, "Privatizing War: How Affairs of State Are Outsourced to Corporations Beyond Public Control," *Nation*, July 28, 1997.

19. Ibid.

20. UN Development Programme, *Human Development Indicators*, 1994, http://hdr.undp.org/en/media/hdr_1994_en_indicators1.pdf.

21. Barlow, *Executive Outcomes*, 319.

22. Singer, *Corporate Warriors*, 112. The author also goes on to add in his footnotes that the claim of being paid in the form of diamond profits is still disputed to the current day.

23. Ibid, 114.

24. The $35 million mentioned to restore Sierra Leone translates to eight M1 Abrams main battle tanks for the U.S. Army with a replacement cost of $4.3 million. See M1 Abrams Main Battle Tank, *GlobalSecurity.org*, http://www.globalsecurity.org/military/systems/ground/m1-specs.htm

25. Singer, *Corporate Warriors*, 114; and Barlow, *Executive Outcomes*, 386.

26. Ibid.

27. Ibid.

28. Ibid.

29. Human Rights Watch, "Summary," *Sierra Leone: Getting Away with Murder, Mutilation, Rape* 11, no. 3(A) (July 1999), http://www.hrw.org/legacy/reports/1999/sierra/SIERLE99.htm#P2_0.

Chapter 4. The Perfect Storm

1. General Shinseki said the following when appearing before the Senate Armed Services Committee on February 25, 2003, just prior to the invasion of Iraq: "I would say that what's been mobilized to this point—something on the order of several hundred thousand soldiers are probably, you know, a figure that would be required. We're talking about post-hostilities control over a piece of geography that's fairly significant, with the kinds of ethnic tensions that could lead to other problems. And so it takes a significant ground force presence to maintain a safe and secure environment, to ensure that people are fed, that water is distributed, all the normal responsibilities that go along with administering a situation like this." See also Eric Schmitt, "Pentagon Contradicts General on Iraq Occupation Force's Size," *New York Times*, February 28, 2003, http://www.globalpolicy.org/component/content/article/167/35435.html; and Alyssa Fetini, "Secretary of Veterans Affairs: Erik Shinseki," *Time*, December 2, 2008, http://www.time.com/time/specials/packages/article/0,28804,1863062_1863058_1865215,00.html.

2. This 1991 quotation from Secretary of Defense Dick Cheney came from David Green's story "Cheney's Policy Influence Is Unabated," *All Things Considered*, August 26, 2005. Transcripts of the interview (his comments are about a half-dozen paragraphs in) are available at http://www.npr.org/templates/story/story.php?storyId=4818130.

3. Coalition Provisional Authority, "Memorandum #4: Contract and Grant Procedures Applicable to Vested and Seized Iraqi Property and the Development Fund for Iraq," August 19, 2003. For more information, see http://www.sigir.mil/reports/pdf/audits/cpaig_audit_cpa_contracting_processes.pdf, 10.

4. Committee on Government Reform, U.S. House of Representatives, *Rebuilding Iraq; U.S. Mismanagement in the Middle East* (New York: Coismo Reports, 2005), 10–11.

5. Special Inspector General for Iraq Reconstruction (SIGIR), *Quarterly and Semiannual Report to the United States Congress* 58 (July 30, 2004).

6. Federal Reserve Bank of New York, *Summary: Special Currency Shipments to Iraq*, Letter from Federal Reserve Bank of New York to Minority Staff (February 15, 2005).

7. SIGIR, *Quarterly and Semiannual Report*.

8. Federal Reserve Bank of New York, *Summary*.

9. Committee on Government Reform, *Rebuilding Iraq*, 8, 11–12.

10. Frank Willis, testimony, "An Oversight Hearing on Waste, Fraud and Abuse in U.S. Government Contracting in Iraq," Senate Democratic Policy Committee, February 14, 2005.

11. Ibid.

12. Deborah Hastings, "Prosecutor Alleges Money Laundering," Associated Press/ *Washington Post*, August 4, 2006, www.washingtonpost.com/wp-dyn/content/.../AR2006080400978_pf.html.

13. Michael O'Hanlon and Adriana Lins de Albuquerque, *Iraq Index: Tracking Variables of Reconstruction & Security in Post-Saddam Iraq*, updated June 21, 2004, http://www.brookings.edu/fp/saban/iraq/index20040621.pdf.

14. According to *Wiser in Battle: A Soldier's Story*, the autobiography of Lt. Gen. Ricardo S. Sanchez (with Donald T. Phillips)—as quoted by Michael Abramowitz in "McClellan Recounts Administration's Missed Chances after '04 Election," *Washington*

Post, June 2, 2008—Bush was incensed by the murder of the four contractors. Sanchez quoted the former president as saying the following during a national security videoconference: "Kick ass! If somebody tries to stop the march to democracy, we will seek them out and kill them! We must be tougher than hell! This Vietnam stuff, this is not even close. It is a mind-set. We can't send that message. It's an excuse to prepare us for withdrawal." The president then went on to proclaim, "There is a series of moments and this is one of them. Our will is being tested, but we are resolute. We have a better way. Stay strong! Stay the course! Kill them! Be confident! Prevail! We are going to wipe them out! We are not blinking!" The *Washington Post* article can be found at http://www.washingtonpost.com/wp-dyn/content/article/2008/06/01/AR2008060101961_2.html.

15. Philip Seib, *The Al Jazeera Effect: How the New Global Media Are Reshaping World Politics* (Washington, DC: Potomac Books, Inc., 2009).

16. Ibid. Having been in Baghdad during the fearsome summer of 2004, I personally noticed the dramatic difference between Al Jazeera and CNN. While neither network was, in my opinion, totally accurate, the Arab version was certainly both bloodier and more hateful. Al Jazeera was far closer to propaganda than reality on many days, and it is my personal opinion that it inflamed the situation on the ground. Four years later, while I was deployed to Kenya, Al Jazeera, along with the BBC, were the only news available. Both the theme and the tone of the Arab network were far more muted than they had been three years earlier. And although there was still occasionally an anti-American bias, it was nowhere near as bad as it had once been. The TV station has matured dramatically since the invasion of 2003.

17. The U.S. casualty figures show the seriousness of the insurgency. O'Hanlon and Lins de Albuquerque's *Iraq Index* shows the figure of 33 U.S. soldiers killed in action in Iraq in March 2004. The number for April nearly quadrupled to 122 the next month, but April saw the battle of Fallujah by the 1st Marine Division and, on the ninth, the attack on the KBR convoy.

18. Jennifer K. Elsea, Moshe Schwartz, and Kennon H. Nakamura, *Private Security Contractors in Iraq: Background, Legal Status, and Other Issues* (Washington, DC: Congressional Research Service, August 25, 2008), http://fas.org/sgp/crs/natsec/RL32419.pdf.

19. See Coalition Provisional Authority, "Order #17."

20. The Iraq Development Fund was a fund totaling over $22 billion—all of it Iraqi money—which was frozen by the United States upon taking Baghdad. The CPA spent Iraqi money, and nearly $9 billion remain unaccounted for to this day. See "Development Fund for Iraq," *Global Policy Forum,* http://www.globalpolicy.org/iraq/humanitarian-issues-in-iraq/development-fund-for-iraq.html.

21. SIGIR, *Quarterly and Semiannual Report,* Appendix J updated; Jeremy Scahill, *Blackwater: The Rise of the World's Most Powerful Mercenary Army* (New York: Nation Books, 2007), 133–34; and the author's personal interviews with individuals on Bremer's protection team.

22. Paul Bremer, *My Year in Iraq: The Struggle to Build a Future of Hope* (New York: Threshold Editions, 2007), 391. I was in Baghdad during the last days of June 2004 and lived through many of the events described in Bremer's book. Suffice it to say, my recollections of some of these events differ from his.

23. Hannah Arendt, *The Origins of Totalitarianism* (New York: Harcourt, Brace and World, Inc., 1950), 348–49.

Chapter 5. Anatomy of a Disaster

1. Tristan is a pseudonym.
2. Mark is also a pseudonym.
3. The Foreign Claims Act (10 U.S.C. § 2734-2736) is the statute that covers the payment to foreign civilians for accidental death or damage caused by U.S. forces; however, the bar to collection can be formidable. The victim must know the specific unit (or PMC) that killed his or her relative, *have a claim form filled out by the PMC admitting its responsibility* (author's emphasis), and produce two witnesses and appropriate medical reports. Clearly, in Baghdad in 2004, few Iraqis had the intestinal fortitude to approach armed PMCs with copies of the paperwork necessary for filing a claim.

Chapter 7. SATMO: Doing It Right

1. Kenya surreptitiously provided support for the American military by authorizing a small, highly covert unit to be based near the island of Lamu, practically astride the Somali border. There is considerable speculation through open sources that the base, along with naval forces, has served as a springboard for highly classified missions into Somalia. Kenya is also strategically placed in the geopolitical sense, with Somalia to the northeast, Sudan to the northwest, and the Congo within striking distance.

Chapter 8. Ten Minutes on Ambush Alley

1. The incident described in this chapter occurred in the summer of 2004. Engagements of this sort were fairly routine back then, and this one merited no special coverage. It was considered "normal," if one can use that word when describing close combat. Dan Tucker is the actual name of the individual who performed so heroically. I was to serve with him the next year in South Africa, Zimbabwe, Central America, Colombia, and the United States. A finer man I could not find. Although we spoke of the particular incident described here, there was no serious effort to put it into this book for several years. The actual series of interviews with Dan and the other team members occurred from 2006 to 2007. As is the norm in combat, each person had a slightly different view of the events that transpired. This re-creation of that horrible day has been made to the best of my ability to sort out facts from fear and from objective recollections versus biased tale telling. If there are any mistakes in its telling here, they belong to me and not to the men who suffered so much during that broiling summer of '04 in Baghdad.
2. PSD teams are a subelement of particular types of private military companies, but *only* these elements are what I have chosen to classify as "operational," meaning they engage in combat operations. In this case two contractors, Dan and George, were tapped to protect a group of American civil engineers who were tasked with rebuilding the Baghdad power grid.
3. A VS-17 panel is a bright orange marker, roughly the size of a tablecloth. It is equipped with tie downs on the sides and corners so it can be attached to vehicles. It is primarily designed to identify friend and foe from the air. It became so commonplace in Iraq that all Coalition members universally accepted it as a friendly marker.

Chapter 10. The Big Fix

1. Almost all big-league contractors work for either the Department of Defense (DOD) or the Department of State (DOS). For example, Blackwater in Iraq worked for the

State Department, as they were contracted to protect DOS individuals. The ten advisers in Kenya were under DOD's umbrella. Are there small, fly-by-night operations that still conduct business for commercial organizations unrelated to the military? Yes. But they are shrinking rapidly in number as the industry continues to streamline itself. The U.S. government is the world's largest paymaster, and by logical inference, he who has the money can dictate the terms. If DOD and DOS implemented mandatory guidelines for any organization wishing to enter the PMC business, the industry would adopt them in a day. They would protest but would do it, for to fight it risks losing the most lucrative contracts of all—those of the federal government.

2. Department of the Army, Headquarters, *Field Manual 3-07.22: Counterinsurgency Operations* (Washington, DC: Department of the Army, 2004).

3. See chapter 3 of this volume, "A History of Violence."

4. Halliburton fraud ranges from individuals within its employ to allegations against the company itself. For one example, see Griff Witte, "Former KBR Worker Admits to Fraud in Iraq," *Washington Post*, August 23, 2005, http://www.washingtonpost.com/wp-dyn/content/article/2005/08/22/AR2005082201435.html. See the U.S. House of Representatives, Committee on Government Reform, Minority Staff, Special Investigations Division, and the U.S. Senate, Democratic Policy Committee, "Halliburton's Questioned and Unsupported Costs in Iraq Exceed $1.4 Billion," June 27, 2005. The report's conclusion is self-explanatory: "The favoritism shown Halliburton appears to be continuing. Despite the auditor finding of over $1.4 billion in questioned and unsupported costs in Iraq, Halliburton has recently received two new contract awards" The full report can be found at http://dpc.senate.gov/hearings/hearing22/jointreport.pdf.

5. Coalition Provisional Authority, "Order #17."

6. See Karen Houppert, "KBR's Rape Problem," *Nation*, May 5, 2008, http://www.thenation.com/doc/20080505/houppert; and James Risen, "Limbo for U.S. Women Reporting Iraq Assaults," *New York Times*, February 13, 2008, http://www.nytimes.com/2008/02/13/world/middleeast/13contractors.html.

7. Unknown to most of the world, there are in fact thousands of foreign citizens serving in the ranks of the U.S. armed forces. See Anita U. Hattiangadi et al., "Non-Citizens in Today's Military: Final Report" (Alexandria, VA: Center for Naval Analyses, April 2005), http://www.cna.org/documents/D0011092.A2.pdf.

Selected Bibliography

Barlow, Eeben. *Executive Outcomes: Against All Odds.* Alberton, South Africa: Galago Press, 1999.

Bremer, Paul. *My Year in Iraq: The Struggle to Build a Future of Hope.* New York: Threshold Editions, 2007.

Committee on Government Reform, U.S. House of Representatives. *Rebuilding Iraq: U.S. Mismanagement in the Middle East.* New York: Coismo Reports, 2005.

Department of the Army, Headquarters. *Field Manual 3-07.22: Counterinsurgency Operations.* Washington, DC: Department of the Army, 2004.

Fainaru, Steve. *Big Boy Rules: America's Mercenaries Fighting in Iraq.* Cambridge, MA: Da Capo Press, 2008.

Hoare, Michael. *Congo Mercenary.* London: Robert Hale Ltd., 1967.

Miller, T. Christian. *Blood Money: Wasted Billions, Lost Lives, and Corporate Greed in Iraq.* New York: Little, Brown, 2006.

Rasor, Dina, and Robert Bauman. *Betraying Our Troops: The Destructive Results of Privatizing War.* New York: Palgrave Macmillan, 2007.

Scahill, Jeremy. *Blackwater: The Rise of the World's Most Powerful Mercenary Army.* New York: Nation Books, 2007.

Singer, P. W. *Corporate Warriors: The Rise of the Privatized Military Industry.* Ithaca, NY: Cornell University Press, 2003.

Stephenson, James. *Losing the Golden Hour: An Insider's View of Iraq's Reconstruction.* Washington, DC: Potomac Books, Inc., 2007.

Index

About the Author

Shawn Engbrecht is the founder of the Center for Advanced Security Studies, one of the premier training facilities for protection officers in the world. He has worked as a private contractor in Iraq on multiple occasions and has been deployed to the European Union and Africa. A veteran of the American 75th Ranger Regiment, he spent six years in the 1st Ranger Battalion of Special Operations Command. He lives in Florida. For more information, visit his website, www.americascovert warriors.com.